ANIMATING FACIAL FEATURES & EXPRESSIONS

SECOND EDITION

ANIMATING FACIAL FEATURES & EXPRESSIONS

SECOND EDITION

DAVID KALWICK

CHARLES RIVER MEDIA

Boston, Massachusetts

Cover Design: Tyler Creative

CHARLES RIVER MEDIA
25 Thomson Place
Boston, Massachusetts 02210
617-757-7900
617-757-7969 (FAX)
crminfo@thomson.com
www.charlesriver.com

This book is printed on acid-free paper.

David Kalwick. Animating Facial Features & Expressions, Second Edition.
ISBN: 1-58450-474-9

All brand names and product names mentioned in this book are trademarks or service marks of their respective companies. Any omission or misuse (of any kind) of service marks or trademarks should not be regarded as intent to infringe on the property of others. The publisher recognizes and respects all marks used by companies, manufacturers, and developers as a means to distinguish their products.

Library of Congress Cataloging-in-Publication Data
Kalwick, David J.
  Animating facial features & expressions / David Kalwick. — 2nd ed.
     p. cm.
  Includes index.
  ISBN 1-58450-474-9 (pbk. with cd-rom)
  1. Computer animation. 2. Facial expression in art. I. Title. II.
Title: Animating facial features and expressions.
  TR897.7.K357 2006
  006.6'96—dc22
                          2006009634

06 7 6 5 4 3 2 First Printing

CHARLES RIVER MEDIA titles are available for site license or bulk purchase by institutions, user groups, corporations, etc. For additional information, please contact the Special Sales Department at 800-347-7707.

Requests for replacement of a defective CD-ROM must be accompanied by the original disc, your mailing address, telephone number, date of purchase, and purchase price. Please state the nature of the problem, and send the information to CHARLES RIVER MEDIA, 25 Thomson Place, Boston, Massachusetts 02210. CRM's sole obligation to the purchaser is to replace the disc, based on defective materials or faulty workmanship, but not on the operation or functionality of the product.

I'd like to dedicate this book to all of the new 3D animators
trying their hand at this wonderful craft.
It is the eager, enthusiastic youth that pushes the software
enabling this emerging art form closer to reality.
Rock on!

CONTENTS

ACKNOWLEDGMENTS

It's been said countless times and in as many ways, but it holds forever true. Behind every success, there is a team of supportive staff that brings an idea to reality. I'd like to thank Jenifer Niles for the opportunity to expand on an existing success, and for the groundwork laid out by Bill Flemming and Darris Dobbs.

I'd also like to acknowledge and thank Bryan Davidson and Lance Morganelli for their help in the production and editing of this book, as well as the unnamed staff at Charles River Media and Thomson Learning for putting this book together.

INTRODUCTION

There are many aspects to 3D graphics but none are more fascinating and complicated than facial animation and expression. Creating emotion can be challenging, but the reward clearly outweighs the effort. To be successful at facial animation, one must study and understand the underlying structure of the head, as well as the ability of humans to express emotions.

There are many possibilities for facial animation, and they aren't simply limited to the human head. You can animate cartoon characters, animals, alien creatures, and talking trees if you get the urge. But, no matter what character you are animating, facial expression becomes a critical part of the project. Nothing is quite as disappointing as a wonderfully modeled and surfaced character that appears lifeless because it has poorly animated expressions. Creating believable and emotive facial expressions brings your character to life, no matter how fictional it may appear.

OVERVIEW OF THE BOOK AND TECHNOLOGY

New technology is steadily being developed that expands the capabilities of 3D products. Even the most basic 3D programs possess many of the essential tools for creating amazing facial expressions and animations. While the capabilities of 3D programs will continue to grow, the principles of 3D facial expression and animation will always remain constant because they are based on physical principles of musculature, bone structure, and emotional expression. This book covers countless universal techniques for creating inspirational facial expression and animation. These techniques are not fixed to any one specific program, but rather apply to nearly every 3D program on the market.

If you use any of the following programs you should read this book: Maya®, 3ds Max®, SoftImage®, Alias®, LightWave®, Animation: Master™, or any other 3D program that offers any form of facial animation techniques.

How This Book Is Organized

This book is divided into three parts that will take you logically through the process of developing facial expressions and animations. Each part is a complete concept, allowing you to reach closure at the end. You don't have to read one part to understand another, though the best results are achieved by reading the entire book. If you are only interested in how to animate your facial expressions with morph targets, you can read Part 2 and skip the other parts of the book, for example.

Part 1–The Human Head

Chapter 1–Anatomy of the Head

This chapter will start by taking a look at the anatomy of the human head. To explore facial animation we must first start below the skin where all the expression is created. While not a medical anatomy book, most of the major bone structure and musculature are identified here. While this chapter contains a lot of anatomical information, it is imperative to understand that the different muscles in the head affect particular regions of the face. The key to creating believable expression is to first understand the mechanisms behind them. After grasping the skeletal structure of the human head, move to one of the more daunting aspects of human head modeling—proportions.

Chapter 2–Proportions of the Head

Creating the proper proportions for the head is essential if we want the facial expressions and animation to appear convincing. Because real facial expressions are so familiar to the everyone who can see, there is no more difficult task than creating believable human facial animation and expression. In our exploration of proportions, we will cover every detail of the ideal human head. The important point to remember is that this discussion is merely to serve as a foundation for you own head modeling. Some proportions of the head remain constant in most humans, making them a necessity to include in your model if you want your audience to believe your animation has emotions.

Once we have a handle on the physical proportions of a human head, we'll take a look at the mechanism behind facial expression and animation–facial muscles.

Chapter 3–Facial Muscles

The facial muscles drive expression and animation. Knowing how each of the facial muscles works will give you a distinct advantage when creating facial expressions and animation. In this chapter, we'll explore each of the facial muscles and view examples of them in action. You'll see many example images as well as animations that show the actual facial muscles moving.

After we've satisfied our craving for human head anatomy, we'll take a look at how facial expression is used to set the stage for an image or animation.

Part 2–Expression

Chapter 4–Facial Features and Expressions

It's been said, "Every picture tells a story." With facial animation, the picture is the character's face. Without the proper expression the scene may not evoke the emotions that are intended in the script.

In this chapter, we'll explore a few case studies of facial expression in 3D images to gain a better understanding of their impact on the message of the scene. Once we've had a little fun with expression, we'll get our hands dirty in Part 3–Animation.

Part 3–Animation

Chapter 5–Speech/Lip Synch

In this chapter the principles of lip synch will be introduced. We'll learn the phonemes necessary for lip synch, how to break down a sound file, and how to create a timing chart. We'll also explore straight morphing, the most common technique for creating lip synch animation. Then using the straight morph technique, we'll walk through creating a short dialogue animation.

After we have a handle on straight morphing, we'll take a look at the advanced morphing system, weighted morph, which is used to integrate emotions with lip synched dialog.

Chapter 6–Weighted Morphing Animation

In this chapter, we get neck deep in facial animation. Morphing animation is the backbone of character facial animation and in this chapter we explore that and another technique of facial animation: segmented morphing. This chapter ends with a look on how facial animation is created using weighted morph targets, including an insightful section on changing facial expression during the phoneme synching process.

Chapter 7–Animating Facial Expressions Using 3ds Max

In this chapter, you'll use the information you've learned in the previous chapters while working in 3ds Max. This chapter is software specific and

3ds Max has been chosen for its popularity and ease of use. For the most part, the tools used can be used in any version of 3ds Max greater than version 4.0. In addition to using morph targets, you will also learn how to use XForms, Physique, and Spline IK for facial animation. You will also learn how to incorporate sound for lip synching your facial animation in 3ds Max, as well.

Chapter 8—Facial Animation with Maya

As with the 3ds Max chapter, this chapter uses the knowledge gained in Chapters 1 through 6 and puts them in practice in the Maya animation environment. In this chapter, you'll learn how to apply facial animation principles using Joints, Clusters, and Lattices. You will also use the IK tools within Maya to animate a tongue as well as sound utilities to import sounds for lip synching.

Appendices

Appendix A—Typical Human Expression Weighted Morph Targets

In this section you'll find a visual reference for the human expression morph targets used for the segmented morphing style described in Chapter 6. In the top half of the image is the head in a neutral pose, with the expression pose in the lower half. This appendix is used with Chapter 6.

Appendix B—Typical Human Visual Phonemes

In this section you'll find a visual reference for common phoneme morph targets to be used with human models, regardless of the 3D program used.

Appendix C—Typical Cartoon Expression Weighted Morph Targets

In this section you'll find a visual reference for cartoon character expression morph targets used for the segmented morphing style described in Chapter 6.

Appendix D—Typical Cartoon Visual Phonemes

In this section you'll find a visual reference for common phoneme morph targets used with cartoon character models.

Appendix E—Facial Expression Examples

In this section you'll find reference material for 40 facial expressions, including front and profile image of each expression, as well as a detailed description of the distinguishing aspects of the expression. Outlining how the four major parts of the face are changed: brow, eyes, mouth, and chin. You're provided with examples for both a human and a detailed cartoon character.

In addition to the expression description, you'll also find a list of the common morph targets used for the expression and their morph percentages. While the exact morph values may vary with each program, they will get you started with the expression.

Appendix F—Just for Fun—Cartoon Expressions

In this section you'll find several examples of cartoon character expressions. A cartoon character has fewer emotional expression, but it is more exaggerated than a human or detailed character.

Who Should Read This Book

This book is for any 3D artist looking to improve their facial animation skills. As the art of 3D animation progresses, those who lack this skill will be left behind in the industry. With the proliferation of 3D animation in both animated and live action films, it is inevitable that in order to be competitive, a 3D artist must have some facial animation skills in their portfolio.

Tools You Will Need

To get the most from this book, a 3D program will be helpful, although in the first few chapters on bone structure, musculature and proportions, no computer is necessary. For the chapters that delve into the 3D modeling aspect of facial animation, a 3D program is definitely highly recommended. In today's market, 3D options encompass a wide range of programs ranging from very inexpensive (such as Animation:Master) and the higher end, all encompassing packages, such as my personal favorites, 3ds Max and Maya.

The most important tool however comes from within. Without dedication all the training in the world won't make a difference. Take your time and practice, practice, practice. Every man (or woman) was once a baby and even the greatest of artists didn't know how to draw at some point in their lives.

What's on the CD

Included with this book is a companion CD-ROM that contains a variety of support material for each chapter. The support materials are provided in common formats that are compatible with all computers and 3D programs. Below you'll find a detailed description of the contents on the companion CD-ROM.

Chapter 1

Movies
> **Jawmovement.mov:** An example of jaw movement
> **Jawrotation.mov:** An example of jaw rotation
> **Mandiblemove.mov:** An example of mandible motion
> **Mandiblerotation.mov:** An example of mandible rotation
> **Noselock.mov:** An example of nose lock
> **Supraorbital.mov:** An example of supraorbital motion

Chapter 2

DXF Models
> A female skull, head modeling template
> A male skull, head modeling template

Chapter 3

Movies
> QuickTime movies demonstrating movement of the following muscles: corrugator, depressor, frontalis, levator, masseter, mentalis, obicularis oris, obicularis oculi, platysma, triangularis, and zygomaticus.

Chapter 4

Movie
> An animation of Papagaio demonstrating facial expression and emotion

Chapter 5

Movies
> **Knuckles1.mov:** The first pass at lip synching Knuckles
> **KnucklesFix.mov:** The improved Knuckels animation
> Sound file
> **Knuckles.wav:** Knuckles dialog

Chapter 6

Movies
  2TargetMorph.mov: An example of weighted morphing
  Ptest1.mov: The first pass of lip synching Guido
  Guidofinal.mov: The second pass at lip synching Guido
  Sound file
  Youwant.wav: Guido's dialog

Expression Templates

Modeling templates for forming facial expressions.

Phoneme Templates

Modeling templates for forming basic phonemes.

Figures

All of the figures referenced within the text, in JPEG format. Each figure is organized by chapter, is full sized, and in 32 bit color.

Getting Started

Hardware/Software Requirements

To view the animated reference files, you'll need a QuickTime player. A free QuickTime player can be downloaded from *http://www.apple.com/quicktime*, although most systems come with QuickTime installed. The sound files can be viewed either by using QuickTime, Windows Media Player or any other program capable of playing WAV files. All of the figures are in JPEG format and can be viewed by any image viewer capable of handling .jpg format. Most internet browsers by default can handle viewing JPEG formatted images.

HUMAN HEAD

ANATOMY OF THE HEAD

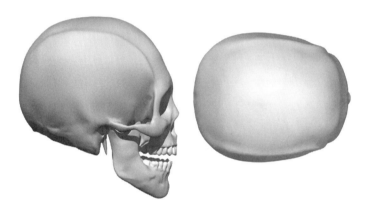

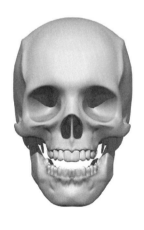

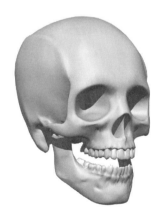

C reating a human head requires a thorough understanding of the skull, which is the foundation of any head and defines the shape of muscles and skin. If you want to create a properly proportioned head, you must intimately know the skull's form. It provides you with the rough outline of the head's shape, and the placement of the major facial features such as the nose, mouth, and eyes. Figure 1.1 shows a human skull from several perspectives.

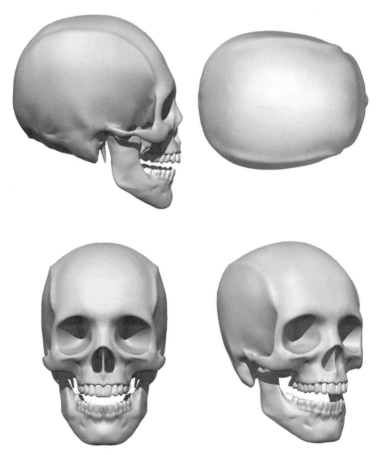

FIGURE 1.1   The human skull.

Looking at the skull, you can see there are many prominent features, such as the nose and mouth, and some more subtle features, such as the temporal ridge depicted in Figure 1.2. The temporal ridge runs along the side of the skull and defines the width of the skull.

FIGURE 1.2   The temporal ridge of the skull.

The temporal ridge defines the sides of the head, as it is more vertical than the top portion. Many 3D artists overlook the temporal ridges when building a 3D head model, resulting in heads that look somewhat egg shaped. Notice the head in Figure 1.3. The temporal ridge isn't actually visible, but the results can plainly be seen in the flatter portion on the sides of the head.

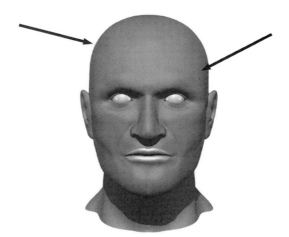

FIGURE 1.3   The temporal ridge of the human head.

CRANIAL SUBSTRUCTURES

The temporal ridge is just one of the many cranial features that create the foundation for external details of the head. This section outlines and identifies the cranial substructure necessary to build the ideal human head. The components are listed here and identified in Figure 1.4. A detailed explanation follows.

A. Frontal bone
B. Temporal ridge
C. Parietal bone
D. Nasion
E. Supraorbital margin
F. Nasal bone
G. Orbital cavity
H. Infraorbital margin
 I. Zygomatic bone
J. Maxilla
K. Mandible
L. Mental protuberance

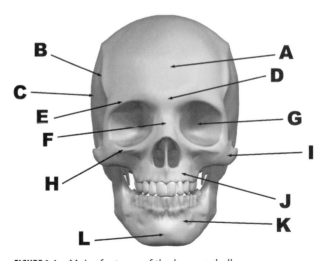

FIGURE 1.4   Major features of the human skull.

Frontal Bone

The frontal bone forms the structure of the forehead, and is slightly curved toward the back of the head and the sides. The frontal bone is rather thick and terminates at the brow, just above the nose and at the temporal ridge on the sides.

Temporal Ridge

The temporal ridge runs along the side of the upper skull. It's subtle on the skull and nearly unperceivable on the finished head, but is responsible for creating the square-shaped appearance of the upper skull.

Parietal Bone

Derived from the Latin "parietalis" meaning "belonging to the wall," the parietal bone makes up the side of the head. It's a smooth curved bone that extends outward until it lines up with the back of the jawbone. Along the side of the head, the parietal bone is between the frontal bone and the occipital bone on the back of the head.

Nasion

The nasion is the area where the frontal bone meets the nasal bone. Basically, it's the little dip at the top of the nose, just before the brow ridge, as shown in Figure 1.5.

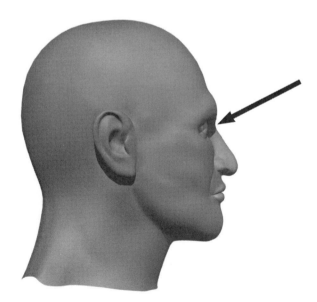

FIGURE 1.5 The nasion.

Supraorbital Margin

The supraorbital margin defines one of the most distinctive facial features. It creates the ridge above the eyes, as shown in Figure 1.6. The supraorbital margin is the bone directly under the eyebrows creating the upper portion of the eye sockets. When animating facial expressions, the skin moves over the supraorbital margin. A common mistake is to move the supraorbital margin, which tends to make the effect unrealistic because this bone is part of the skull structure that doesn't move. The best approach is to move the physical tissue on the upper portion of the supraorbital margin, keeping the lower portion locked in place as shown in Figure 1.7.

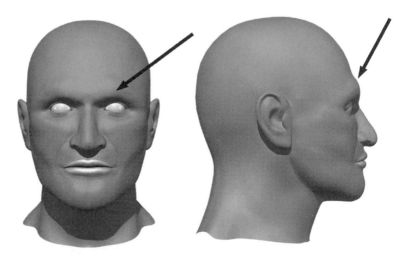

FIGURE 1.6   The supraorbital margin.

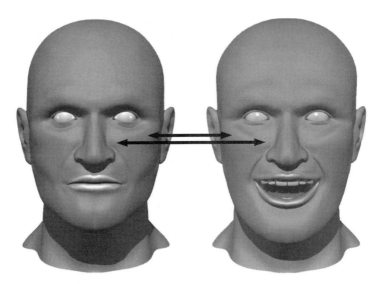

FIGURE 1.7   Moving the eyebrows.

Observe yourself raising your eyebrows in a mirror. Notice how most of the eyebrow across the middle is moved, but the sides stay locked. That is because they are resting on the supraorbital margin. To get a better feel for the movement of the eyebrow, look at the Supraorbital.mov movie file in the Chapter 1 folder on the companion CD-ROM. Notice how the tissue just above the upper eyelid is pulled upward. This isn't the supraorbital margin moving, but rather the sagging skin tissue that surrounds it. When you raise your eyebrows, this tissue is pulled taught over the supraorbital margin. When you are animating facial expressions, you'll want to keep the sides of your supraorbital margin region fixed so your model doesn't look like a cartoon character.

ON THE CD

Nasal Bone

The nasal bone is comprised of two small oblong bones, side by side, starting at the nasion, and continuing down the face essentially forming the bridge of the nose. The point where the nasal bone terminates usually creates a small bump in the nose as seen in Figure 1.8.

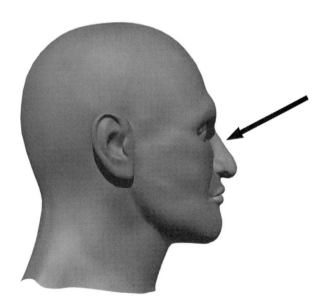

FIGURE 1.8   The nasal bone.

The cartilage that forms the tip of the nose is connected to the nasal bone. A common mistake in facial animation is to move the tip of the nose during facial expression. While subtle movement in the nose does occur, it's due to the skin covering being stretched. For the most part, the nose is fixed and stable, as shown in Figure 1.9.

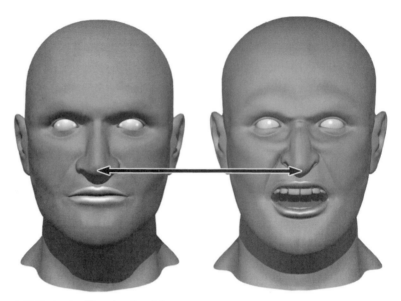

FIGURE 1.9 Locking the tip of the nose.

Making grimacing faces in the mirror, you can see that the tip of the nose moves very little and is a result of the surrounding tissue moving. You can also look at Noselock.mov located in the Chapter 1 folder on the companion CD-ROM. In this animation, you'll see the tissue surrounding the tip of the nose change shape without affecting it. In most cases, you will want to lock down the tip of the nose to prevent it from moving directly, and add some influential controls for some of the subtle movement. More about that in a later chapter.

ON THE CD

Orbital Cavity

The orbital cavity is the large hole where the eye is located. It is much larger than the actual eye, which sits rather high in the orbital cavity.

Infraorbital Margin

The infraorbital margin is the lower portion of the orbital cavity and the upper portion of the cheekbone. It creates the ridge under the eye as shown in Figure 1.10.

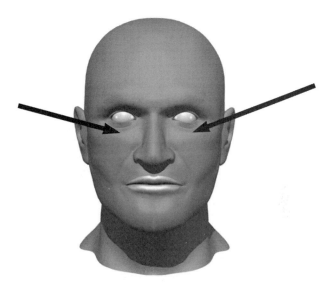

FIGURE 1.10   The infraorbital margin.

The infraorbital margin is directly responsible for creating bags under the eyes. It supports the excess fluids and tissue to create the bags. One of the common mistakes made in facial animation is to move the infraorbital margin. When the cheeks are raised, the tissue rides up and over the infraorbital margin, collecting under the lower eyelid, forcing it to puff up. Since the muscle tissue can't move over the infraorbital margin, it collects under it and creates the puffy cheeks as shown in Figure 1.11.

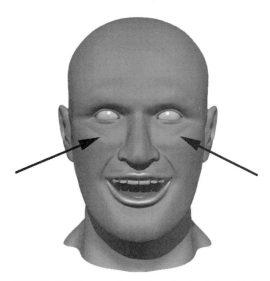

FIGURE 1.11   Tissue collected under the infraorbital margin.

When animating facial expressions, you'll want to move tissue up and over the infraorbital margin, but still keep the rise of the infraorbital margin intact. To see this, make a big smile or wink while looking in a mirror. Be sure to wink one eye at a time. You can see how the tissue moves up and collects under the lower eyelid, while the muscle tissue collects under the infraorbital margin. During each expression, you can see the infraorbital margin bulge.

Zygomatic Bone

The zygomatic bone is the cheekbone that lies directly under the infraorbital margin as shown in Figure 1.12.

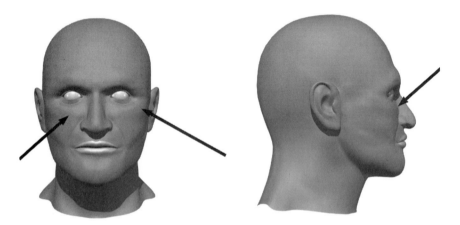

FIGURE 1.12   The zygomatic bone.

The zygomatic bone is obscured by the infraorbital margin from the front view, but is visible on the outer edge where it protrudes from the face, creating the common cheekbone. When you smile, the tissue collects in front of the zygomatic bone, which pushes it outward to create puffy cheeks.

Maxilla

The maxilla is the upper jawbone, directly under the nose, as shown in Figure 1.13. The maxilla is stationary and holds the gums and upper row of teeth.

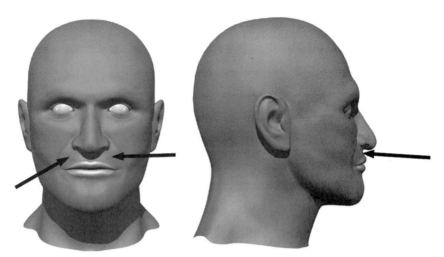

FIGURE 1.13   The maxilla.

Mandible

The mandible consists of the complete lower jawbone and defines the contour of the face. It's the largest facial bone and is the only movable bone on the skull. The mandible can be seen in Figure 1.14.

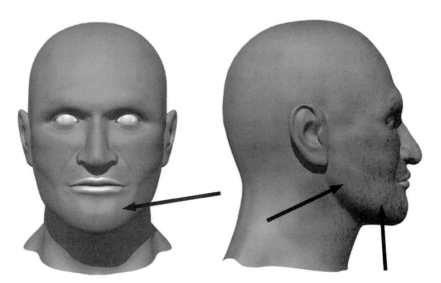

FIGURE 1.14   The mandible.

The placement of the jawbone is crucial when working with facial animation and expression. A common mistake in facial animation is rotating the jaw from the wrong point. To understand the proper axis for jaw rotation you need to know the shape and placement of the mandible, which is one of the major reasons why the study of the human skull is necessary to properly animate the face.

The axis for jaw rotation is located at the tip of the condyle, just behind the earlobe. An exterior reference for a rotational axis would be the base of the antihelix (the upper inner portion of the ear) where it meets the lobule (the lower, fleshy portion of the ear), as shown by the axis designation in Figure 1.15.

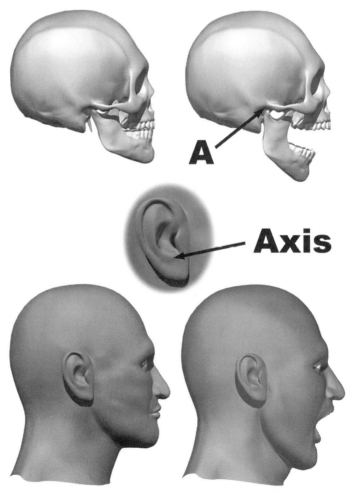

FIGURE 1.15   The jaw rotation axis. The condyle is identified by the letter A.

When rotating the jaw, pick the center of this point in the ear as a pivot point. If you put your fingers in your ears and open your mouth wide, you can feel where the jaw rotates. See Jawrotation.mov in the Chapter 1 folder on the companion CD-ROM for an animation of the jaw's rotation on a completed head model. You can also load the Mandiblerotation.mov file, which illustrates the proper movement of the jawbone on a skull.

ON THE CD

In addition to rotational movement, the jaw also moves from side to side. The side-to-side motion is not rotational; the jawbone actually shifts its position horizontally as shown in Figure 1.16.

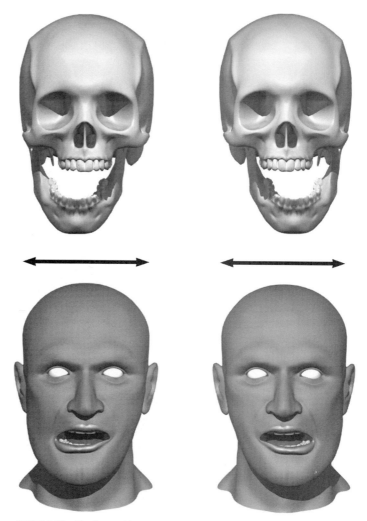

FIGURE 1.16   Horizontal jaw movement.

The movement of the jaw seems quite dramatic in the skeletal model, but not as dramatic in the actual head because there is an abundance of tissue covering the movement. Figure 1.17 illustrates the extent of the jaw movement limits.

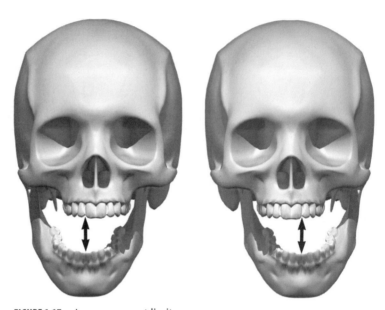

FIGURE 1.17   Jaw movement limits.

The teeth provide an easy guide to determining the movement limits. At the jaw's maximum movement, the gap between the two lower front teeth lines up with the outside edge of the incisor. In other words, the horizontal movement of the lower jaw is about equal to one tooth's distance in either direction. Of course, if your character is toothless, you'll need to use the gums as the guide. The gum tissue raised up between the two lower teeth will serve as the guide. As always, observe this movement while looking in a mirror, or load the Jawmovement.mov and Mandiblemove.mov files in the Chapter 1 folder on the companion CD-ROM. The movement may look rather excessive because so much movement isn't always obvious, but you will find cases where this movement is necessary to achieve certain facial expressions, such as when chewing or looking dumbfounded and confused.

ON THE CD

Mental Protuberance

The mental protuberance is the very tip of the lower jawbone. This bone forms the chin of the human head shown in Figure 1.18.

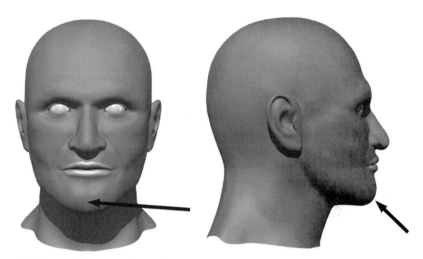

FIGURE 1.18   The mental protuberance.

As you can see, several skull structures define the visible facial features, and how they animate. When modeling a human head, you need to consider the proper proportions and placement of the skull features to properly animate the face.

SKULL PROPORTIONS

It's critical that proportions are correct on the skull so the entire head, including skin tissue and musculature, is correctly proportioned and positioned. Part of creating the proper proportions is to know how the mass of the skull is distributed. Figure 1.19 shows the distribution of skull mass.

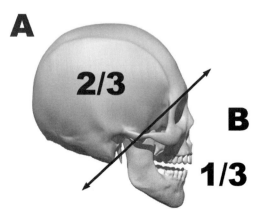

FIGURE 1.19   Skull mass distribution.

The skull is divided into two main masses, cranial and facial. The cranial mass consists of the top and back of the skull and makes up two-thirds of the total skull mass. The cranial mass gives the head its shape, although it has less detail than the facial mass. While it only makes up one third of the total mass of the head, the facial mass is the most detailed and critical portion of the skull.

SKULL SHAPE

From a side view, a human skull fits perfectly in a square. Its height and depth are relatively equal in dimension, as shown in Figure 1.20.

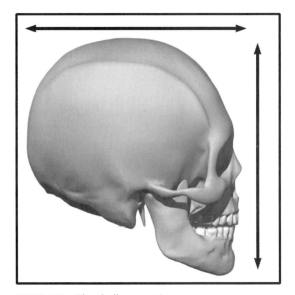

FIGURE 1.20   The skull proportions.

The distance from the chin to the top of the head is equal to that of the brow to the back of the head. It is a common error to model heads to be somewhat shallow. Some tend to make the head shorter from front to back because it looks awkwardly large otherwise. This isn't as noticeable in real humans, because the hair balances out the shape of the head.

When modeling human heads, create a square in the background for proportioning the model, as shown in Figure 1.21. Although a simple technique, it will help gauge whether you have created the proper proportions from the side view of the head. Proportioning the model from the front is a bit more complicated and is addressed in Chapter 2, "Proportions of the Head."

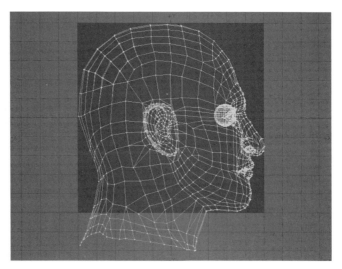

FIGURE 1.21   Proportioning the head.

Another proportion to consider is the vertical proportion of the facial mass. Vertically, the front view of the head can be evenly divided by drawing a horizontal line through the orbital cavity as shown in Figure 1.22.

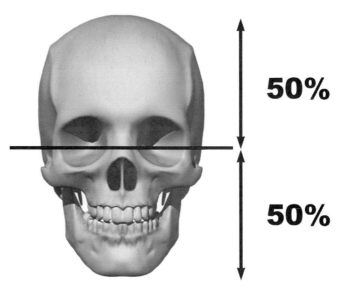

FIGURE 1.22   Skull mass distribution.

The distance from the chin to the center of the orbital cavity is roughly equal to the distance from the center of the orbital cavity to the top of the skull. With this measurement and the skull proportions measurement, you can accurately develop the general shape of the head so it's proportional to a human head.

Conclusion

Understanding cranial anatomy will give you the knowledge needed to properly model and animate a human head. Even though most animators don't normally build a skull for their characters, learning and understanding the skull is important when modeling and animating any head. Because the underlying skeletal structure determines the outer appearance, understanding the foundation of the human skull will pay big dividends when modeling and animating any character head.

PROPORTIONS OF THE HEAD

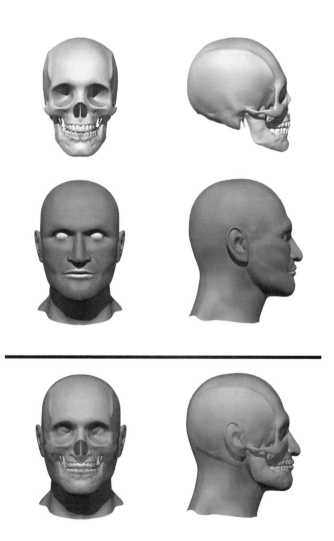

If there are any doubts as to the importance of the underlying structure and proportions of a skull when modeling a correct head, consider the fact that forensic anthropologists can reconstruct a model of a human from just the skull. The detail of their reconstruction is not limited to the head, but also includes facial features, the age, sex, stature, and even ancestry. All this information is derived by understanding the bone structure of the skull. For example, the sex of the subject can be determined by the shape of the cranial features listed here and shown in Figure 2.1.

A. Cranial mass
B. Supraorbital margin
C. Zygomatic muscle attachments
D. Mandible
E. Cranial mass depth
F. Superciliary arch
G. Canines

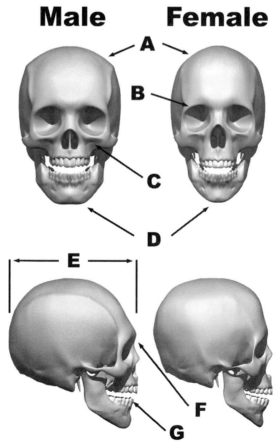

FIGURE 2.1   Determining sex through skull features.

CRANIAL COMPONENTS

The differences between the male and female skull are prominent enough to make identifying gender easier. Because of these differences, if you build all heads (male and female) the same way, your character won't look believable. In the following sections, each of the differences is discussed in more detail.

Cranial Mass

The male cranial mass is larger than that of the female and tends to be a bit blockier. The female head is more rounded and tapers at the top. When modeling, use a circle as a guide for building a male head, and an ellipse when building a female head.

Supraorbital Margin

The supraorbital margin is the upper area around the eye sockets. The supraorbital margin of a female skull is sharp on the underside, while the male's is rather round and dull. This along with the superciliary arch will affect the appearance of the eye sockets.

Zygomatic Muscle Attachments

The zygomatic muscle attachments make up the cheeks. The muscle attachments on the zygomatic bone are more pronounced on a male skull. Because of evolution, the male head is more muscular, which makes for a stronger looking jaw and fuller looking face.

Mandible

The mandible (or lower jaw) of a female is like a rounded "V," narrower at the chin, while the male mandible is squared.

Cranial Mass Depth

From a side perspective, the mass of the male and female shows a considerable difference. The male skull has a deeper cranial mass, with the depth being approximately equal to that of the entire height of the head. On a female head, the depth is about 83% of the height of the skull.

Superciliary Arch

The superciliary arch is the mass of bone above the eyes creating the eyebrow ridge. The superciliary arch on a male is large and pronounced. It protrudes from the forehead and overhangs the ocular cavity. In females, the superciliary arch is barely noticeable.

Canines

The canines are the longest and strongest of all the teeth, and contribute to the size and shape of the jaw. In males, the canines are significantly larger than in females.

HEAD CONSTRUCTION

As mentioned in the previous section, several differences between male and female skulls aid the forensic anthropologist or 3D animator in constructing a head. The structural differences between male and female skulls must be considered when constructing an appropriate head for a character.

The science of recreating a person's appearance from a skull is called *forensic craniofacial reconstruction*. Using fossil fragments, plaster, clay, and epoxy putty, the anthropologist creates a lifelike reconstruction of the head. The process begins by creating a plaster cast of the skull and placing depth markers in strategic locations, as seen in Figure 2.2.

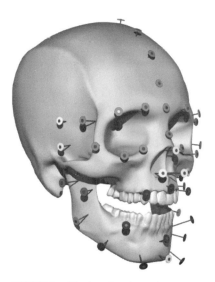

FIGURE 2.2   Placing depth markers.

A tissue thickness chart is used based on the race, gender, and size of the person (thin or obese). The depth markers are color coded or marked for tissue depth, and placed at key locations to ensure a consistent topology along the surface. The tissue depth is determined by several factors, although primarily, the shape of the skull's features is used to determine depth. We know that the skin is very thin over the bony ridges such as the supraorbital and infraorbital margins. It's also rather thin along the frontal bone. The shape of the mental protuberance gives clues as to how much of a chin the person had, while the size of the nasal bone suggests the size of the nose and the distinguishing bump on the middle of the nose. In addition to cranial evidence, the anthropologists use bone analysis to determine the age of the person, which also helps to identify an approximate tissue depth, as tissue depth changes with age. In younger children, tissue depth increases with age. With older adults, tissue depth varies greatly, and consequently there is no definitive standard for determining tissue depth precisely.

Once all the appropriate depth markers have been placed on the model, clay is added to the plaster cast skull as shown in Figure 2.3.

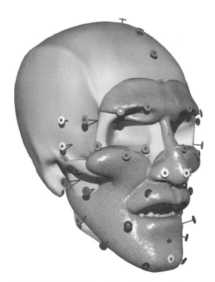

FIGURE 2.3   Adding clay to the plaster skull.

Clay is continually added, using the depth pins to direct the depth of the tissue until the head is completely covered in clay, like the one shown in Figure 2.4. Some features, such as lips and ears, require a little more artistic license, but are based on race and size of the skull.

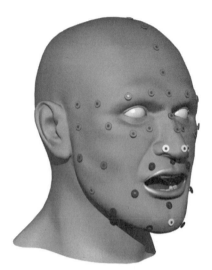

FIGURE 2.4 The reconstructed head.

Since the maturity of 3D technology, forensic anthropologists are starting to use 3D software for forensic reconstruction. They start by digitizing a clay cast of the skull and then place virtual depth indicators on the head model using the 3D software. The virtual depth indicators represent control points for splines to be wrapped around the skull.

While the work of a forensic anthropologist may seem like overkill for building a 3D head, the process is similar. Just like an illustrator, having a good knowledge base on the components that make up a skull will aid when building heads for any character you create.

Building a skull is a great way to start your 3D head models. The 3D skull can be used as a template for ensuring the proportions and features of the head are accurate. While a new skull isn't required for every head you build, having a standard male and female skull is a great starting point for building any 3D head. In Figure 2.5, the skulls and heads are shown separately, and then superimposed to show the correlation.

The skull was modeled first, and then the head was modeled over it, using the skull's shape and proportions. It can be very challenging to properly shape a 3D head without a template, and using a 3D skull is an excellent way to help ensure proportions and shape of the head. You can find low-resolution (10,000-point) male and female skulls in the Chapter 2 folder on the companion CD-ROM, appropriately named maleskull.dxf and femaleskull.dxf. Using these skulls as a template for shaping your head and placing details will greatly simplify your head construction. We typically start by building the basic head shape, then load the skull template in the background, and fine-tune the shape of the head as shown in Figure 2.6.

ON THE CD

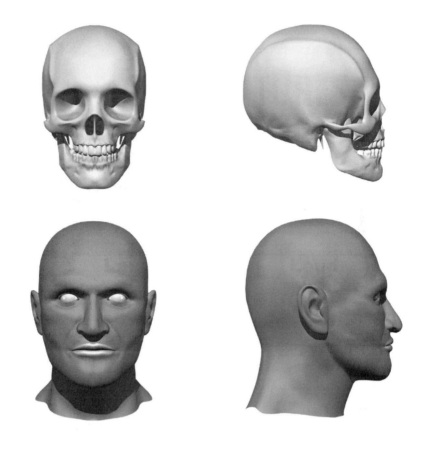

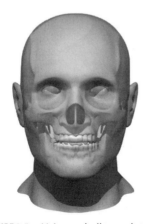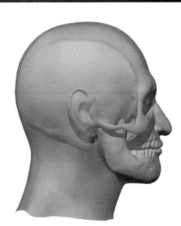

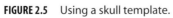

FIGURE 2.5   Using a skull template.

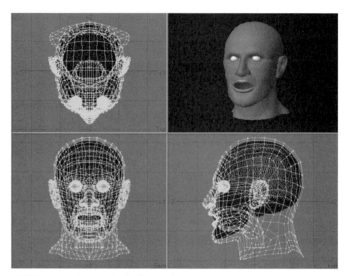

FIGURE 2.6   Using a 3D skull template.

Using a 3D skull template makes a significant difference in shaping the head. Without it, one could spend significantly more time trying to get the right shape. Even when creating fantasy creature heads, proportions are important.

Of course, not all heads are shaped the same, but using the template skulls provided is a great start. The next phase of head construction is determining facial feature proportions and placement.

EXTERNAL FACIAL FEATURES

Creating properly proportioned facial features is essential if you want your head to be convincing, even when creating fantasy and cartoon characters. There are eight major facial features to consider when creating your heads:

- Brow ridge
- Eyes
- Nose
- Cheekbones
- Mouth
- Chin
- Lower jaw
- Ear

In this section, each of these facial features and the method for determining its proper proportions and placement is discussed. The techniques outlined are simple and don't require much experience to apply, but the results are a 3D head that has proper proportions.

Proportional Units

To make a head proportional, relative units are used. In other words, when measuring the head, the typical height is three-and-one-half units, while the width is typically three units wide. Regardless of how big each unit is, the proportions are the same. Once you memorize all the proportions, building proportionately correct heads will become second nature.

The Brow Ridge

The center of the eyes is the vertical midpoint of any head. The brow ridge is above the midpoint by about one eyeball's height. A common technique for determining the width of the brow ridge (and other key facial components) is to use eye lengths. The head width along the brow ridge is five eye lengths wide as shown in Figure 2.7. The brow itself is four eye lengths wide, as shown in Figure 2.8.

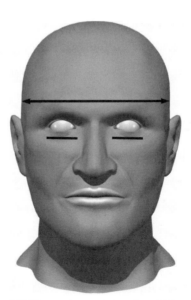

FIGURE 2.7 Determining the width of the head.

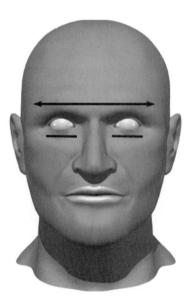

FIGURE 2.8   Determining the brow ridge size.

Another thing to note when creating your brow ridge is to dip the center of the brow where it lies over the glabella, just above the nasion. A common mistake with 3D head models is that a brow runs straight across the forehead, making the character look like a troglodyte.

The Eyes

One of the most complicated features on the face is the eyes. The eyelids, tear ducts, and skin surrounding the eyes require intricate detail to be modeled. Before starting any of the detail, placement of the components in the correct proportions is the priority.

The eye socket, or ocular cavity, extends halfway down the length of the nose, terminating at the top of the cheekbone (zygomatic bone). The eye itself is roughly one-and-a-quarter inches in diameter and nearly perfectly round, with the exception of the conjunctiva and cornea, which form the bulge in front of the iris. The shape of the eye mass is very important since it's the center of our focus when we view the face. Poorly modeled eyes are a common problem found in 3D human head models. They suffer from many issues, such as exposed upper eyelids as shown in Figure 2.9.

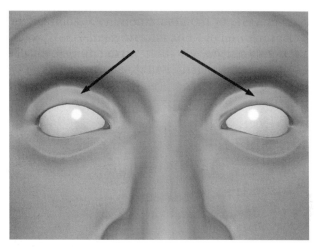

FIGURE 2.9   The exposed eyelids of incorrectly modeled eyes.

Notice how the eyelid is clearly visible. This is nearly impossible on a human head because the supraorbital margin hangs over the upper eye. It can happen in rare cases, but because it's uncommon, eyes modeled this way will not look correct. The proper formation of the upper eyelid has the tissue under the supraorbital margin covering the upper eyelid as seen in Figure 2.10.

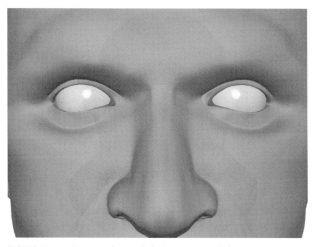

FIGURE 2.10   A properly modeled upper eyelid.

Another common problem in 3D human head models is floating eyelids, which can cast shadows on the eyeballs, as shown in Figure 2.11. In reality, the eyelids form a seal over the eyes, so proper 3D eyelids should lay flush against the eye.

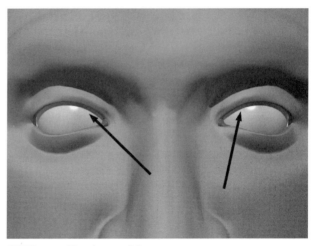

FIGURE 2.11   Floating eyelids.

Equally important to the detail of the eyes is the placement. A common mistake is having eyes either too close together or too far apart. Because we are accustomed to seeing several sets of eyes during the course of the day, incorrect placement of the eyes will detract from the modeled head. While it may not be readily apparent, there will be a subconscious feeling of something not being quite right when viewing the head. The center of the eye should be positioned about one third in of the entire head width. The inside corner of each eye is one eye width apart as shown in Figure 2.12.

In addition to poor eyelid shape and position, another commonly overlooked aspect is the shape of the eye opening. Many 3D models tend to have an oval eye opening, which is close, but subtle nuances in the shape of the eyelids make the eye more detailed and interesting. The eye opening is not a symmetrical oval, but rather oblique, somewhat almond shaped, caused by the eyelid wrapping around the round eyeball. The high point of the upper eyelid is close to the inside of the eye, while the low point of the lower eyelid is close to the outside of the eye, as shown in Figure 2.13.

You can determine the high and low points of the eye by measuring in about one third of an eye width from each end of the eye. Remember that the high point is toward the inside on the upper edge and toward the outside of the lower edge of the eye.

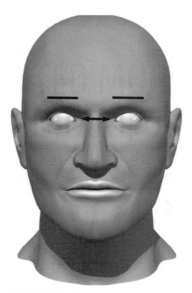

FIGURE 2.12   Proper eye placement.

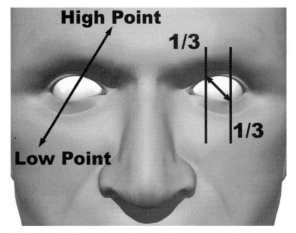

FIGURE 2.13   The proper shape of an eye opening.

Eyeballs and Irises

After creating the eye opening, we still need to create the eyes. The iris is the most prominent feature of the eye, and its placement is essential for proper facial expression. It appears to hang from the upper eyelid, hovering just above the lower eyelid, allowing a sliver of the eye white to be visible between the bottom of the iris and the lower eyelid as shown in Figure 2.14.

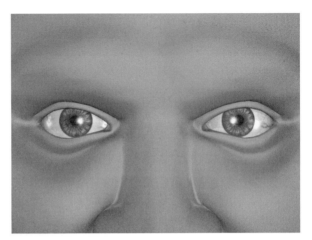

FIGURE 2.14   Proper placement of the iris.

The eyes change greatly depending on the expression of the character. For a static nonexpressive pose, the iris hangs from the upper eyelid. On heavier or older people, the eyelids tend to close around the iris more, covering both the top and bottom edge. Younger eyes tend to expose more of the iris, and there is a clear separation between the iris and the lower eyelid. The more the iris is covered, the more depressed the character will appear.

The Iris

The size of the iris can reflect the demeanor of the character you are creating, so be sure the size is measured properly. As a rule, the pupil is roughly one-half the width of the eye opening, as shown in Figure 2.15.

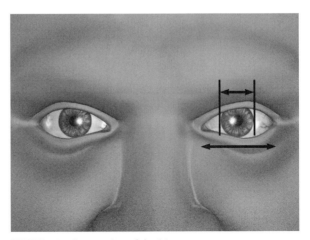

FIGURE 2.15   Proper size of the iris.

By now, you may realize that the eye is quite elaborate and requires a lot of detail to fit the type of character you are building. Spending the time to make the eyes correct for your character will be well worth the effort and make your character more believable.

The Nose

The nose divides the facial mass down the middle, and its length covers half the distance of the facial mass, as shown in Figure 2.16. The distance from the nasion to the tip of the nose is about the same as the distance from the tip of the nose to the bottom of the chin (mental protuberance). The base of the nose is the same width as the eye, as shown in Figure 2.17.

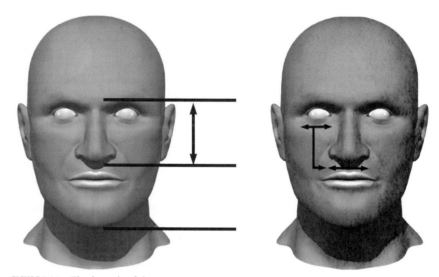

FIGURE 2.16   The length of the nose.   **FIGURE 2.17**   The base of the nose.

The nose is divided in the middle where the nasal bone terminates, thus creating the nasal hump (the bump on the bridge of the nose). A side view of the nose is shown in Figure 2.18, which illustrates the position of the nasal hump.

The last measurement for the nose is the bridge between the eyes. The distance between both eyes is one eye width across, as shown in Figure 2.19.

The nose, like the eyes, is simply a matter of common proportions. By using relative measurements and standard proportions, it becomes much less difficult to create a proportionate nose.

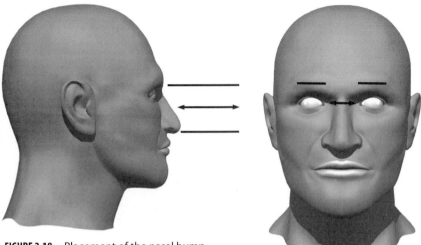

FIGURE 2.18 Placement of the nasal hump.

FIGURE 2.19 The width of the nose bridge.

The Cheekbone

The cheekbone is a vital part of the facial structure, and gives your head personality and character. Placement is crucial for proper facial animation, since the cheek muscles play a major role in facial expression. The baseline of the cheekbone lines up with the base of the nose as shown in Figure 2.20.

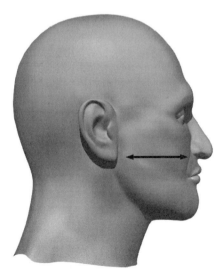

FIGURE 2.20 The baseline of the cheekbone.

A good source of reference for the cheekbone is to measure a diagonal from the nasion. The cheekbone starts at the top of the nasal bone and runs 30 degrees diagonally from the corner of the eye socket to the angle of the jaw as shown in Figure 2.21.

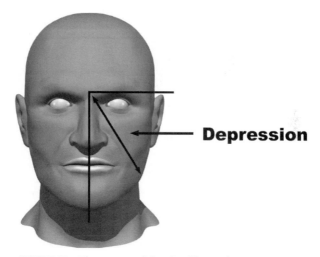

Depression

FIGURE 2.21   Placement of the cheekbone depression.

The depression of the cheekbone is along the midpoint of the diagonal line from the nasion. The last element of the cheekbone is the arch, or top, of the cheekbone. This starts at the infraorbital margin and lines up with the termination of the nasal bone, or midpoint of the nose, and ends roughly in the middle of the ear as shown in Figure 2.22.

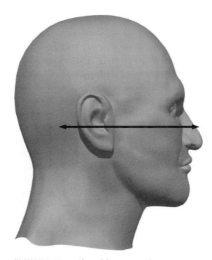

FIGURE 2.22   Cheekbone arch.

The Mouth

The mouth is one of the more complicated facial features because it has both an internal and external structure that is instrumental in facial animation. The entire mouth occupies two-thirds of the lower half of the face (the space from the tip of the nose to the chin), as shown in Figure 2.23.

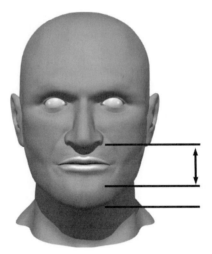

FIGURE 2.23 The mass of the mouth.

As a rule, the corners of the mouth typically extend horizontally to the center of the eyes, as shown in Figure 2.24. Often, the mouth is drawn too narrow because the mouth doesn't extend out far enough.

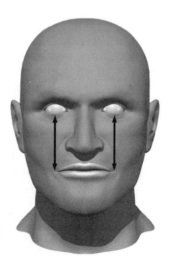

FIGURE 2.24 Aligning the corners of the mouth.

Vertically, the corners of the mouth are aligned with the angle of the lower jaw (from a side view), as shown in Figure 2.25. Measuring from the chin to the base of the nose, the corners of the mouth are about two thirds of the way up.

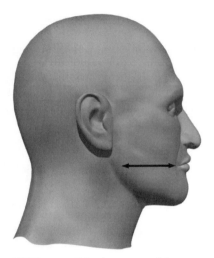

FIGURE 2.25   Side alignment of the jaw corner.

Viewing a head from the side, notice how the upper lip extends beyond the lower lip. The upper lip overhangs the lower lip slightly, due to the upper teeth overlapping the bottom teeth. The angle between the upper and lower lip is approximately a 7.5-degree angle, as shown in Figure 2.26. Failure to build a mouth and lips this way could lead to mouths that don't animate properly or begin to intersect with the upper teeth.

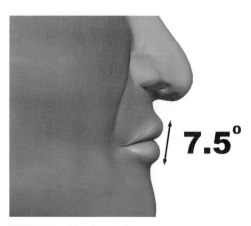

FIGURE 2.26   The lip angle.

The Mouth Interior

The interior of the mouth is significantly more complicated than the exterior; it's also one of the major problem areas seen in 3D human heads. One of the common problems is inflated cheek tissue as shown in Figure 2.27.

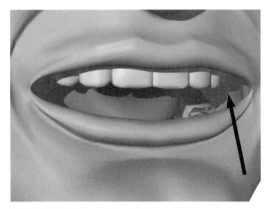

FIGURE 2.27   Inflated cheek tissue.

You can see how the cheek tissue is drawn away from the gums, making the mouth interior more like a balloon. In reality, the cheek tissue is drawn tightly against the gums, as shown in Figure 2.28.

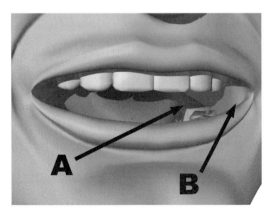

FIGURE 2.28   Proper cheek tissue placement.

In your own mouth, you should be able to feel the inside of your cheeks against your teeth. Be sure to extend the inside of the 3D model's cheeks inward as well. The tissue should also fold in a bit just after the corner of the mouth as indicated by B in Figure 2.28. This also helps to prevent the "barrel mouth" effect.

Another common mistake is to make the lips too parallel, where the contour of the gums is ignored, as shown in Figure 2.29.

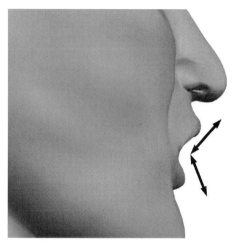

FIGURE 2.29   Parallel lips.

The lips should contour around the form of the gums, pulling the sides of the mouth back into the head as shown in Figure 2.30.

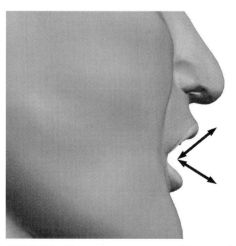

FIGURE 2.30   The proper curvature of the mouth.

Placement of the gums and teeth is also crucial. Two dental arches, the maxillary and the mandibular, form the substructure of the mouth. The maxillary arch holds the upper teeth, while the mandibular arch holds the lower teeth. The point where the teeth meet in the middle is directly behind the seam between the lips as shown in Figure 2.31.

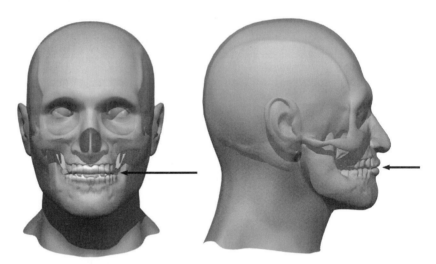

FIGURE 2.31   The placement of the teeth.

The gums are also pressed tightly up against the back of the lips, although they don't actually touch the lips, whereas the teeth are more inclined to touch the lips. One of the more challenging aspects of creating teeth for 3D characters is selecting the proper size. If you make them too big, the character will look goofy, and if they are too small, the character appears unrealistic. Sizing the teeth is relatively simple. The first measurement is the width of the dental structure. The sides of the teeth align with the center of the ocular cavity as shown in Figure 2.32.

Determining the size of the teeth can be complicated, but there is an easy reference for the front teeth, shown in Figure 2.33. In most cases, the back teeth and molars are barely visible, so you don't need to be quite as precise in their sizing.

The four teeth in the center of the upper jaw are equal to the width of the lower nose. The gaps between the upper and lower teeth in the center of the jaw are aligned, and the lower canines line up with the outer incisors of the upper jaw.

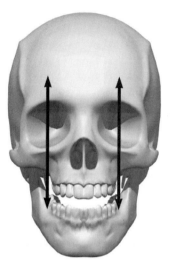

FIGURE 2.32 Sizing the width of the dental structure.

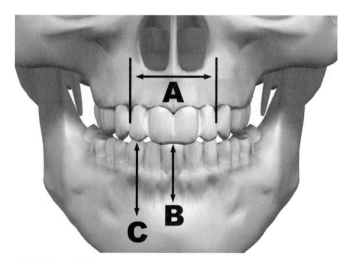

FIGURE 2.33 Sizing the teeth.

Average adults have 32 teeth by the time they are 20 years old, although the teeth in the front are the most relevant for facial animation. Directly behind the teeth is the tongue. The tongue is thicker than most people realize, and is quite fat, as shown in Figure 2.34.

The tongue is a very flexible muscle that stretches quite a bit during facial animation. If you want to properly animate the face, you'll need to create a thick tongue for those times when the mouth is open and the tongue is resting on the lower pallet, such as during a yawn.

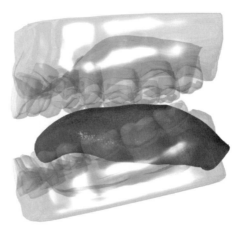

FIGURE 2.34   The proper thickness of the tongue.

Another measurement to consider is the width of the tongue. In its resting position, the tongue fills the lower gums, pressing up against the teeth as shown in Figure 2.35.

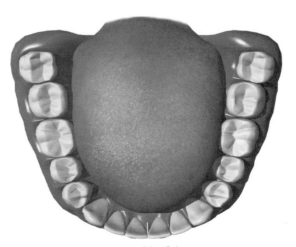

FIGURE 2.35   The proper width of the tongue.

The Chin

The chin comprises one-third of the mass below the nose. At its widest point, it aligns with the sides of the mouth and the center of the eyes, as shown in Figure 2.36.

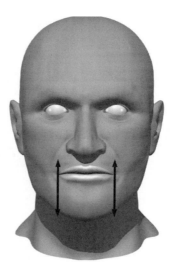

FIGURE 2.36   Proper chin width.

There is a lot of flexibility when modeling a chin. A character's chin is useful in conveying a sense of the character's personality. Use thin chins for weaker or spindly characters, and thicker chins for more masculine or menacing characters.

The Lower Jaw

The lower jaw defines the profile of the head. It's a very distinguishing element of the facial structure in that it also defines the character. The angle of the lower jaw aligns with the corner of the mouth, as shown in Figure 2.37.

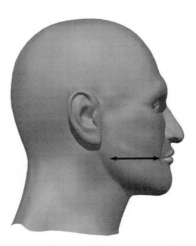

FIGURE 2.37   The angle of the lower jaw.

From the front view, the widest point of the jaw is aligned with the outside edge of the supraorbital margin, as seen in Figure 2.38.

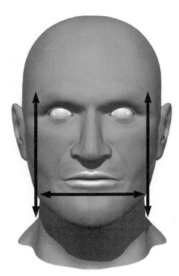

FIGURE 2.38 The width of the lower jaw.

The Ears

The vertical placement of the ear lies between the eyebrow and the base of the nose as shown in Figure 2.39.

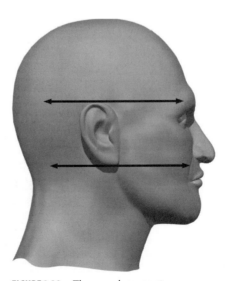

FIGURE 2.39 The ear placement.

The horizontal placement of the ear is roughly in the middle of the head (from a side view). Actually, the curved edge of the tragus is lined up with the vertical centerline of the head, as shown in Figure 2.40.

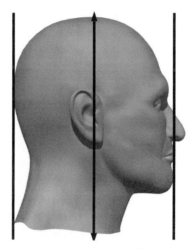

FIGURE 2.40   The horizontal placement of the ear.

One common mistake made in 3D heads is to place the ear along a vertical line on the head. In reality, the rear is rotated back 15 degrees, as shown in Figure 2.41.

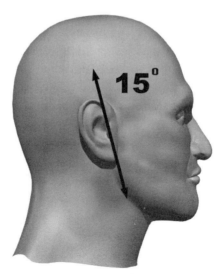

FIGURE 2.41   The angle of the ear.

The ear's angle is pretty much in alignment with the angle of the lower jaw; a line drawn along the length of where the ear attaches to the head would lead directly into the jawbone. The ear itself requires a bit of thought since it's a rather complicated shape. An easy way to determine the size of the actual ear features is demonstrated in Figure 2.42.

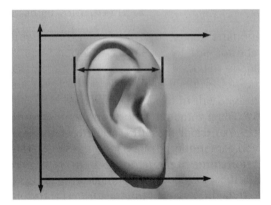

FIGURE 2.42   Sizing the ear details.

The width of the ear is half its height. The widest point of the ear is across the outer rim of the helix. The concha, or hole in the ear, is equal to one-third the height of the ear and is centered vertically as shown in Figure 2.43.

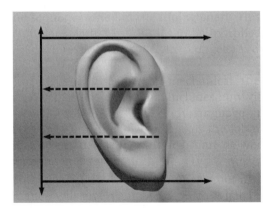

FIGURE 2.43   Placing the hole in the ear.

The earlobe is one-third the height of the ear, as shown in Figure 2.44.

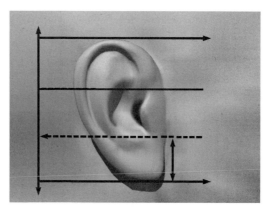

FIGURE 2.44   The earlobe size.

The width of the earlobe at its widest point is equal to half the width of the ear, as shown in Figure 2.45.

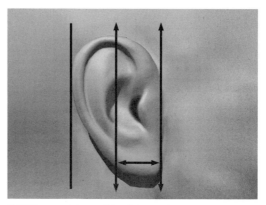

FIGURE 2.45   The width of the earlobe.

The last element of the ear is the antihelix, which is two-thirds the height of the ear and extends from the top of the earlobe to just under the helix as shown in Figure 2.46.

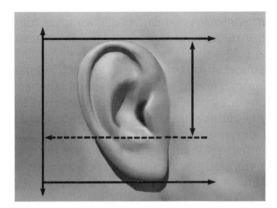

FIGURE 2.46   The antihelix size and placement.

CONCLUSION

The process of creating realistic human heads can be daunting at first, but after you've created a few, it quickly becomes second nature. For the most part, once you create a good neutral male and female model, you can modify them to fit the needs of other characters.

That being said, no two human heads are alike, so consider the dimensions shown in this chapter as guidelines or the foundation for the ideal head. Given the differences in head shapes and sizes, consider the character's build, personality, ethnicity, age, and weight prior to building the head. You will also want to consider what level of facial animation the character will have, as this could affect how components are built.

In the next chapter, you'll learn about the mechanisms behind facial expression—the facial muscles and the actions they perform.

3

FACIAL MUSCLES

Laughter   Smiling

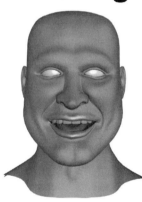

Facial expressions are created by using facial muscles. That's an easy concept to comprehend, but the difficulty is in understanding the facial muscles themselves. Once a thorough understanding of the facial muscles is achieved, one can animate a character much easier and with greater effect. For example, if you didn't understand the movement of the cheek muscles, you would not realize that they collect under the zygomatic bone when raised, rather than traveling over it.

While facial muscle anatomy is a complex topic, the movement of the facial muscles is essential when creating facial animation. The important thing to take away from this chapter is how muscle movement affects the facial tissue. If you understand the facial muscle, you'll find creating facial expressions a great deal easier.

The following sections explore the 11 major facial muscles that control facial expression.

The Facial Muscles

Eleven facial muscles are responsible for facial animation. There are actually more than 20, but most of them tend to be supporting muscle rather than instigating muscles. The facial muscles are divided into four muscle masses: the jaw muscles, mouth muscles, eye muscles, and brow/neck muscles. By dividing the muscles into these four groups, it will be easier to determine how they affect the facial movement.

The 11 major muscles are listed here, and Figure 3.1 identifies the location of the different facial muscles.

- A. **Masseter:** The clenching muscle
- B. **Levator labii superioris:** The sneering muscle
- C. **Zygomaticus major:** The smiling muscle
- D. **Triangularis:** The facial shrug muscle
- E. **Depressor labii inferioris:** The lower lip curl muscle
- F. **Mentalis:** The pouting muscle
- G. **Orbicularis oris:** The lip tightener muscle
- H. **Corrugator:** The frown muscle
- I. **Orbicularis oculi:** The squinting muscle
- J. **Frontalis:** The brow lifting muscle
- K. **Risorius/Platysma:** The corners of the mouth

ON THE CD

We'll look at each muscle and explore its involvement in facial expression and animation. Each of the muscles covered is featured in full color on the CD-ROM. Each plate features a skinless head on the top with the muscle indicated in a light color and with arrows. On the bottom are heads showing the external effect of the muscle's movement. On the left is

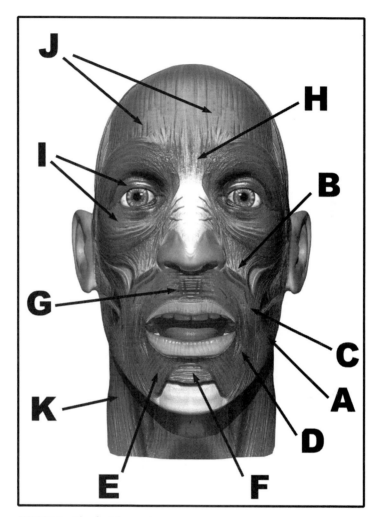

FIGURE 3.1   The facial muscles.

a neutral head with no muscle movement; on the right is the same head showing the result of muscle movement. The plates are referred to frequently throughout this chapter.

Jaw Muscles

The lower cranial muscles can be categorized into jaw muscles and mouth muscles. The jaw muscles control the jawbone, while the mouth muscles control the lips and chin.

The Masseter

The jaw muscles include one major muscle and several smaller supporting muscles. The main muscle is the masseter, which is used to clench the teeth and raise the jaw. The masseter is located at the base of the jaw as shown in Plate 1 in the Chapter 3 folder on the CD-ROM.

The masseter plays a major role in any movement where the lower jaw is dropped wide open. Some of the expressions created by the masseter muscle are fear and yawning, which are both shown in Figure 3.2. In both expressions, the masseter muscle is used to raise the jaw to the neutral position. To see the masseter muscle in motion, load the Masseter .mov movie file from the Chapter 3 folder on the companion CD-ROM.

ON THE CD

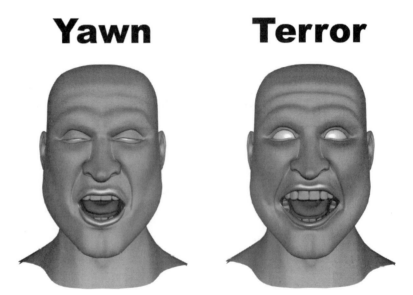

FIGURE 3.2   Expressions created with the masseter muscle.

Any time the mouth is clenching, chewing, or biting down, the masseter muscle is used. While the jaw contains the least number of muscles in any of the facial groups, the mouth contains the most.

Mouth Muscles

The mouth muscles consist of six groups to control the lips, mouth, and chin. This group contains the largest number of muscles and is used extensively during lip synching animation.

Levator Labii Superioris—For Sneering

ON THE CD

The levator labii superioris raises the upper lip beneath the nostrils, and is located around the upper and lower lips as shown in Plate 2 in the Chapter 3 folder on the CD-ROM. This muscle is one of the least-used mouth muscles, because very few expressions involve raising the upper lip under the nostrils. Of course, it plays a major role in creating the disgust and disdain facial expressions shown in Figure 3.3. In both expressions, the levator labii superioris muscle is used to raise the upper lip. To see the levator labii superioris muscle in motion, load the Levator.mov movie file from the Chapter 3 folder on the companion CD-ROM.

ON THE CD

Disgust   Disdain

FIGURE 3.3   Expressions created with the levator labii superioris muscle.

Zygomaticus Major—For Laughing

ON THE CD

The zygomaticus major muscle raises the mouth upward and outward. It's located around the upper and lower lips and attaches just before the ear as shown in Plate in the Chapter 3 folder on the CD-ROM.

This muscle is one of the more frequently used, particularly when animating a jovial character. It's used for any expression that requires the upper lip to be raised up and out, such as smiling and laughing, as shown in Figure 3.4.

Laughter Smiling

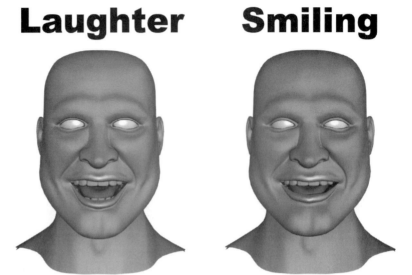

FIGURE 3.4 Expressions created with the zygomaticus muscle.

In both expressions, the zygomaticus major muscle is used to raise the upper lip, pulling it outward in the process. To see the zygomaticus major muscle in motion, load the Zygomaticus.mov movie file from the Chapter 3 folder on the companion CD-ROM.

ON THE CD

Triangularis Major—For Facial Shrugging

Located around the upper and lower lips, the triangularis muscle pulls the corner of the mouth downward. As shown in Plate 4 in the Chapter 3 folder on the CD-ROM, it attaches just before the ear and to the mandible.

ON THE CD

While this muscle is not used as frequently as others are, it is crucial for creating sadness or frowning, as shown in Figure 3.5.

In these expressions, the triangularis muscle is used to pull the corners of the mouth. To see the triangularis muscle in motion, load the Triangularis.mov movie file from the Chapter 3 folder on the companion CD-ROM.

The Depressor Labii Inferioris—For Lip Curling

The depressor labii inferioris muscle pulls the lower lip down and out. It's located around the upper and lower lips and attaches to the mandible as shown in Plate 5 in the Chapter 3 folder on the CD-ROM.

ON THE CD

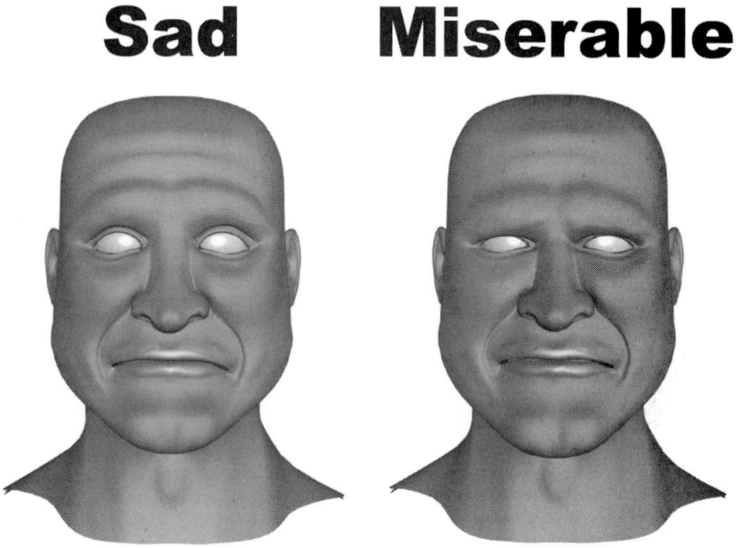

Sad   Miserable

FIGURE 3.5   Expressions created with the triangularis muscle.

Again, this muscle is not frequently used, but is crucial (along with the frontalis muscle) for creating expressions like surprise, shown in Figure 3.6.

Surprise

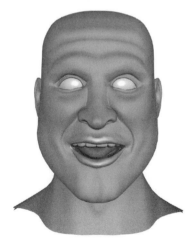

FIGURE 3.6   An expression created with the depressor labii inferioris muscle.

ON THE CD

To see the depressor labii inferioris muscle in use, load the Depressor .mov movie file from the Chapter 3 folder on the companion CD-ROM.

The Mentalis—For Pouting

ON THE CD

The mentalis muscle is located on either side under the lower lip, as shown in Plate 6 in the Chapter 3 folder on the CD-ROM. It raises and tightens the chin while pushing the lower lip upward and outward. This muscle is used to create expressions such as suppressed sadness and fear, shown in Figure 3.7.

Suppressed Sadness   **Afraid**

FIGURE 3.7   Expressions created with the mentalis muscle.

In these expressions, the mentalis muscle is used to push the lower lip upward and outward. Of course, as you can see in the "afraid" example, this doesn't always mean the mouth will be sealed tight. To see the mentalis muscle in action, load the Mentalis.mov movie file from the Chapter 3 folder on the companion CD-ROM.

ON THE CD

Orbicularis Oris—For Pursing Lips

The orbicularis oris is the last of the major muscles in the mouth muscle mass. It is located around the entire mouth like a ring that encompasses the mouth, as shown in Plate 7 in the Chapter 3 folder on the CD-ROM, and is used to narrow or compress the mouth or purse the lips.

This muscle is used to create expressions such as disdain and repulsion, as shown in Figure 3.8.

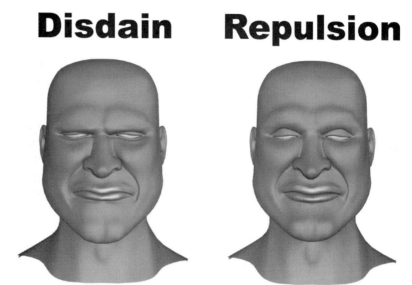

Disdain   Repulsion

FIGURE 3.8   Expressions created with the orbicularis oris muscle.

In these expressions, the orbicularis oris muscle is used to purse the lips. In both expressions, the orbicularis oris is used in conjunction with the levator labii superioris, which is used to lift the upper lip. You'll find that many muscles often work in conjunction to move the facial tissue. To see the orbicularis oris muscle in action, load the OrbicularisOris.mov movie file from the Chapter 3 folder on the companion CD-ROM.

ON THE CD

As you can see, the mouth requires a greater number of muscles, because it can take on a variety of distinct shapes. The mouth is the most expressive muscular element of the face. It's been said that the eyes are the most expressive, but eyes have fewer muscles, meaning they can't achieve as many variations as the mouth can. We'll get into this topic in more detail in Chapter 4, "Facial Features and Expression." For now, let's continue our exploration of the facial muscles around the eyes.

Eye Muscles

The Corrugator Muscle—For Frowning

ON THE CD

The corrugator muscle compresses the skin between the eyebrows, creating a frown. It's located directly between the eyes as shown in Plate 8 in the Chapter 3 folder on the CD-ROM. Normally, the corrugator muscle works with the depressor supercillii and the procerus, two smaller nearby muscles.

The corrugator muscle is used to create expressions such as intense concentration and disgust, as shown in Figure 3.9.

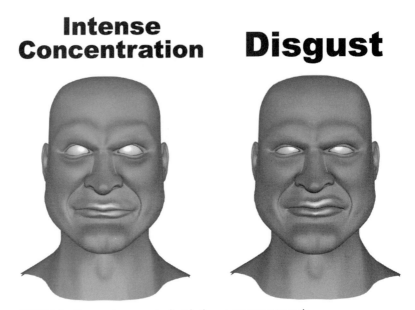

FIGURE 3.9   Expressions created with the corrrugator muscle.

In these expressions, the corrugator muscle is used to compress the skin between the eyebrows, making the character appear angered. To see the corrugator muscle in motion, load the Corrugator.mov movie file from the Chapter 3 folder on the companion CD-ROM.

ON THE CD

Oricularis Oculi—For Blinking and Squinting Eyes

The orbicularis oculi muscle closes the eyelids and compresses the eye opening, and is the only muscle that does so. It encircles the eye as shown in Plate 9 in the Chapter 3 folder on the CD-ROM.

ON THE CD

The orbicularis oculi muscle is used to close the eyes and make the character wink or squint. Common expressions using the orbicularis oculi muscle would be asleep or drowsy and tired, as shown in Figure 3.10.

In these expressions, the orbicularis oculi muscle is used to compress the eyelids and close them. This is probably the most relevant muscle in facial animation. It doesn't play a major role in expressions, but it does add that hint of realism by making the character blink occasionally. To

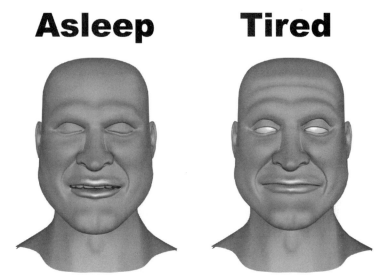

Asleep   **Tired**

FIGURE 3.10   Expressions created with the orbicularis oculi muscle.

ON THE CD

see the orbicularis oculi muscle in motion, load the OrbicularisOculi.mov movie file from the Chapter 3 folder on the companion CD-ROM.

Brow/Neck Muscles

The Frontalis—For Lifting the Brow

ON THE CD

The frontalis muscle draws the scalp down and up, wrinkling the forehead skin, and covers the forehead as shown in Plate 10 in the Chapter 3 folder on the CD-ROM.

The frontalis muscle is actually two distinct muscles, one on either side of the head, which makes it possible to move the eyebrows independently. The actor Jim Carey has incredible control of his frontalis muscles. The frontalis is one of the most frequently used facial muscles, and is a part of nearly every facial expression. Some common expressions that use the frontalis are fear and a charming smile, both of which are shown in Figure 3.11.

In these expressions, the frontalis muscle is used to pull the forehead skin upward, creating wrinkles. To see the frontalis muscle in motion, load the Frontalis.mov movie file from the Chapter 3 folder on the companion CD-ROM.

ON THE CD

The Risorius/Platysma—For Stretching the Lower Lip

The risorius/platysma muscle is a unique facial muscle because it's primarily a neck muscle, although it does draw the lower lip downward and outward. In effect, it controls the corners of the mouth. It covers the

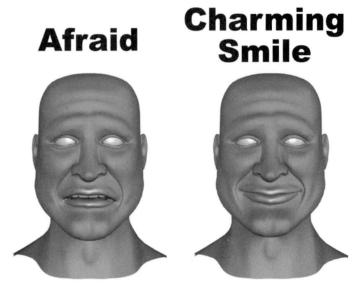

FIGURE 3.11 Expressions created with the frontalis muscle.

ON THE CD

neck, mandible, and parts of the mouth as shown in Plate 11 in the Chapter 3 folder on the CD-ROM.

The risorius/platysma is one of the most frequently used facial muscles, and is a part of nearly every facial expression. Some common expressions that use the risorius/platysma are terrified and crying, which are shown in Figure 3.12.

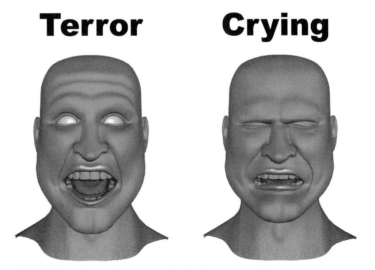

FIGURE 3.12 Expressions created with the risorius/platysma muscle.

As you can see, the lower lip has been pulled downward in both expressions. To see the risorius/platysma muscle in action, load the Platysma.mov movie file from the Chapter 3 folder on the companion CD-ROM.

SAMPLE EXPRESSION—CRYING

As you can see, several muscle groups play a major role in facial animation and expression. To get a better idea of just how many muscles are involved in creating a facial expression, the following section is a study of a crying expression. Figure 3.13 identifies the muscles used in this expression.

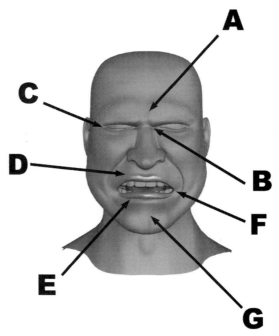

FIGURE 3.13   The muscles used in a crying expression.

As with most expressions, multiple muscle groups are used. For a typical crying expression, eight muscles or components need to be animated. Here are the muscles and what they do to make this emotion:

A. **Lowered brow:**   The corrugator muscle lowers the inner eyebrow.
B. **Furrowed nose:**   The procerus muscle assists in tightening the inner eye.
C. **Tightly closed eyes:**   The orbicularis oculi muscle tightly closes the eyes.

D. **Drawn upper lip:** The levator labii superioris pulls the upper lip upward.

E. **Curled lower lip:** The triangularis pulls the lower lip downward, curling it slightly.

F. **Stretched out mouth:** The risorius muscle pulls the corner of the mouth sideways.

G. **Crumpled chin:** The mantalis muscle tightens the chin, creating a bulge.

By identifying the muscles used in any emotion, you can animate the proper muscle groups to create an animation that conveys the proper emotion. In addition to facial muscles, there will also be corresponding body actions that help portray an emotion. One must always consider the body language and pose of the character when showing emotion, although that's outside the scope of this book.

CONCLUSION

Facial muscles drive our expressions and speech, and a thorough understanding of them is important for conveying the right emotion. You need to understand which muscles are used with each expression, and know the limits of their movement for that expression. Moving the wrong muscles or having them move incorrectly or too much for a particular expression will reduce the believability of an animated expression. The animations on the companion CD-ROM should give you a solid idea of how the facial muscles move and provide good reference material when creating animation targets.

ON THE CD

This completes Part I of this book. Now that cranial anatomy has been covered, Part II will delve more deeply into facial expression. Before moving to the next section, be sure you understand the musculature and bone structure of the head. As an exercise, look at your own face in a mirror while making different expressions. See if you can identify all the muscle groups of your own face.

EXPRESSIONS

4

FACIAL FEATURES AND EXPRESSIONS

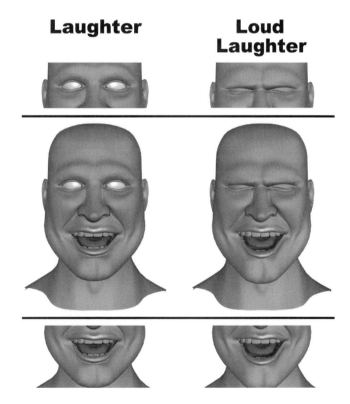

Laughter **Loud Laughter**

The first step in facial animation is to determine what the appropriate expression is going to be. Does the expression fit the pose? Do the expression and pose fit the mood of the character? Does the mood of the character fit the shot? These questions should be part of the story development, but in many cases, the nuances of an expression may be up to the animator. Either way, building your skills as an animator includes being able to determine appropriate expressions. Within the expression itself, subtle nuances can either add or detract from your expression.

Before working on a character's facial expression, determine the type of expression. Expressions can be categorized into three types: questions, answers, and statements. By categorizing expressions, it will be easier to determine if the expression is right for the action of the character. For example, if your character were puzzled, you would choose a question expression, not a statement or answer expression. Categorizing the expressions into general groups makes it easier to determine which expression *not* to use.

Let's look at each of the types of expressions and the role it plays in facial animation.

QUESTION EXPRESSIONS

Question expressions are typically those that show puzzlement, concern, or concentration, as if to say "Is it safe?" or "Huh, what's, going on here?" Figures 4.1 and 4.2 show examples of concern and concentration.

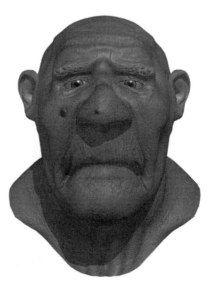

FIGURE 4.1   A concern question expression— worried.

FIGURE 4.2   A concentration question
expression—thinking or making a decision.

Notice how both expressions seem to be posing a question to the
viewer. They also cause the viewer to question what the character is thinking about. Another good example of a question expression would be a
charming smile, which poses the question, "Did I do something wrong?"
Figure 4.3 shows a charming or bashful smile.

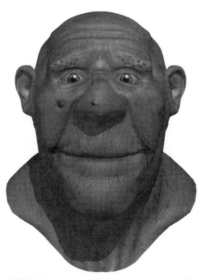

FIGURE 4.3   A bashful or charming smile.

Notice how the eyes are wide open, a common trait of a question expression. Raised eyebrows denote confusion. The eyes play a major role in creating question expressions. We'll be talking about the significance of the eyes in creating facial expressions later in this chapter.

Okay, so what defines a question expression? Well, if the expression doesn't denote a statement or answer to a question, then it's a question expression. For example, when you're confused, you may state that you're confused (e.g., "I don't understand"), but your expression is that of questioning, as if to say, "What are you talking about?"

When determining the expression group, it's important not to confuse what the character may be saying with what it is expressing with its face. While these may often go hand in hand, there are also times when nothing is explicitly stated. If a character is handed a small, gift-like box, the character may not say anything. Depending on the situation, the character may be surprised (unexpected gift), thrilled or excited (at a birthday celebration), or even annoyed (the box represents trouble or drudgery). The character may also say something completely different from what it is feeling, as in betrayal, overconfidence or even being deceitful. The facial expressions of your character typically portray its real feelings, regardless of what it is saying. One of the most exciting and challenging aspects of facial expression is to have your character say one thing and express another.

Common Question Expressions

Some common expressions are typically used as question expressions. The following list gives you a starting point for selecting an expression for your animation. Some common question expressions include:

- Concentration
- Confusion
- Worry
- Fear
- Smirk
- Devious smile

It's important to note that these expressions may not always be posed as question expressions. For example, a smirk or devious smile can also be an answer expression, depending on the situation and how it's used.

STATEMENT EXPRESSIONS

Statement expressions are the instigators, and are used to tell the viewer or another character in the animation how the character feels. They tend to be more of the emotional category rather than expressive, as with the question expressions. Common statement expressions include anger, misery, and joy. Notice in Figures 4.4 and 4.5, how Papagaio is telling you how he feels through the expression. The yawning expression in Figure 4.6 conveys more of the state of the character (tired or exhausted) as opposed to an emotion, such as anger.

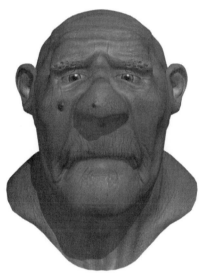

FIGURE 4.4   Statement expression—misery.

FIGURE 4.5   Statement expression—anger.

FIGURE 4.6   Statement expression—yawning.

The statement expressions are the feeling expressions and, like any other expression can betray the spoken word. As with all facial expressions, use the character's true emotional state to dictate the expression, not necessarily what is spoken. Some common statement expressions include:

- Rage, enthusiasm
- Sternness
- Shouting
- Misery, sadness, dazed
- Exertion
- Sleep, yawn, drowsiness
- Intensity, passion

Not all statement expressions are limited to feelings; shouting isn't a feeling, but it's a variation of rage or anger, which are both statement expressions.

ANSWER EXPRESSIONS

Answer expressions provide the viewer with a visual response to a question or action, although the question need not be audible. For example, wincing, laughing, and crying are answer expressions. Samplees of these are shown in Figures 4.7 and 4.8.

FIGURE 4.7   Laughter—an answer expression.

FIGURE 4.8   Repulsion—an answer expression.

Laughter, smiling, and grinning are common answer expressions. When someone tells a joke or something funny happens, your face answers with a laugh or involuntary smile. The answer expressions are facial responses to situational stimuli. Some additional answer expressions include:

- Crying
- Surprise
- Laughter
- A phony smile or laughter
- Terror, disgust
- Disdain, repulsion
- Smiling, facial shrug

Answer expressions often follow question expressions. For example, an expression of fear (question expression) could be followed by crying, surprise, or laughter (answer expression).

The three expression types are used as a basis for analyzing the appropriate expression for a character in any given situation. To truly understand which expression is to be used, animators study acting. By learning which actions and emotions evoke which expressions, you will create better animation. The focus of this chapter is to teach you the basics of recognizing the different facial expressions. Your animated facial expressions are successful if your audience can understand the mood you are trying to convey even without sound.

Consider the expressions in the following scenario. A child character is sitting on a park bench watching an ice cream vendor selling ice cream to other children. His expression is one of despair (statement expression), since he has no ice cream. With a glum look on his face, he rests his head on his fists, obviously unhappy. His eyes look to the sidewalk where he sees a dollar bill on the ground. The character's expression transforms to one of surprise (answer expression), and then excitement (statement expression). He picks up the dollar bill and uses it to buy an ice cream cone from the vendor. The camera shot is that of a close-up of the character's face, and he has an obvious expression of joy (answer expression). With an expression of anticipation (question expression), he sits back down on the bench to enjoy his prize, but as he licks the ice cream, it falls off the cone and to the ground, causing a look of disbelief (answer expression), and then anger (statement expression).

In the preceding scenario, the facial expressions play an important role in communicating to the audience the mood of the character. Using appropriate and varied expressions are what make the animation more believable, and more exciting. Typically, a character's expression changes regularly, which makes for a more interesting story. By constantly analyzing the scenario, the story, the character's reactions and intentions, and what the story is trying to tell the audience, you can more effectively communicate that concept.

In animation or even filmmaking, it's just as important to keep the audience in mind as it is to consider the character's emotional state. The audience will only know what's going on through the actions and emotions of the characters. For that same reason, characters in film and animation usually have exaggerated gestures and posturing—it simply makes the character's actions more telling, and more exciting. It also may give the audience some subtle clues about subplot or anticipation for an upcoming event. Understanding expressions and gestures enables you to add more life to your characters. To do so, you'll need to know and understand the individual elements of the face and the role each plays in facial animation. In the following section, you'll learn and understand what defines an expression.

EXPRESSION FEATURES

Each portion of the face plays a role in facial expression, and some play greater roles than others do. Although there are many muscles in the face, three major features of the face define facial expression: the brow, the eyes, and the mouth. These features are broken into two categories, the foundation (the mouth) and the modifiers (the eyes and brows). The role of the foundation is to set the expression, while the modifiers enhance the foundation to achieve a wide variety of expressions.

The Foundation—The Mouth

As stated earlier, the mouth is the foundation of every expression. The shape of the mouth in any pose is consistent in its meaning, while the eyes can portray many meanings in the same pose.

Notice in Figure 4.9 that the face has been separated into three segments, the whole face, the eyes above, and the mouth below. Look at the eyes at the top and you'll see that by themselves, they don't reveal the emotion of the character. In fact, the eyes are identical on both characters, while the facial expressions are different. Now, look at the mouths on the bottom and you'll see they are different. This is an example of how the mouth is the foundation of the expression. In an expression, closed eyes could mean a number of things, such as sleep or straining. Because there are many possible expressions with eyes closed, the eyes are incapable of reflecting the true facial expression alone.

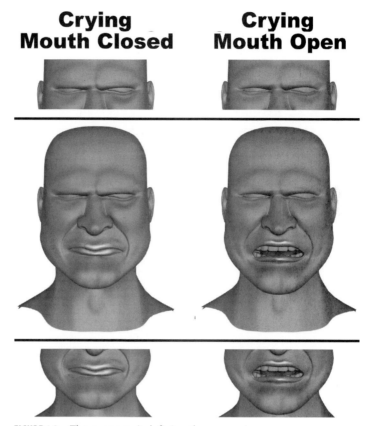

FIGURE 4.9   The eyes aren't defining the expression.

While the expression in the previous example was similar (crying with mouth open or closed), Figure 4.10 shows how crying and laughter compared this way will also show similar eyes with very different mouth poses.

In both of the previous examples, notice how the eyes remained the same but the mouth changed dramatically. That's because the eyes do not define the expression. The mouth, however, was different in both examples because the mouth is the foundation and defines the emotion. For example, a smiling mouth always depicts happiness, and a drooped mouth depicts sadness.

To reinforce the point, compare the mouth and eyes of Figure 4.11. In both poses, the mouth is happy. As a result, the eyes are modifying that happiness pose to be either jovial laughter or loud laughter. Either way, the base emotion is the same—happiness. Because it is capable of a

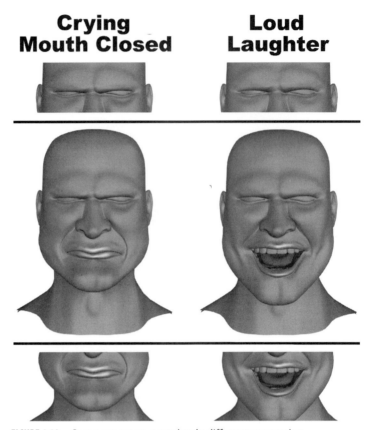

Crying Mouth Closed   **Loud Laughter**

FIGURE 4.10   Same eye pose, completely different expression.

wider range of movement than any other feature on the face, the mouth can assume more poses and therefore becomes the foundation of all expressions. The eyes, however, build on that foundation and can greatly alter the degree of the emotion portrayed by the mouth.

The Eyes as a Modifier

The eyes are the lead modifier and take a close second to the mouth in defining a facial expression. They are used to reinforce, and in many cases modify, the facial expression created by the mouth. In the previous example, the mouths were the same, depicting laughter, but the eyes were different. The open eyes softened the laughter, while the closed eyes amplified the effect. The eyes have a tremendous impact on the expression.

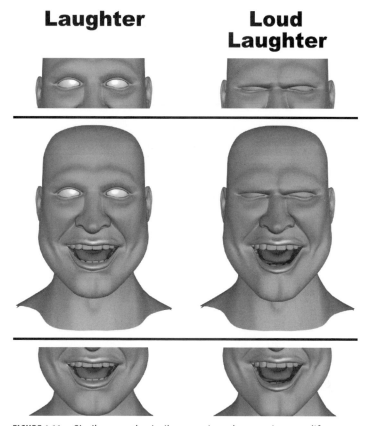

FIGURE 4.11   Similar mouth, similar emotion; the eyes just modify.

In addition to the size of the ocular gap (how wide the eyes are opened) affecting the expression, the focus of the eyes also defines the expression. In fact, the direction the eyes are looking has the greatest impact on defining the expression.

In Figure 4.12, notice the eyes of the Papagaio character. In this pose, Papagaio has an expression of exhaustion. Notice how the eyes are hanging under the eyelids and looking forward. Hanging the eyeballs on the eyelids (figuratively speaking) reinforces the tired expression.

Figure 4.13 shows the same expression except that the eyes are focused downward. With the eyes looking downward, the character has a more depressed or defeated look. While exhaustion and defeat are similar in muscle pose, they evoke different emotions. By merely changing the rotation of the eyes, we have created two different expressions.

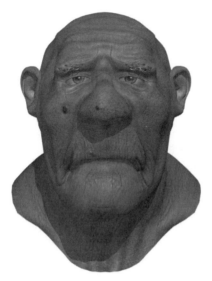

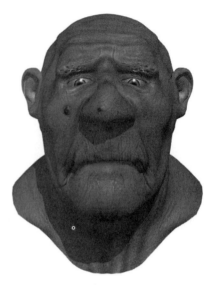

FIGURE 4.12   An exhausted expression—eyeballs hang from eyelids.

FIGURE 4.13   A defeated expression—eyes focus downward.

As you can see, while not the foundation of either of the previous expression examples, the eyes are an essential element of facial expression. In fact, they are paramount when it comes to creating expressions for characters that aren't human. In the Disney film *Bambi*, the animators had a very difficult time animating expression because of Bambi's mouth; it simply wasn't built to talk or to create the foundation for human emotions. As a result, the animators had to rely more on the eyes and had to make the eyes more expressive.

To get an idea of how important the eyes are in creating creature expressions, look at Figure 4.14.

Here we have the Munch character from the Komodo Empire film *Dwellers*. This pose has Munch feeling rather stern. His mouth is clenched, and he's looking right at us, defiantly.

In Figure 4.15, we have a similar pose, but this time the eyes are focused away from the camera. This is Munch's pouting pose, yet the only significant difference is the eye rotation.

In Figure 4.16, Munch is in the same pose, but the eyes have been rotated upward, giving him a mischievous expression. As with all three examples, the eyes are the significant factor in creating facial expressions for creatures. By putting the emphasis on where the eyes are looking, you can give your expression dramatic impact, with little or no change to the other facial features.

FIGURE 4.15   A pouting Munch.

FIGURE 4.14   A stern Munch.

FIGURE 4.16   A mischievous Munch.

The Brows as a Modifier

As with the eyes, the brows have a tremendous impact on the facial expression, and are modifiers to an expression, not the foundation. Notice in Figure 4.17 how little impact the brows have in defining the two very different expressions.

While these poses are distinctly different, they both have identical brows. This illustrates that the brow doesn't define the expression but merely enhances it.

The brow works in conjunction with the eyes to create variations of the expression defined by the mouth. What's wonderful about the brow is that it can create numerous, subtle variations that add diversity to expressions and can completely change the emphasis.

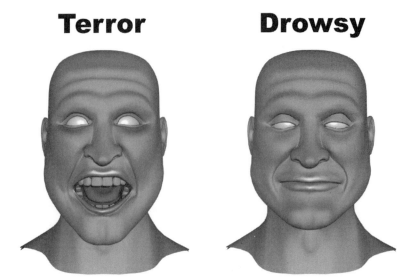

FIGURE 4.17   The minimal impact of the brows.

In Figures 4.18 and 4.19, the facial expressions are somewhat similar. In the yawning pose, the brows are lowered over the eyes and are relatively parallel. In the angry expression, the brows are turned upward in the middle, giving the pose a look of irritation or annoyance. This subtle detail transforms the character's expression from a potential yawn into one of anger.

FIGURE 4.18   A yawning expression.   **FIGURE 4.19**   An angry expression.

ANIMATING FACIAL EXPRESSIONS

Understanding facial muscles and how they act in each expression is one thing; animating facial features is something else. While the most challenging aspect of character animation, it is arguably one of the most rewarding. Seeing your character acting and expressing emotion based on your efforts can be quite rewarding.

Animating facial expressions require an analysis of the character's personality, its mood, and the action in that shot. Consider the personality of Knuckles, another character from the *Dweller* film. Knuckles is a gruff brute and typically carries a stern expression. His facial features and personality give the impression that he is always angry, as seen in Figure 4.20.

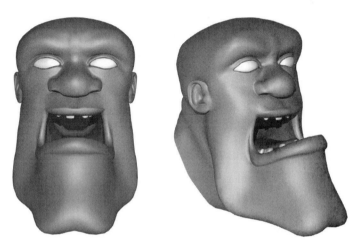

FIGURE 4.20   The perpetually irritable Knuckles.

Knuckles' large chin, heavy brow, missing teeth, and small ears combine to make him an intimidating character. Even when creating expressions of joy, one needs to overcome the physical characteristics for a character's head.

Appendix C, "Typical Cartoon Expression Weighted Morph Targets," features Knuckles in 40 common expressions. You'll see that he tends to look irritated in nearly every pose, which is a matter of character design. Intimidating characters are built with physical features that make them intimidating, just as cute and cuddly creatures have softer features. What makes for great animation (and great story telling) is turning an ugly, intimidating ogre character like Shrek™ (from the movie of the same name from DreamWorks) into a character the audience loves and embraces. When creating facial expressions for a character, consider the personality of the character, as it will both define and potentially limit the flexibility of your character's visible emotions.

Of course, even grumpy characters are not relegated to looking mean or angry in every expression. The Papagaio character is a grumpy old man, but he is also capable of very pleasant and endearing expressions. In Figure 4.21, his demeanor is more inviting with that enormous smile and those soft eyes. He's normally a grumpy character, but with the proper attention to expression detail, he can become soft and lovable.

FIGURE 4.21   An inviting demeanor.

Giving characters a wide range of emotion requires an understanding of facial expressions and how to control them to transform a character's disposition. While it's not always easy, the reward is a character that is more fully developed, and animation that is much more believable and interesting.

ON THE CD

The Papagaio.mov animation in the Chapter 4 folder on the companion CD-ROM features Papagaio making several facial expressions that cover a wide range of emotions. Although a character doesn't typically go through all emotions in 30 seconds, this sample animation illustrates the transitioning effect the face has on each expression.

The Rules of Facial Animation

As with any discipline, there are three basic rules to follow for success. Use these rules as guidelines until you understand the concepts of facial animation, and then experiment by bending them to expand your own animation capabilities.

- Keep the head moving.
- Move the eyes.
- Move the mouth.

Keep the Head Moving

One common mistake made in character animation is keeping the head still. In reality, the head moves quite a bit. It's not always dramatic movement, but there is plenty of subtle movement. Incorporating this movement into your animations will add a tremendous amount of depth to the character, making it more believable and more interesting.

Move the Eyes

Steady eyes are boring and show a lack of life. Eyes have a tendency to continually search for something interesting to focus on. The eye movement doesn't need to be dramatic, but frequent, subtle movement will keep the eyes looking real. Depending on the type of thinker the character is, the eyes will move up, down, or side to side.

There are three modes of thinking and storing information—visually, audibly, and kinesthetically. Different personalities use different modes, some using more than one. A visual thinker stores information as pictures, as in a photographic memory. An audible type thinker stores information with words, recalling memories in words, as well. Typically, audible type thinkers are heavy readers. A kinesthetic thinker stores information emotionally—feeling everything, which consequently makes information retrieval challenging. Decide which method suits your character and use that when the character is talking or thinking. Some studies suggest that people may use all three modes at different times, thereby validating the use of all three eye movement types as appropriate.

When thinking and searching our brains for information, our eyes move based on our type. A visual thinker will look up when recalling information. An audible thinker's eyes will move from side to side (or just one side), and a kinesthetic will look down, as if looking toward the heart. These visual patterns are a necessary part of facial animation. By matching the thinker type to the personality of your character, you will introduce subtle nuances that will add dimension to your animation.

For real life examples, study those around you and notice how their eyes move when they are thinking or talking. In addition, study the eyes in classic animated features, such as *The Incredibles*, *Toy Story I & II*, and *A Bug's Life*, all from Pixar. In DreamWorks' *Shrek 2* are some great shots of Puss In Boots that feature an intense use of eyes for facial expression.

In each example, real or animated, notice how the eyes spend some time searching, then focus on the viewer, then go back to searching, and so on. This is more realistic, and makes the shot (and the character) more interesting. You'll also notice that the head will lead the eyes when he turns his head. There is a common misconception that the eyes lead the head. While the eyes may pick up on items in their peripheral vision, the head initiates the move before the eyes lock onto the target.

Move the Mouth

This rule applies to when the character isn't speaking. Obviously, the mouth will move when speaking, but there is also movement when the character isn't speaking. Subtle mouth movements are natural in humans, particularly when they think. They will quite often bite the inside of their cheeks, move their tongues, lick their lips, roll their lips inward, or even bite their lips, literally. While they may be nervous habits, they all add to the character's personality and again, make the animation more believable.

Swallowing is another mouth movement that is often overlooked. Having a character swallow due to fear or excitement is an obvious mouth (and throat) movement. Adding subtle versions of this also adds to the depth of your facial animation.

CONCLUSION

Although there are only three simple rules to apply in facial animation, the breadth of what's implied covers a large range of emotion. What's important to remember about facial expressions is that there are many subtleties to every expression. As with any art form, implementing those subtleties will add much more depth to your work, and in turn make your animation a more rewarding experience for your audience.

After giving your character more dimension through facial expressions, it's time to give him a voice. In the next section, you'll learn about lip synching and how it applies to facial animation.

ANIMATION

SPEECH/LIP SYNCH

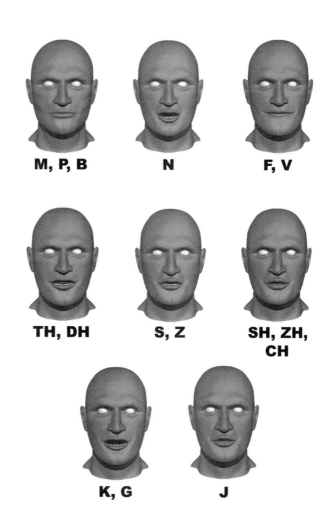

M, P, B   N   F, V

TH, DH   S, Z   SH, ZH, CH

K, G   J

In this chapter, we concentrate on matching a character's facial movement to recorded dialogue. The process involves a few steps:

1. Model the facial expression for each phoneme.
2. Translate the recorded dialogue to a timing chart of phonemes.
3. Animate the facial expressions from one phoneme to the next, in synch with the recorded voice over track.

Our first step is to build a library of facial variations that depict the basic mouth shapes necessary for each of the sounds (phonemes) in speech. Since each sound or phoneme is created by shaping the mouth in a particular way, a limited number of facial expressions are needed to create all the sounds of a particular language. In the English language, there are 40 audible phonemes (more on phonemes later), yet only 16 visual phonemes. That means only 16 different facial expressions need to be modeled to animate speech. Once all the phonemes have been modeled for your character, they are used for targets in animation through different means, most commonly morphing.

The second step is to translate the recorded dialogue track to a timing chart of phonemes that is synchronized to the recorded speech. The timing chart will indicate the time, phoneme, and corresponding facial expressions that, when run in sequence, will create the illusion of the character speaking.

The third step is to animate the pre-built facial expressions. There are several methods for this, although the most common is using morph targets, a process discussed in more detail in Chapter 6, "Weighted Morphing Animation."

Finally, the facial shapes that were built in the first step are arranged according to the sequence listed in the timing chart. This can be done by supplying the software with a list of files to be morphed, or by building the phonemes and expressions with weighted targets, as discussed in more detail in Chapter 6.

Although the steps may seem a bit mechanical, there is art in how your character delivers its dialogue. That includes how visually expressive the character's facial expressions and body language are. Lip synching is only part of the act. And that's what makes the job of the director so important—being able to decide that the actors are delivering the dialogue in the appropriate manner for the scene.

PHONEMES AND LIP SYNCHING

The first step in the lip-synch process is to understand the foundation of speech—phonemes. A phoneme is the smallest sound component of a spoken language. In phonetic speech, combining phonemes, rather than the actual letters in the word, creates words. For example, in the word "foot," the "oo" sound would be represented by the "UH" phoneme. The phonetic spelling of the word would be "F-UH-T."

When synching animation to speech, the facial expression of the character is synched to the recorded dialogue. When the phonemes are spoken, the mouth changes shape to form the phonemes that are heard, not specifically the words that are spoken. There are 41 phonemes in the American English language, which are listed in Table 5.1.

TABLE 5.1   American English Phonemes

ARTICULATION	PHONEME	EXAMPLE	VISUAL PHONEME	ARTICULATION	PHONEME	EXAMPLE	VISUAL PHONEME
Vowels	IY	B**ea**t	1	Nasals	M	**M**aim	9
	IH	B**i**t	2		N	**N**one	10
	EY	B**a**y	2		AN	Ba**ng**	2
	EH	B**e**t	2	Fricatives	F	**F**luff	1
	AE	B**a**t	2		V	**V**alve	11
	AA	H**o**t	3		TH	**Th**in	1
	AO	B**ou**ght	3		DH	**Th**en	1
	OW	B**oa**t	4		S	**S**ass	1
	UH	F**oo**t	5		Z	**Z**oo	13
	UW	B**oo**t	4		SH	**Sh**oe	1
	AH	B**u**t	2		ZH	Mea**s**ure	14
	ER	B**i**rd	5		H	**H**ow	2
	AX	Ab**ou**t	4	Plosive (Stops)	P	**P**op	9
Diphthongs	AY	B**uy**	2		B	**B**ib	9
	OY	B**oy**	4		T	**T**op	7
	AW	H**ow**	2		D	**D**id	7
	YU	B**eau**ty	4		K	**K**ick	15
Glides	Y	**Y**ou	6		G	**G**ig	15
	W	**W**ow	4	Affricatives	CH	**Ch**urch	14
Liquids	L	**L**ull	7		J	**J**udge	16
	R	**R**oar	8				

The phonemes don't mimic the printed word, but when spoken, they sound identical. What determines a phoneme? A unit of speech is considered a phoneme if replacing it in a word results in a change of meaning.

For example, "pin" becomes "bin" when we replace the "p"; therefore, the "p" is a phoneme. Other examples include the "Ch" in "Chat" or the "o" in "Cot."

The phonemes in Table 5.1 apply only to American English. When it comes to international phonemes, things get very complicated. Because there is a lack of correspondence between letters and sounds, a symbolic system was created that better represents sounds—the International Phonetic Alphabet (IPA). The IPA assigns a set of symbols to phonemes. Some symbols are not available on an ordinary typewriter, so the IPA has been converted to English letters. The IPA is basically the same as the English phonemes, except that the YU phoneme (as in beauty) has been dropped. You can find the IAP phonemes in Table 5.2.

TABLE 5.2   International Phonetic Alphabet (IPA)

ARTICULATION	IPA CODE	EXAMPLE	ARTICULATION	IPA CODE	EXAMPLE
Vowels	EY	G**a**te	Fricatives	F	**F**ault
	EH	G**e**t		V	**V**ault
	AE	F**a**t		TH	E**th**er
	AA	**Fa**ther		DH	Ei**th**er
	AO	L**a**wn		S	**S**ue
	OW	L**oa**n		Z	**Z**oo
	UH	F**u**ll		SH	Lea**sh**
	UW	F**oo**l		ZH	Lei**s**ure
	AH	B**u**t		HH	**H**ow
	ER	M**ur**der		WH	**Wh**ere
	AX	Ab**ou**t	Plosives	P	**P**ack
Diphthongs	AY	Hi**d**e		B	**B**ack
	OY	T**oy**		T	**T**ime
	AW	H**ow**		D	**D**ime
Glides	Y	**Y**oung		K	**C**oat
	W	**W**ear		G	**G**oat
Liquids	L	**L**augh	Affricatives	CH	**Ch**urn
	R	**R**ate		J	**J**ar
Nasals	M	Su**m**			
	N	Su**n**			
	NG	Su**ng**			

VISUAL PHONEMES

Visual phonemes are the mouth positions that represent the sounds in speech, and are the building blocks for lip-synch animation. As mentioned earlier, lip-synch animation starts with the modeling of the facial poses for each of the phonemes. While simple lip-synch animation can be achieved with 9 visual phonemes, there are actually 16 distinct visual phonemes, illustrated in Figures 5.1 and 5.2.

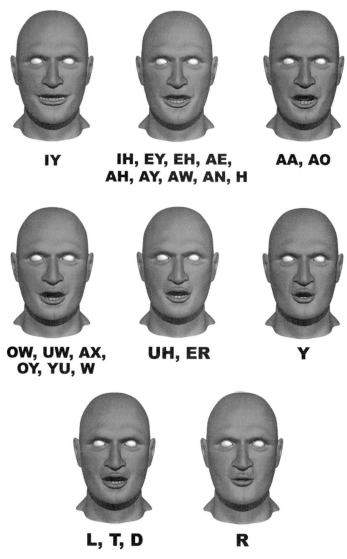

IY   IH, EY, EH, AE,   AA, AO
            AH, AY, AW, AN, H

OW, UW, AX,   UH, ER   Y
OY, YU, W

L, T, D   R

FIGURE 5.1   Visual phonemes.

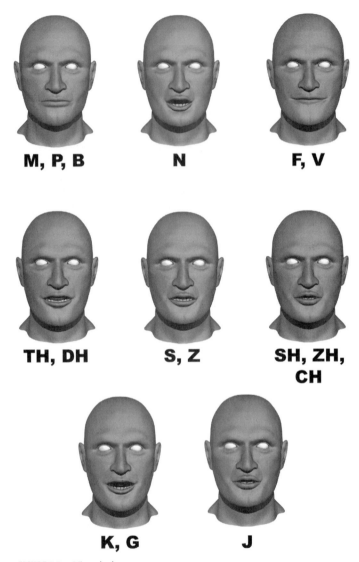

FIGURE 5.2 Visual phonemes.

Under each visual phoneme are the audible phonemes associated with that mouth expression. Although some look identical, there are subtle differences, such as the position of the tongue. To see the tongue positions more clearly, refer to Appendix B, "Typical Visual Phonemes," which features larger images of each phoneme and illustrates the actual tongue position for each.

The tongue may seem an insignificant element in lip synch, but it's important with close-up shots and especially in understanding how the mouth creates each phoneme. In most cases, the tongue isn't animated in any detail, but understanding its position will add to the realism of lip-synched animation. If the lip synch doesn't have to be realistic, a shorter list of phonemes can be used. The short list of phonemes, comprised of 10 general phonemes, instead of 16, is shown in Figure 5.3.

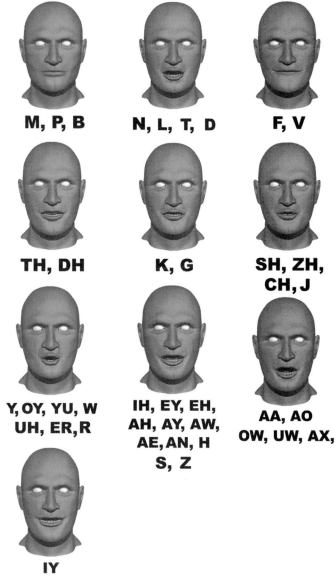

FIGURE 5.3   The visual phoneme short list.

In the short list, several of the visual phonemes with similar exterior appearances have been combined. By using the general phonemes, tongue movement will not be as accurate, but that isn't always important, particularly if the shot isn't a close-up. Using only 10 phonemes will help expedite the animation process for times when budget and time do not permit the more extensive phoneme list. By understanding phonemes, an animator can decide when it's appropriate to substitute the short list of phonemes without a noticeable loss in lip-synch animation quality. To better understand each of the phonemes, one must understand their classifications.

PHONEME CLASSIFICATION

The classification of a phoneme plays a vital role in lip-synch animation. When trying to synch animation to dialogue, one needs to fully understand the duration and inflection of the phonemes to make an informed decision as to which phoneme to use and when. Classifying the phonemes makes this task easier.

There are generally eight classifications of phonemes, which break the phonemes down into logical groups, making them easier to understand and apply. For example, in Table 5.1, one classification is the column labeled "Articulation." Understanding the classification of phonemes greatly increases an animator's ability to lip synch animation.

POINT OF ARTICULATION

Phonemes are classified based on several characteristics, one of which is the point of articulation. The point of articulation is the place in the mouth (on the palate) where the air stream is obstructed by the tongue. In speech, after the air has left the larynx, it passes into the vocal tract. The constriction of airflow determines whether the phoneme is a vowel or consonant. If the air, once out of the glottis, is allowed to pass freely through the resonators, the sound is a vowel. If the air, once out of the glottis, is obstructed in one or more places, either partially or totally, the sound is a consonant. These obstructions can occur in a number of places known as the articulators, several of which are indicated here:

- Lips (labial)
- Teeth (dental)
- Hard palate (palatal)
- Soft palate (velar)
- Back of throat (uvula/glottis)

The point of articulation is essential to creating truly realistic dialogue. The 16 phonemes are based on the different points of articulation. While the facial expression may be the same on the exterior, the tongue is positioned differently to create each unique sound. For this reason, when shooting close-ups of your characters, it's strongly recommended that you use the long list of visual phonemes.

MANNER OF ARTICULATION

Equally as important as the *point* of articulation is the *manner* of articulation. Since manner of articulation is based on the type of obstruction, it relates only to consonants. Speak the words "line," "dine," and "nine." The only audible difference between the three is the first consonant. However, pay close attention to the position of your tongue when you speak each word. Each position is distinctly different, especially between "line" and "nine." This is referred to as consonant constriction.

Consonant Constriction

Four types of consonant constriction often occur in English:

- Fricative
- Plosive
- Affricative
- Nasal

Fricative

A fricative is the type of consonant that is formed by forcing air through a narrow gap, creating a hissing sound. Typically, air is forced between the tongue and the point of articulation for the particular sound. Say the "f" in fun, the "v" in victor, and the "z" in zoo. You should be able to feel the air turbulence created by the sounds. The fricative sounds are "F," "V," "TH," "DH," "S," "Z," "SH," "ZH," and "H."

Fricative consonants are held for a longer duration than any other consonant, and the sound continues as long as air passes through the mouth. For example, say the word "shoe." Notice how the "sh" sound last longer than the rest of the word. The same applies for the "h" in help and "z" in zoo. When creating the timing sheet for lip-synch animation, mark the fricative phonemes so a longer frame count can be given to those sounds during the animation.

Plosives—Drop Consonants

Plosives involve the same restriction of the speech canal as fricatives, but are fueled by a burst of air, rather than a steady stream. As a result, a resonant sound is produced at the point of articulation. Fricatives develop from tense articulations, while plosives develop when articulation is loose. When the articulation is loose, a spirant occurs. During a plosive phoneme, the speech organs are substantially less tense during the articulation of a spirant. For example, try to slowly say "p." You should feel the buildup of air that bursts into the "p" sound when you open your lips. Of course, you cannot prolong a spirant because it's fueled by a burst of air. The plosives in the English language are "P," "B," "T," "D," "K," and "G."

Plosives are commonly referred to as "drop consonants" in lip-synch animation. These sounds are uttered quickly and abruptly, meaning they are quite often passed over by the visual phonemes. Due to the short time span for plosives, the next visual phoneme needs to be animated before the plosive phoneme can be expressed. It's important to realize that not all consonants need to be reflected with visual phonemes, particularly if they are plosive.

Affricative

An affricative is a plosive immediately followed by a fricative in the same place of articulation. To clarify, say the word "jump." The "J" is an affricative created by combining a plosive "D" immediately followed by a fricative "Z." There are two affricatives in the English language: "CH" and "J."

Affricative phonemes are strong sounds; therefore, be sure to use a visual phoneme each time they occur. The affricatives can cause the entire jaw to move, and dropping these phonemes will definitely be noticeable when lip synching animation.

Nasal

A nasal consonant is a consonant in which air escapes only through the nose. For nasal sounds, the soft palate is lowered to allow air to pass by it. At the same time, a closure is made in the oral cavity to stop air from escaping through the mouth. The three nasal sounds in the English language are "M," "N," and "AN."

VOICING

Phonemes are either voiced or voiceless. Voiced phonemes produce a more prominent visual phoneme than a voiceless phoneme will. A sound is described as voiceless when the vocal cords do not vibrate during its articulation, such as in a whisper. If the vocal cords vibrate, the sound is called voiced, as in normal speech. All vowels are voiced sounds.

The vocal cords are folds of muscle located at the level of the glottis (the space between the vocal cords). The vocal cords vibrate when they are closed to obstruct the airflow through the glottis. They vibrate under the pressure of the air being forced through them by the lungs. Technically, only consonants are classified as voiced or voiceless, as all vowels are voiced.

The easiest example of a voiceless phoneme is to whisper. During a whisper, the glottis is wide open, meaning all the sounds produced are voiceless. However, if the vocal cords are very close together, the air will blow them apart as it forces its way through, making the cords vibrate, producing a voiced sound. To feel the distinction between voiced and voiceless, place your finger and thumb lightly on your throat. Then say "FFFFF" to yourself. Now say "ZZZZ." Notice the vocal chord vibrating during the "ZZZZ" sound, but there was no vibration during the "FFFF" sound.

It is also possible to hear the vibration. Instead of putting your fingers on your throat, put your index fingers in your ears and repeat the sounds. You should hear a low buzzing sound when you articulate "ZZZZ," but almost nothing for the "FFFF."

The important thing to remember about voicing is that the voice phonemes are more likely to be represented visually. Because vowels are always voiced phonemes, they are accentuated with visual phonemes. As a result, vowels should always be animated during lip-synch animation.

PHONEME VOWELS

Vowels differ from consonants in that there is no noticeable obstruction in the vocal tract during their production. When a vowel is spoken, the vocal tract is wide open and the vocal chords are vibrating. When saying "AAAA," "EEEE," "IIII," "OOOO," or "UUUU" aloud, you should be able to feel the vibration. Vowels are determined by changes in position of the lips, tongue, and palate. While the tongue changes position to make each of the vowels, it never actually obstructs the airflow.

Changes in tongue position can be very slight and difficult to detect. There are several variations and types of sounds. For example, vowels can be unitary or glide into one another to form diphthongs.

UNITARY SOUNDS

A unitary sound is a single syllable sound with no change in articulator position. The unitary vowel phonemes are "IY," "EY," "EH," "AI," "AA," "AO," "OW," "UH," "UW," "AH," and "AX."

DIPHTHONG

A diphthong is a gliding, single-syllable vowel sound that starts at or near one articulator position and moves to or toward the position of another, such as the "eau" in the word "beauty." Diphthongs are often referred to as semivowels and are relatively slow transitions. They are those sounds that consist of a movement or glide from one vowel to another. The first part of a diphthong is always longer and stronger than the second part; as the sound glides into the second part of the diphthong, the loudness of the sound decreases. In the word "beauty," the "eau" is a "YU" diphthong and takes up more audio time than all the other sounds of that word combined. One of the most frequent errors made by people doing lip-synch animation is to use unitary vowels instead of diphthongs, which tends to make the animation choppy, particularly since a diphthong is slower than a unitary vowel. When lip synching animation, the diphthong phonemes require a higher frame count to prevent the animation from appearing choppy. For example, dropping the "YU" in "beauty" would leave you with "BTY," which sounds like "Betty." The English language diphthong phonemes include "AY," "OY," "AW," and "YU."

GLIDE

Glides are a subclass of diphthongs and are even slower in their transition. As such, glides require even more time when lip synching a glide phoneme. For example, the "Y" in "You" is a glide that lasts much longer than the "OU." The English language glide phonemes include "Y" and "W."

LIQUIDS

Liquids are another subclass of diphthongs and tend to be more like a rolling or trilling sound. The liquid phonemes are "L" and "R." A liquid phoneme is pronounced rather quickly and requires fewer frames to animate than a glide does. If a liquid phoneme is dropped or not animated properly, the entire meaning of the word is lost. For example, in the word "lots," if the liquid phoneme "L" weren't animated, the visual phonemes for the rest of the word, "ots," would not translate well.

The subtleties of phonemes can become extensive. Once you have a basic understanding of the phoneme and the sound types, lip synching becomes easier. In the next section, you'll learn a few simple rules that will aid in producing consistently higher quality animation.

Record the Dialogue First

While it may seem obvious, some animators will begin animating before the voiceover track has been recorded. There are two reasons to record the dialogue before animating:

Easier to match expressions: It's far easier to match a character's facial expressions to the dialogue than it is to find voice talent that can accurately dub an existing animation. Additionally, animation studios will videotape the voiceover talent while recording so facial expressions can be matched even closer.

Easier to match inflections: The recorded voiceover track will help you determine where the keyframes and inflections occur in the track. By using sound editing software with visual sound representation, the stronger points of the sound can be easily determined by identifying the high points in the sound graph.

Animate Phonemes Based on Their Articulation

The articulation of a phoneme determines how much emphasis the visual phoneme will receive, and the duration. Table 5.1 can be used for visual phoneme reference, and for articulation.

Vowels—Unitary Vowels

Strong vowels are the vowels that are also the strongest sound within that word (e.g., the "EA" in "beat," the "O" in "hot"). Unitary vowels should not be missed when lip synching and should be emphasized with the visual phonemes. When animating unitary vowels, give the visual phoneme the strongest morph target value possible to accentuate that sound.

Consonants

The consonants are described by four different types: nasals, fricatives, plosives, and affricatives. Each consonant should be identified during lip synching to ensure the mouth movement accurately matches the type of sound. The four consonant types are described in more detail here.

Nasal Consonants

The nasal phonemes are held for a longer period than most consonants, since they involve passing air through the sinuses. A nasal phoneme starts slow and ends on a high note. For example, in the word "mother," the "M" is started softly and slowly, and then builds in tempo and volume until a sharp "M" sound is uttered. When animating nasal phonemes, morph them gradually, to not lead the sound.

Fricative Consonants

Fricative consonants can go either way, as far as animating the visual phoneme. In some cases, they need to be accentuated, while in others they are hardly noticeable. In the word "evolve," for example, the first "v" needs to be accentuated, while the second "v" is barely perceivable. Say "evolve" aloud while looking in a mirror to see how different each "v" phoneme is.

Plosives

Plosives are the stop consonants, so they are never emphasized in lip-synch animation, unless they are at the start of a word. For example, in the word "talk," the "T" and "K" are both plosives, meaning they are abrupt. Since "K" falls after the diphthong "AW," which tends to be slow and drawn out, it should be dropped to prevent the mouth from popping open and closing too rapidly. As a rule, you should drop plosives at the end of a word but never at the beginning.

Affricatives

Affrictive phonemes should never be dropped. They are the strong accent of the word, and feature two phonemes combined. Sounds such as the "J" sound in "jump" or "soldier" and the "CH" sound in "cello" or "church" are very noticeable visual phonemes. Removing these visual phonemes from animation will leave a large gap in the mouth movement. They are also long phonemes, so provide more time for them.

By learning to identify the articulation of the phonemes in the voiceover and marking them on the timing chart, lip synching will become much easier and more accurate. Create a timing chart of each of the 16 visual phonemes in the recorded track as a guide. With the timing charts of the visual phonemes and the entire track, synching up the animation to the voiceover track will be much easier.

Never Animate Behind Synch

There are occasions when lip synch will look better if it is actually one or two frames ahead of the dialogue, but never when the facial expression is after the dialogue. In reality, the mouth can be positioned for a sound prior to making that sound, but the sound will never happen before the mouth is positioned. For example, you can form your mouth into an "o" shape and then say "oh," but you can't say "oh" before you shape your mouth. It is best to start by animating exactly on synch. Then, if necessary, you can always move parts of the animation forward a frame and see if it works better.

Don't Exaggerate

This is another important rule that is often overlooked. Study your own mouth while talking; the actual range of movement is fairly limited. Unless your subject is supposed to be a zany cartoon-type character, overly pronounced poses will look forced and unnatural. It is far better to underplay it than overdo it. You'll find that the mouth doesn't open very much at all during speech, so you don't want your visual phonemes to be exaggerated.

Keep a Mirror on Your Desk

When it comes to lip synching animation, having a mirror handy is a requirement. To animate visual phonemes, it's always best to have a good source of reference. For reference, speak the dialogue aloud and watch yourself in the mirror while talking.

Animate Phonetically

Many consonants, and occasionally vowels, are actually pronounced in the transition between the preceding and following sounds. As a result, the full pose for that sound never occurs. Since consonants are often held for only one frame, there can be a major change in mouth position before and after the consonant. In these cases, it's best to drop the consonant pose or intermediate pose.

As an example, some dialects in any language tend to abbreviate their speech. Depending on local dialect, syllables are often slurred or deleted entirely. Let the character's personality and the voice pronunciation dictate the visual phonemes. The key to good lip synching is to animate phonetically, not verbally. For instance, in Kansas, where Darris Dobbs was raised, the phrase "That was a good rain we had the other night" would often be pronounced in casual conversation as something like "'ad'z uh gud rain wee'ad thuther nite." In some cases, consonants and entire syllables can be eliminated.

You will find similarly abbreviated speech patterns in other areas, particularly in the South and Southwest. In the New England area, speech is more clipped and precise, but vowels are often held longer than usual. The important thing is to pay attention to the dialogue and the dialect. Listen for the sounds, not the words. When lip synching, animate the sounds, not the words. Create a phonetic dialogue sheet, identify the visual phonemes, and then animate those. Try to hear the dialogue not as words, but as sounds.

Remember, the goal is to make the movements of the mouth appear natural and lifelike. Concentrate on smooth transitions between each pose. If you need to skip a consonant to maintain the tempo and avoid contorting the mouth, it will be far better than forcing the mouth into unnatural poses or losing the rhythm of the dialogue.

THE LIP-SYNCH PROCESS

The first step before animation can commence is to build variations on your original character model that correspond to the basic phonemes. This is where you put the knowledge you gained in the first part of this book to work. It's imperative that you properly model the phonemes, taking into consideration the muscle movements, or you'll end up with a very awkward animation, no matter how well you synch the dialogue. Basically, if the phoneme poses are incorrect, the lip synch can never be right.

To make the process of developing the phoneme morph target easier, you'll find charts in Appendices B and D that illustrate the visual phonemes for both humans and cartoon characters. In addition to the visual reference of the appendices, you'll also find image templates of each phoneme in the PhonemeTemplates folder on the companion CD-ROM.

ON THE CD

You are provided with a front and side image of each phoneme to be used as a background template for creating your character's phonemes. While your heads will likely not match the ones in the images, they should be close enough to help you determine the shape of each visual phoneme expression. Use these as a guide until your experience increases and you become intimately familiar with all the phonemes.

Once the visual phonemes have been built, the lip synching is just a matter of timing. Using the phoneme chart in Table 5.1, translate the dialogue into a phonetic script. Add to that the visual phonemes and match the timing to the voice track—it's that simple.

THE STEPS TO ANIMATING LIP SYNCH

To get started, use a simple short sound byte. Once you understand the process, it's just a matter of staying on track. The steps of lip-synch animation are listed here. A detailed description of each step follows.

1. Record the dialogue—use video if possible as additional reference for facial expressions.
2. Transcribe the dialogue to phonetic speech on a timing chart.

3. Identify the visual phonemes on the timing chart.
4. Set the keyframes.
5. Add Articulation—transitional poses.

For the purpose of illustration, these examples use a piece of dialogue from the living Toon character Knuckles, which was created for the Komodo Empire film *Dwellers*. Knuckles' exaggerated features and slurred speech make for an interesting example.

Step 1: Record the Dialogue

When recording the dialogue, use a video camera with a straight-on head shot of the voiceover talent if possible. If possible, use multiple cameras (one on either side, and one straight on) to record both sides of the face or to capture facial expressions that may occur with the head turned away from a straight-on camera. Using a video camera adds another excellent source of reference material against which to check your character's visual phonemes.

Step 2: Transcribe Dialogue to Phonetic Speech

After recording the dialogue, the next step in lip synch is to transcribe the speech to phonetic reference. In the sample phrase, "That was a good rain we had the other night," the phonetic translation sounded more like "'ad'z uh gud rain wee'ad thuther nite." If the dialogue were animated based on the words in the sentence, versus what is heard, the visual phonemes wouldn't match the spoken dialogue.

ON THE CD

Let's see how this is accomplished with a piece of dialogue from Knuckles. In the Chapter 5 folder on the companion CD-ROM, you'll find an audio file named Knuckles.wav. Take this opportunity to load the file and play it a few times.

Notice how Knuckles tends to slur his speech, skipping the majority of the consonants. Converting the actual dialogue to a phonetic translation results in what is shown in Figure 5.4.

Notice how the phonetic translation doesn't necessarily match the actual words. This is an important element, since we need to assign phonemes to the actual sounds we hear, not the words we understand the sounds to mean. You can see how Knuckles has slurred the words "shouldn't ought to" into a single word "shudnada." If we were to transcribe the words "shouldn't ought to" into phonemes, it wouldn't match the actual dialogue as you can see in Figure 5.5.

Comparing the actual sounds to the intended speech, you can see there certainly are some major differences. In fact, everything after "sh uh d n" is completely different. If we were to use the text phoneme translation, we would end up with something reminiscent of those classic

Text: **You shouldn't ought to talk to me like that.**

Phonetic: Ya   shudnada   tak tuh me like   dat

FIGURE 5.4   A phonetic translation of Knuckles' dialogue.

Dialog:	**shouldn't**	**ought**	**to**
Phoneme:	SH UH D N T	AA T	T UW

Dialog:	**shudnada**
Phoneme:	SH UH D N AA D AH

FIGURE 5.5   A comparison of the written and phonemic phonemes.

Kung-Fu theater movies where the lip synch was completely off. In any lip-synching project, it's imperative to phonetically translate the text before you actually start assigning the phonemes.

Transcribing the sounds phonetically is best done in an audio program. Any decent audio program will have a visual graph of the sound wave and a timeline or counter depicting the time code for any specific moment in time. This takes the guesswork out of timing, since you can simply identify the start and end times of each sound within the software. Software that can display SMTPE time code is preferable for the most accurate timing. In addition, be sure you can set the frame rate to match the animation output frame rate. Figure 5.6 shows what you should end up with when the knuckles.wav file has been transcribed phonetically.

Dialog:	**Ya**	**shu**	**dn**	**ada**	**tak**	**tuh**	**me**
Phoneme:	Y AH	SH UH	D N	AA D AH	T AA K	T AH	M IY

Dialog:	**like**	**dat**
Phoneme:	L AY K	D AE T

FIGURE 5.6   The phoneme breakdown.

Figure 5.7 depicts a visual representation of a portion of the sound file. As you listen repeatedly to small portions of sound, you will come to recognize them in the visual representation, which in turn will assist you in pinning down a phoneme's location. The high points in the file represent words, and the low points the space between words. For example, the sound burst at "A" is the word "should," at "B" the word "talk," and at "C" the word "that."

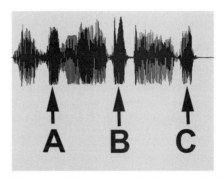

FIGURE 5.7 The Knuckles visual wave analysis.

Step 3: Identify the Visual Phonemes

Once the speech has been transcribed to phonetic speech in step 2, the visual phonemes can be identified much easier. Along with the transcribed timing sheet and listening to the recorded dialogue in a sound editing program, identify all the visual phonemes for the spoken dialogue. This begins by looking at the phonetic translation, and the audio sound wave display.

On closer inspection of the sound wave display, you'll see that distinct phonemes stand out in the wave file. For example, the high peaks indicated in Figure 5.8 are plosives, or stop consonants.

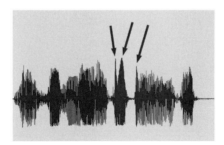

FIGURE 5.8 Plosive peaks.

The first arrow points to the "t" in "talk," the second to the "k" in "talk," and the third to the "t" in "to." Plosives always will be the highest peaks in your wave file, since they are a burst of air. This is an important distinction when selecting your visual phonemes, because you'll want to give priority to the strongest sounds in the dialogue.

Other phonemes that will register as high peaks in a wave file are vowels because they are voiced. The airflow isn't obscured by the articulation so they tend to be louder. Figure 5.9 shows some distinct vowels in the Knuckles wave file.

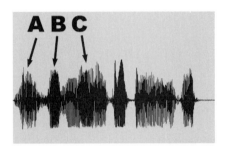

FIGURE 5.9   Vowel peaks. A, the "AH" in Ya; B, the "UH" in shu; C, the "AA" in ada.

All three of these are single syllable unitary vowels, meaning they are hit hard in dialogue; therefore, they need to be represented clearly with the visual phonemes. One distinction to make with Knuckles is that he slurs his vowels. In normal speech, the vowels are accentuated hard and abruptly, unless they are diphthongs. This is another reason why we must start by analyzing the speech pattern of the dialogue so we are prepared to compensate for accents and speech impediments.

The visual representation of phonemes in the wave file is very helpful since it gives us a visual means for identifying the location of phonemes. By scrubbing smaller intervals around the peaks, we can extrapolate the precise location of each phoneme that goes into building up the phrase.

Once the dialogue track has been broken down into its component phonemes, they should to be entered into a chart along with the exact times at which they occurred. The chart should show the phonetic translation, the actual phoneme, and the time when the phoneme occurs. Figure 5.10 shows the timing chart for Knuckles' dialogue.

As you can see, in addition to the phoneme and the frame, the timing chart also has the visual phoneme target listed. Once you have identified a phoneme, you enter the designation for the visual phoneme target to be used. In Appendix B, you will find a list of realistic human visual phonemes, and Appendix D contains a list of 10 visual phonemes built for a human-like cartoon character. The cartoon visual phonemes were used for Knuckles' timing chart.

When you do the breakdown for the first time, be sure to enter the time for every phoneme. While it's likely you will be dropping plosives, you still want to add them in the initial pass in case they play a role in the visual lip synch. Dropped plosive phonemes can easily be deleted later.

PHONEME	Target	Frame		PHONEME	Target	Frame
Y	7	2		L	2	53
AH	8	6		AY	8	57
				K	5	61
SH	6	10				
UH	7	15		D	2	62
D	2	19		AE	8	63
N	2	20		T	2	66
AA	9	25				
D	2	30				
AH	8	32				
T	2	37				
AA	9	38				
K	5	42				
T	2	45				
AH	8	46				
M	1	48				
IY	10	50				

FIGURE 5.10   The complete timing chart.

Step 4: Setting the Keyframes

Timing charts make setting keyframes for lip synch a trivial process. Once the dialogue has been translated into visual phonemes and the frames identified for each, all that needs to be done is to morph the visual phonemes from one pose to another at the appropriate time in the animation.

When setting up the morphing, initially use the model poses for each of the visual phonemes at the time listed on the timing chart. This sets up the rough animation from one visual phoneme to the next.

There are two types of morphing, straight and weighted. Straight morphing simply morphs the object in a linear progression from one object to another. The morphing can be any value from 0 to 100%, and in many cases can even exceed 100%. The only issue is that you are limited to a single morph object so you can't introduce subtleties into your animation like the occasional blinking eye without having to build hundreds of morph targets.

Weighted morphing allows you to blend multiple objects in a single morph. This is very useful when adding facial expressions and emotions to your lip-synch animation. You can add subtle eye blinks and complete changes in the character's personality through facial expressions. Of course, this greatly complicates the animation process, but the result is well worth the effort. We'll be taking a close look at animating facial expression with dialogue in Chapter 6, "Weighted Morphing Animation." For now, we'll focus on straight morphing.

ON THE CD
The Knuckles animation came out to be 70 frames in length at 30 frames per second. Load and view the Knuckles1.mov movie file from the Chapter 5 folder on the companion CD-ROM to see the resulting animation.

Step 5: Adding Articulation—Transitional Poses

Don't be discouraged if your facial animations aren't perfect. Lip synching is an art, not an exact science, and as such, there's plenty of room for interpretation. For the most part, this means that the transition between each pose will need to be manipulated. In some cases, the synch may appear more realistic if it's a frame or so ahead of the dialogue, so that the mouth is moving as the viewer's brain is processing the sound rather than when his ear is receiving it.

You'll find that applying the articulation of phonemes to your lip synch will ensure you hit the mark very close every time you do it. Reviewing the Knuckles1.mov file, you may notice that Knuckles' face seems to jitter too much in a few places, which indicates too many visual phonemes. The first step is to go back to our timing sheet and add one more column. We then enter the articulation for each of the phonemes on the column as shown in Figure 5.11.

PHONEME	Target	Frame	Articulation		PHONEME	Target	Frame	Articulation
Y	7	2	Glide		L	2	53	Liquid
AH	8	6	Vowel		AY	8	57	Diphthong
					K	5	61	Plosive
SH	6	10	Fricative					
UH	7	15	Vowel		D	2	62	Plosive
D	2	19	Plosive		AE	8	63	Vowel
N	2	20	Nasal		T	2	66	Plosive
AA	9	25	Vowel					
D	2	30	Plosive					
AH	8	32	Vowel					
T	2	37	Plosive					
AA	9	38	Vowel					
K	5	42	Plosive					
T	2	45	Plosive					
AH	8	46	Vowel					
M	1	48	Nasal					
IY	10	50	Vowel					

FIGURE 5.11   Adding the articulation to the timing sheet.

Adding the articulation is a vital step in lip synch because it identifies the problem areas, eliminating the guesswork. By identifying the articulation, it is much easier to see where the visual phonemes will drop out or be less prominent. The next section examines some guidelines for dropping phonemes.

PHONEME DROPPING GUIDELINES

There are two simple guidelines for dropping phonemes. By following these guidelines, animated lip synch will flow smoother and be more believable. The guidelines are listed here and detailed in the following section.

- Never drop a phoneme from the beginning of a word.
- Drop nasal phonemes for smooth transitions.

Never Drop Beginning Phonemes

Never drop a phoneme at the beginning of a word. Doing so will change the visual phonetic pronunciation for the word. The consonants at the ends of words, however, can be dropped without having much impact on the word. In fact, dropping phonemes at the end of a word usually improves animation because speech tends to trail off at the end of a word. The most common phonemes to drop are the plosives because they are very fast and therefore don't really register visually. If we look at the timing chart annotated with articulation, several plosives are causing some stuttering problems, as shown in Figure 5.12.

PHONEME	Target	Frame	Articulation		PHONEME	Target	Frame	Articulation
Y	7	2	Glide		L	2	53	Liquid
AH	8	6	Vowel		AY	8	57	Diphthong
					K	5	61	Plosive
SH	6	10	Fricative					
UH	7	15	Vowel		D	2	62	Plosive
D	2	19	Plosive		AE	8	63	Vowel
N	2	20	Nasal		T	2	66	Plosive
AA	9	25	Vowel					
D	2	30	Plosive					
AH	8	32	Vowel					
T	2	37	Plosive					
AA	9	38	Vowel					
K	5	42	Plosive					
T	2	45	Plosive					
AH	8	46	Vowel					
M	1	48	Nasal					
IY	10	50	Vowel					

FIGURE 5.12   Selecting consonants to drop.

You can see that we've selected the trailing plosives in the words "talk," "like," and "dat." These are the visual phonemes that made the first animation test choppy. With them removed, the animation will flow smoothly from one word to another.

Drop Nasal Phonemes

Drop nasal visual phonemes to smooth out transitions between other phonemes. Nasals are the anti-visual phoneme. The majority of their sound comes through the nasal passage, so they tend to be quick mouth movements and nearly undetectable, yet the sound lingers well after the mouth has moved. This is a very important issue when animating. The trickiest of the nasal phonemes is the "M," since it requires a closed mouth. Since the time span for the "M" sound can be very short, it may require the mouth to be closed for less than a single frame of animation.

In the Knuckles animation, there are several nasal phonemes, but only one is a problem. Play the Knuckles animation again and you'll see that his mouth jumps closed and open again when he says the letter "M." The movement looks unnatural, yet it's synched perfectly to the sound. The problem is that the mouth has to cover a long range to reach closed from a vowel, and then a long range back to get to a vowel that follows. This created the snapping movement of the jaw, which needs to be fixed. At this point, there are two options: either removing the nasal phoneme or reducing the influence of its keyframe. You'll typically want to drop a nasal when it lands between two vowels since the vowels are voiced, meaning they have the widest mouth gap to allow the free passage of air. Of course, if the nasal visual phoneme is the same as the preceding or following vowel, it won't be necessary to delete it. Figure 5.13 shows the nasal "M" in the Knuckles' animation selected for alteration.

PHONEME	Target	Frame	Articulation		PHONEME	Target	Frame	Articulation
Y	7	2	Glide		L	2	53	Liquid
AH	8	6	Vowel		AY	8	57	Diphthong
					K			Plosive
SH	6	10	Fricative					
UH	7	15	Vowel		D	2	62	Plosive
D			Plosive		AE	8	63	Vowel
N	2	20	Nasal		T			Plosive
AA	9	25	Vowel					
D	2	30	Plosive					
AH	8	32	Vowel					
T	2	37	Plosive					
AA	9	38	Vowel					
K			Plosive					
T	2	45	Plosive					
AH	8	46	Vowel					
M	**1**	**48**	**Nasal**					
IY	10	50	Vowel					

FIGURE 5.13   Identifying the problem nasal phoneme.

With this phoneme dropped, the mouth will flow smoothly from the "AH" to the "IY" visual phonemes so we won't see the sharp snap of his mouth.

Now that we have the problem visual phonemes deleted from our sequence, we can create another animation to see the results. You'll find the corrected Knuckles animation in the Chapter 5 folder of the companion CD-ROM, entitled Knucklesfix.mov. Take a moment to load the file and play it a few times. You'll see that it now flows very naturally, and the missing "M" is hardly discernable.

ON THE CD

By studying phonemes, we've managed to make a very difficult task much easier. Lip synching a cartoon character with an exaggerated face and slurred speech is one of the most challenging lip-synch projects, yet with the proper application of phoneme principles, it can be completed rather quickly.

CONCLUSION

While lip synching animation may not be easy, it can be very rewarding. Adding dialogue to a character gives it life that isn't possible any other way. By carefully following the rules and procedures laid out in this chapter, you should be able to effectively synch your character's animation to its dialogue.

Now that you have a handle on lip synching, the real challenge comes with blending emotions with lip synching to produce fuller, richer, character animation. In the next chapter, you'll learn more about emotion and lip synching by creating complete, animated expressions.

WEIGHTED MORPHING ANIMATION

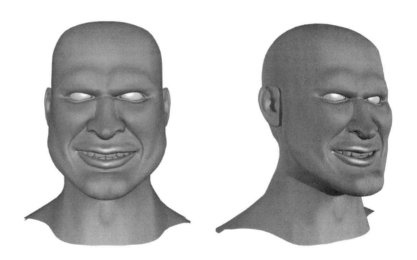

In this chapter, we explore the techniques of animating the face using weighted morph targets and segmented weighted morph targets. The difference between a weighted morph target and a segmented weighted morph target is that the weighted technique morphs between entire models, while the segmented version enables morphing for just a portion of multiple models. Any worthwhile animation package has tools for weighted morphing.

In this chapter, we explore how a short facial animation was made with Guido, a character from the Komodo Empire film *Dwellers*. Guido's animation was created using segmented morphing, which we cover later in this chapter. First, let's take a closer look at weighted morphing.

WEIGHTED MORPHING

Weighted morphing is the ability to morph a base or anchor model into two target models simultaneously. This is a major advantage when you are creating lip-synch animation that includes both dialogue and facial expressions. Figure 6.1 illustrates a simple progression of weighted morphing.

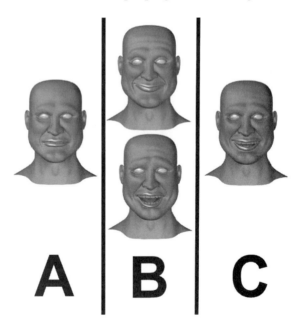

FIGURE 6.1   Two morph targets combined.

In Figure 6.1, the anchor object in column A was morphed 50% of the way toward the model at the top of column B, and 50% of the way toward the model at the bottom of column B, effectively reaching a shape halfway between the two. The result is the model in column C.

Morph targets can be morphed to any percentage; the totals don't even have to add up to 100%. Many programs allow the total to exceed 100%, which produces some interesting results. Additionally, a weighted morphing system will allow you to assign a slider to each target, as Figure 6.2 illustrates.

FIGURE 6.2   A typical weighted morph slider interface.

Within a morph slider interface, a target model is listed next to a percentage slider. Use the slider to give a target more weight or influence in the final pose of the model. In Figure 6.2, the Mouth Crying target is set to 20% and the Mouth Laughter target to 70%. To get a better idea of how weighted morphing works, load 2targetmorph.mov animation file found in the Chapter 6 folder on the companion CD-ROM. This file uses the same anchor and targets shown in Figure 6.1. By using the sliders and creating keyframes, additional poses were possible.

ON THE CD

Weighted morphing is an excellent facial animation tool because a larger number of expressions from a given set of targets can be achieved than with straight morphing. With straight morphing, the percentage of a morph can be set, but multiple targets cannot be morphed simultaneously.

SEGMENTED MORPHING

Segmented morphing allows for morphing separate areas of the model individually. Working with segmented morphs is a little bit like playing with a Mr. Potato Head®, mixing and matching expressions on different areas of the face. You can create separate targets for the eyebrows, eyes, and mouth. If you created only two targets for the brows, eyes, and mouth, you could create eight separate expressions, using combinations of them with 100% morph values.

Additionally, you can combine individual segment targets with weights, making for an astounding variety of expressions with these six simple targets. The term *weight* refers to the percentage of the morph. By using percentages less than 100%, you can create literally thousands of variations from a simple few targets. You can even save combined morph objects as completely new objects that can be loaded into a modeler for tweaking and then loaded back into the weighted morphing system for creating even more combinations. The possibilities are truly limitless.

The real power of segmented morphing, however, is that each facial group can be keyframed individually. This means that the eyebrows can be held in an arched position while the mouth is animated with visual phonemes. This makes the process much easier than with straight morphing, which would require many more morph targets to create all the poses.

Segmented morphing has two advantages over straight morphing: the ability to build a large number of expressions from a smaller set of targets, and to animate a changing expression while the character is talking. Additionally, some interesting benefits from this capability are being able to animate the jaw separately from the lips.

ANIMATING THE JAW WITH SEGMENTED MORPHING

To illustrate for yourself why animating the jaw separately from the lips is a desirable technique, utter the phrase "I climbed the Washington Monument" in a natural speaking voice. Notice that while the lips change shape at least 15 times while forming visual phonemes, the jaw opens and closes a mere 6 times. This indicates that, while jaw motion is driven by the words being spoken, it operates independently from the lips. To achieve this kind of animation control, segmented morphing is required.

For segmented morphing, some separate morph targets need to be created. By creating separate morph targets for the lips and the jaw, each will be given a separate set of sliders that can then be keyframed individually.

In the Guido model, the jaw has been lowered independently of the mouth, allowing for easier selection of the jaw and lips. The jaw will be rotated into proper position prior to animating. Guido's face has been segmented into five groups. Figure 6.3 identifies the position of the five segments listed here:

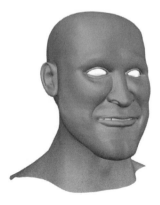

FIGURE 6.3 Guido's face.

The forehead and brows: This group gives Guido the ability to raise and lower the eyebrows independently of the rest of the face.

The eyelids: With this group, one or both eyelids can be opened or closed, making blinking, squinting, and winking possible.

The mouth, nose, and cheeks: The mouth is given a separate group so speech is possible in addition to a wide variety of eye and brow combinations.

The jaw: The jaw is given a separate group so it can operate independently from the mouth as discussed earlier in the chapter.

The tongue: By giving the tongue a separate group, actions such as licking the lips are possible, as well as more detailed representation of the visual phonemes, as we discuss later in the chapter.

Once the segmentation of the character has been identified, the next step is to build a library of morph targets. The morph targets will be used to create the final animation sequence.

CREATING A LIBRARY OF SEGMENTED MORPH TARGETS

In creating the morph targets, three different types are required:

- Expression targets for the expressive poses
- Visual phonemes
- Five tongue targets for the visual phonemes that involve the tongue

CREATING AN EXPRESSION WITH SEGMENTED TARGETS

In Appendix E, "Facial Expression Examples," you'll find a reference of expressions along with morph target weight percentages. These percent-

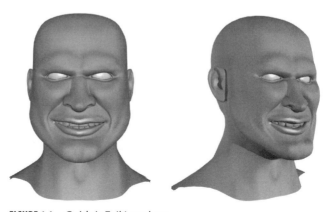

FIGURE 6.4   Guido's Evil Laughter.

ages point to the individual segment targets found in Appendix A, "Typical Human Expression Weighted Morph Targets." Figure 6.4 shows the expression Evil Laughter that will be built in this section.

The first step to creating the Evil Laughter expression is to model the component segmented morph targets. Table 6.1 shows that we'll need to build five targets: two for the brows, two for the mouth, and one for the jaw. We'll start by looking at how the targets for the brows are created.

TABLE 6.1   Evil Laughter Morph Targets

MORPH TARGET GROUP	MORPH TARGET	PERCENTAGE
Brows	Brows angry	70
	Brows compressed	100
Eyes	NONE	N/A
Mouth	Laughter	60
	Smile closed	70
Jaw	Jaw closed	80

Creating the Brow Targets

The first target to build is Brows Angry, shown in Figure 6.5. This is also one of the targets listed in Appendix A.

FIGURE 6.5   The Brows Angry target.

To create the Brows Angry target, start with a neutral pose and pull the points on the inside portion of the brows down toward the eyes to form a bulge in the middle. The Brows Angry pose in Appendix A illustrates the before and after poses. For movement of the brows, refer to Chapter 3, "Facial Muscles." This pose involves just the points of the brow and forehead. Weighted morph systems rely on the principle of vertex location change. The vertices of one model are compared to those of the morph target. When morphing, the vertex positions will move from one target to another based on the percentage values used. If the location of points on the mouth were altered while building a brow target, those points would move toward their new position when the brows were morphed, deforming the mouth when we only wanted to affect the brow. When building segmented targets, be sure to alter only those points that belong to the target group.

Once the Brows Angry target has been created, it is saved as a new model with an appropriate name. The same procedure would be used to create the Brows Compressed target, also found in Appendix A. In this target, the whole brow is lowered, partially obscuring the eyes. Again, this pose should be saved as a new object that will be used as a morph target later.

Creating the Mouth Targets

According to Table 6.1, the mouth requires two targets: Laughter and Smile Closed. Figure 6.6 shows the two morph targets side by side. Eventually, the targets are applied using the percentages shown in the chart to create the expression.

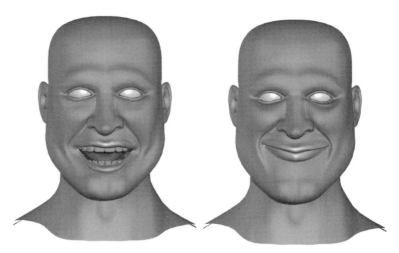

FIGURE 6.6   The two mouth targets.

You may notice that the mouth may penetrate the chin in some of the weighted morph targets. By design, the jaw remained stationary while the mouth was deformed. When these targets are loaded into the weighted morph program, the jaw will be adjusted to its correct position. Working with segmented, weighted morph targets may look odd at first, but the purpose is to isolate specific portions (or segments) of the face. Since individual morph targets are created for each segment, the individual poses may not look correct, but ultimately there is more control over the animation.

In the next section, you'll learn about creating the morph targets for the jaw. While the expression "Evil Laughter" only uses the Jaw Closed target, all five jaw morph targets are discussed.

Creating the Jaw Targets

This section on jaw targets requires you to be familiar with the proper rotation of the jaw, as discussed in Chapter 1, "Anatomy of the Head." It is important that the jaw be rotated at the proper axis point. Starting with the default anchor object (facial pose), the points of the jaw and lower teeth are selected, but not those belonging to the mouth, as shown in Figure 6.7.

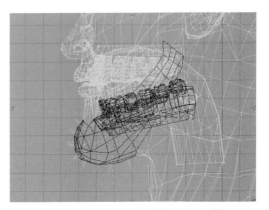

FIGURE 6.7   Select the points of the jaw and lower teeth.

Since in the neutral pose for Guido the jaw is opened to about the halfway point, two jaw rotation targets would be built: Jaw Open and Jaw Closed. The Jaw Open target is built by rotating the jaw from the correct axis at the base of the ear opening to its maximum position as shown in Figure 6.8.

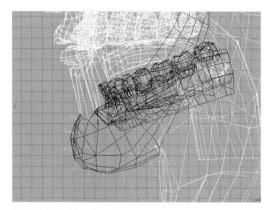

FIGURE 6.8   The Jaw Open target.

Notice that some of the points at the base of the jaw penetrated the neck. These points need to be pulled out to create a little fold where the skin has bunched up. When the jaw opens, the skin underneath the chin bulges out, so those vertices need to be adjusted, as well. Figure 6.9 shows the Jaw Open target after the points have been adjusted. As always, the target is saved as a new object.

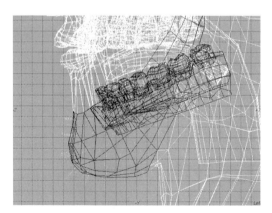

FIGURE 6.9   The Jaw Open target after the chin and neck have been adjusted.

For the Jaw Closed target, the same points of the jaw and lower teeth that were grouped for the Jaw Open target are selected and rotated from the proper axis until the teeth are together in a natural position. Some points of the jaw may penetrate the mouth, but as mentioned earlier, this will be corrected when the morph targets are used with other targets. Figure 6.10 shows the jaw rotated shut.

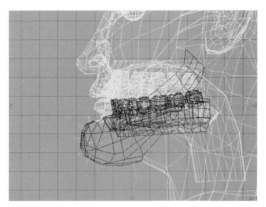

FIGURE 6.10 The jaw rotated shut.

Some of the points of the jaw may have moved dangerously close to points on the cheek. When the jaw opens and closes, the skin of the face naturally stretches and contracts. Vertices need to be adjusted on the side of the jaw to compensate for this movement. Figure 6.11 shows a more natural positioning of points.

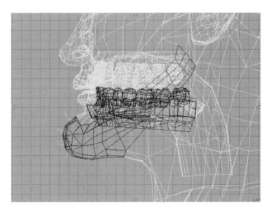

FIGURE 6.11 The Jaw Closed target with vertices adjusted.

While these are the only targets required for this pose, three more targets are necessary for natural jaw motion:

- A target in which the jaw is moved to the right side of the head with the gap between the two front lower teeth lining up with the right side of the upper right incisors.
- A similar target with the jaw shifted to the left.
- A target with the jaw jutting forward.

These three jaw movement targets are created in the same way, by selecting the points of the jaw and lower teeth, moving them left, right, or forward, and adjusting the vertices to simulate natural stretching and contraction of the skin.

Now that the morph targets have been completed, they can be animated. The next section discusses how to combine the segmented targets to create the completed Evil Laughter facial expression.

Combining the Segmented Targets

After creating the morph targets, it's time to put them to work. First, the default head is loaded into the animation software. This will be known as the anchor pose or initial pose, and is the same base model from which the morph targets were created.

Next, three groups of sliders are created: one for the brow targets, one for the mouth targets, and one for the jaw targets. The morph targets are then loaded and assigned to the appropriate sliders prior to animating.

That's all it takes to set up a segmented morph project. The principle is simple, although in very complex models there may be dozens of poses and sliders. For this example, the targets created earlier will be used.

Adjusting the Sliders

Each program works slightly differently when creating and assigning sliders. Consult either the 3ds Max® or Maya chapters in this book for an idea on how to build and assign sliders, unless you are using a different program than those two.

Creating a single expression is achieved by adjusting each slider or the sliders of a particular group. Much depends on setting up the proper group and the morph targets, but with practice, the task becomes easier. For this pose, the following adjustments are made with the sliders of each group:

1. The Brows group is selected, and the Brows Angry slider is moved to 100%. Guido's brows deform smoothly into the target shape, while the rest of the face remains in the strange anchor pose.
2. The Mouth group is selected, and the slider for the Smile Closed target is moved to 100%. The mouth deforms to its target, while the brows remain unaffected in their angry position.
3. The Laughter slider is moved to 100%, and the two mouth targets are combined while, again, the brows hold their shape.

An example of the power of segmented animation is that if the model's jaw is in an incorrect position in relation to the mouth pose, the jaw sliders are moved to open or close it into a more natural position. If the jaw were not a segmented morph target, there would be no control over the jaw only, resulting in some silly poses. If all the weighted morph targets found in Appendix A are created and loaded into an animation program, the possibilities are endless.

CREATING VISUAL PHONEMES FOR SEGMENTED MORPHING

Before Guido can be animated speaking, the visual phoneme targets must be created. For Guido's lip synch, the reduced phoneme list of 10 visual phonemes will be used. The reduced set is used because they represent changes in the mouth only. The remaining six rely on tongue changes, and since the tongue has been assigned to a separate morph group, it can be keyframed separately from the mouth. Because segmented morph targets are used, the reduced set of phonemes can be used. With straight morphing, the full set of 16 visual phonemes would be the better choice to enable the character to have a wider range of emotional facial poses.

Building the 10 visual phonemes shown in Figure 6.12 follows the same procedure as for building the expression targets.

The differences between the phonemes are subtle, but it is important that they be accurately reproduced to create natural and flowing lip synch. Also, while creating visual phoneme shapes for your models, say each phoneme aloud in a mirror for reference. After the 10 mouth shapes have been built, the five basic tongue positions are created.

The Five Basic Tongue Positions

While animating the tongue isn't always necessary, it will add realism when the mouth is open, especially during speech. The decision to animate the tongue depends on several things, including the shape of the mouth and the angle of the shots when the character is talking.

To complete the 16 visual phonemes, six tongue targets are needed. These affect the liquids, nasals, fricatives, spirants, and affricatives, discussed in the previous chapter.

Figure 6.13 illustrates the six basic tongue positions needed to complete the 16 visual phonemes.

The six tongue targets are:

- Floating in the center of the mouth cavity
- The tip pressed against the hard palate just above the upper teeth
- The tip pressed against the lower teeth
- The tongue curled upward
- Between the teeth
- At the base of the mouth

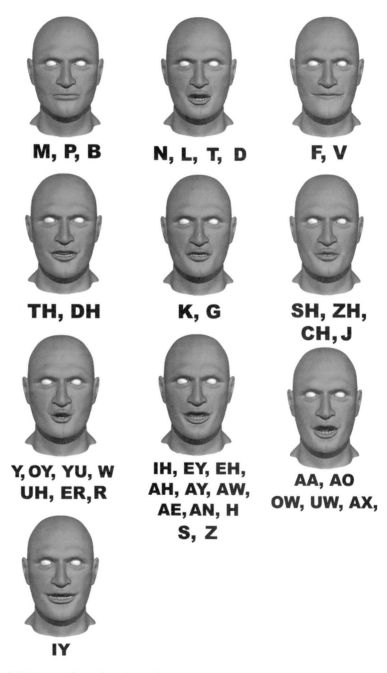

M, P, B   **N, L, T, D**   **F, V**

TH, DH   **K, G**   **SH, ZH,
CH, J**

**Y, OY, YU, W
UH, ER, R**   **IH, EY, EH,
AH, AY, AW,
AE, AN, H
S, Z**   **AA, AO
OW, UW, AX,**

IY

FIGURE 6.12   The reduced set of 10 visual phonemes.

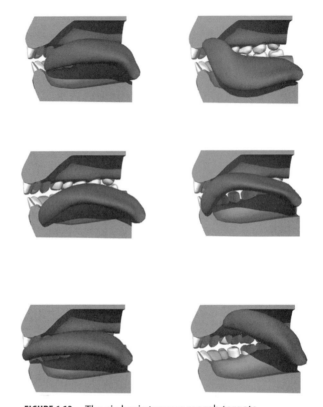

FIGURE 6.13   The six basic tongue morph targets.

Creating these targets is no more difficult than creating the mouth or eyebrow targets. The tongue is simply isolated and rotated section by section until the tongue targets are reproduced.

The tongue position for all 16 visual phonemes can be found in Appendix B. Simply combine the appropriate mouth shape with the tongue shape shown to create the new visual phoneme.

CREATING A FACIAL ANIMATION WITH SEGMENTED MORPHING

ON THE CD

In this section, Guido's face will be animated to the recorded dialogue, "Ya wan't some? Ya want a piece of me? Huh? Do ya?" The audio file entitled Youwant.wav can be found in the Chapter 6 folder on the companion CD-ROM. The targets needed for the walk-through are as follows:

- Brows
- Brows Angry
- Brows Arched

- Eyes
- Left Lid Closed
- Right Lid Closed
- Mouth
- All visual phonemes listed in Appendix B, affecting only the mouth, cheeks, and nose
- Smile
- The five basic tongue positions
- Jaw
- Jaw Open
- Jaw Closed

The preceding morph targets were derived by analyzing the sounds of the dialogue, as discussed in Chapter 5. As with all facial and lip-synch animation, the visual phoneme list must be created prior to the animation so that the proper phonemes, poses, sliders, and morph targets are created. After creating the morph targets and setting them to sliders, they will be loaded and animated. Prior to the facial animation, let's discuss the jaw movement.

The Jaw Movement

Earlier in this chapter, the phrase "I climbed the Washington monument" was muttered aloud, and you noted that while the mouth formed 15 visual phonemes, the jaw opened and closed only six times. Since the reason for creating individual jaw targets is so that the jaw can be moved independently from the lips, when and how far the jaw opens and closes needs to be notated on the chart.

Jaw rotation is notated with numbers ranging from 1 to 10, where 1 signifies the jaw at its closed position, and 10 signifies the jaw opened fully. Figure 6.14 shows the timing chart for the recorded dialogue.

The rotation timing for the jaw is notated in the Jaw column. The rotation values were derived from the dialogue by repeating the voice actor's performance and noting where the jaw opened and closed, how wide it opened, and where it held its position. From here, it's time to set the keyframes.

Keyframing the Segmented Morph Animation

With the timing chart completed, setting keyframes for the dialogue is a simple matter of moving the sliders for the visual phoneme targets listed in the chart at the specified times and setting keyframes. The order of the animated components will make a difference in the animation.

Jaw	PHONEME	Target	Frame	Jaw	PHONEME	Target	Frame
2	YU	4	7	4	(Silence)		75-90
	W	4	10				
3	AA	3		6	AH	2	95-106
1	S	13	14				
	AH	2		2	(Silence)		110-125
4	M	9	20				
				2	D	7	127
	(Silence)		35-50		UW	4	
4				2	Y	6	131
3	YU	4	54	5	AA	3	133-140
	W	4	56				
5	AA	3					
5	N	10	59				
6	AA	3					
6	P	9	61				
	IY	1					
1	S	13	65				
4	AH	2					
3	M	9	69				
4	IY	1	70-74				

FIGURE 6.14   The timing chart for Guido's facial animation.

It's important that the lips be animated before the jaw rotation, because jaw motion is directly related to the mouth shapes. While the jaw rotation levels have been specified in the timing chart, some may need to be adjusted to look more natural, depending on the mouth target used. Only after the mouth targets have been set can one tell how far to open or close the jaw.

Start by setting the keyframes for the mouth as specified in the timing chart, and then animate and set the jaw rotation keys. Next, keyframes are set for the tongue on the visual phonemes that require it. Before adding the brow and smile expressions, check the lip synching against the dialogue. Getting the basic lip synch correct first will save time if corrections need to be made. A test render of the animation at this stage called Ptest1.mov can be found on the companion CD-ROM in the Chapter 6 folder.

ON THE CD

Adding Animated Expressions

Once the timing for speech has been completed, including any dropped phonemes, animated expressions may be added to the face. Expressiveness is an important element of realistic facial animation. Consider the phrase lip synched in the previous section, "Ya wan't some? Ya want a piece of me? Huh? Do ya?" Acting the scenario out and videotaping an actor's performance will give valuable clues to what real facial expressions would look like when speaking this dialogue.

For instance, the brows might be lowered for the first sentence "Ya wan't some?" raised slightly for the sentence "You wanna piece of me?" raised even higher for the "Huh?" and still more for the final "Do ya?" Since timings have already been determined for these phrases, it's easy to see where the brows should be keyframed. They'll be set as follows:

- Brows Angry 20% at frame 1
- Brows Angry 20% at frame 40 (to hold this pose for 40 frames)
- Brows Neutral at frame 20
- Brows Neutral at frame 85 (to hold this pose for 65 frames)
- Brows Arched at frame 90
- Brows Arched 30% at frame 85
- Brows Arched 60% at frame 120

As you see, most of the work of the lip synch is done before the keys are actually set. The sliders are simply keyframed at the indicated percentages at the designated frames. By working out the keys on paper, the process can be expedited and more time can be spent increasing the quality.

During the original voiceover recording, the voice actor smiled between the words "some" and "you wanna" and between the words "me" and "huh." He also smiled somewhat as he spoke the whole phrase, so the mouth smile slider can be set to about 20% for the entire animation and to 60% or 70% for the pauses.

The voice actor who spoke these lines didn't blink once while acting out the lines. If he had, the delivery of the lines wouldn't have been as poignant. The lack of blinking adds a taunting quality to the animation. However, if blinking were to be added, it would be as easy as keying the Eye Lid Closed sliders to 100% on one frame and back to 0% one or two frames later.

ON THE CD

To see the final animation, load the file Guidofinal.mov, found in the Chapter 6 folder on the companion CD-ROM. You can see how Guido has come to life with the addition of the expressive targets mixed in.

CONCLUSION

Both segmented and weighted morphing are extremely powerful techniques, as we've seen in this chapter. Weighted morphing adds the ability to mix morph targets to create large numbers of expressions, and segmented morphing adds the ability to morph separate areas of the face individually, allowing a greater range of expressions. Segmented morphing enables animation of specific features of the face, namely the jaw and mouth, independently making for more realistic facial animation.

Like any animation principle, facial animation isn't difficult if you take the time to study the process. Learn the subtleties of facial expressions and the entire process will be easier. With a little practice and a lot of patience (at first), you'll amaze yourself with the animation you can produce.

ANIMATING FACIAL EXPRESSIONS USING 3DS MAX

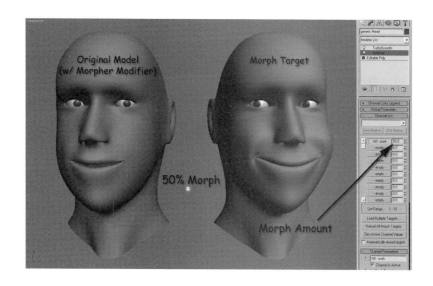

Previous chapters in this book showed you the facial poses for the different phonemes and the underlying structure of the human head. In this chapter, you will learn some of the techniques for applying those in 3ds Max. It is assumed that you have some knowledge of 3ds Max, such as how to use modifiers and basic animation tools.

There are several methods for facial animation in 3ds Max. In this chapter, you will learn:

- Morph target animation
- Linked XForms
- Using Physique for facial animation
- Animating the tongue
- Adding audio to 3ds Max

Deciding which tools to use depends on the type of animation required. Each method has it benefits and limitations, which should be considered when choosing how to rig a character for facial animation.

USING 3DS MAX MORPH TARGETS

In the context of 3D, a morph is a change from one shape to another. Probably the most common method of animating facial features is using morph targets. A morph target is just one model out of a series of models that have been previously posed for the purpose of animation. They are in a sense, key poses of separate, but structurally identical models.

Basically, the Morpher modifier in 3ds Max is a vertex mover. Every mesh object created in 3ds Max has its vertices numbered. Because the models are structurally identical (meaning they have the same number of vertices), the Morpher modifier moves each vertex of one model to the position of the corresponding vertex on the target model. In other words, vertex number one of the original mesh will be moved to the position of vertex number one of each of the target objects. For this reason, it is best to create all morph targets from the same original model.

A Basic Morph

To illustrate how a morph target works in its simplest form, Figure 7.1 depicts a box morphing to a sphere. In the figure, you can see the progression of the box as it changes shape. Each stage shows an increase of 25% more morph weight toward the final stage, which is 100% weighted. In this example, only a single morph target was used, along with the original model of the box.

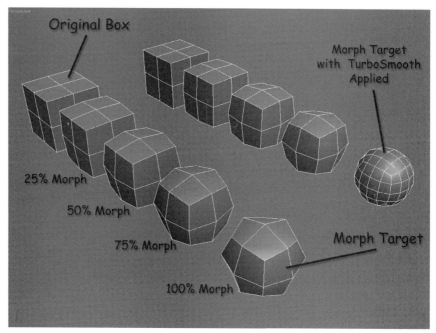

FIGURE 7.1   This box uses a single morph target to change to a sphere over time.

Introducing the Morpher Modifier

One way to perform morphing in 3ds Max is by adding a Morpher modifier to a mesh object. Any two mesh objects with the same number of vertices can be used as part of the morph. One object has the Morpher modifier attached to it. Typically, this is the model in a neutral state. The morph targets are then loaded into the Morpher modifier. By adjusting the weight value of the morph targets, an almost infinite number of combinations between the morph targets can be created.

To use the Morpher modifier, it must first be applied to a mesh object. After applying a Morpher modifier, the Modify panel displays many options as shown in Figure 7.2.

Once applied to a mesh object, the modifier needs to be populated with targets. The Morpher modifier can accommodate as many as 100 target objects, each with its own influence weight controls. Each target object is loaded into its own channel. Each channel has a percentage spinner that is used to control the amount of influence that target has in changing the original mesh.

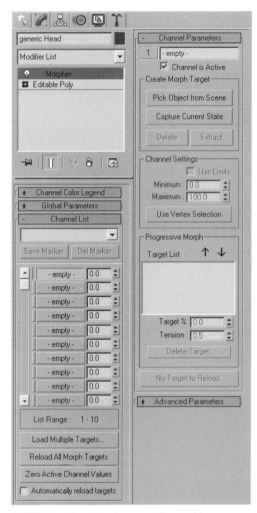

FIGURE 7.2   The Morpher modifier and its parameters.

Creating Morph Targets

While morphing a box to a sphere may be a simplistic example, the process is the same for more complex meshes, such as character faces. The real work is in creating the accurate and convincing morph targets. Use the expressions and phonemes discussed earlier in this book as reference when building the morph targets for facial animation. Remember, because morph targets must have the same number of vertices, it is essential to start with a single mesh, and then clone and edit it for each pose that makes up the morph targets. This ensures compatibility between the morph targets.

Figure 7.3 depicts three heads, each in a slightly different pose. From left to right is the mouth slightly open pose (a semi-neutral pose), mouth agape pose, and on the right a smirking pose. The head models in the center and on the right were cloned from the head on the left. The vertices of each model are then manipulated to the desired pose.

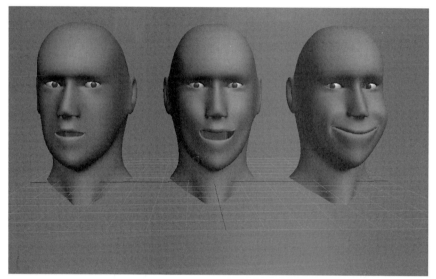

FIGURE 7.3   The original mesh and three morph targets.

When building morph targets, do not add smoothing to the target models. Smoothing can cause the morph targets to become incompatible or cause vertices to move incorrectly. A smoothing modifier, such as TurboSmooth or MeshSmooth, can be added to the original model after the Morpher modifier for better results.

Applying the Morpher Modifier

To use the Morpher modifier, start with a neutral model. In this example, we'll use the generic head character. Figure 7.4 depicts the neutral model and morph targets without a smoothing modifier being applied.

After applying the Morpher modifier, morph targets are added. Notice that the Channel List is empty. To add a morph target, click the Pick Object from Scene button in the channel Parameters section (shown in Figure 7.5). Alternatively, you can right-click on the empty channel button and choose Pick Object from Scene from the short pop-up menu. Click the morph target to load it into the selected channel.

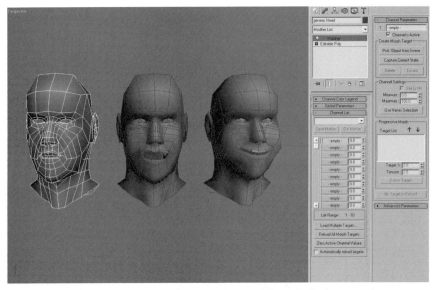

FIGURE 7.4 The neutral model with the Morpher modifier installed.

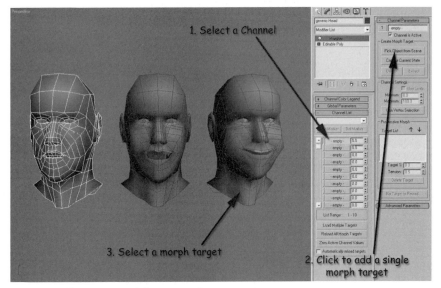

FIGURE 7.5 The steps to adding a morph target.

The Actual Morph

Once morph targets have been applied to the model, the original mesh object can be morphed to any of the morph targets. The original mesh can be made to morph instantly, or it can be animated. Intermediate targets can also be used, but more on that later. The morph is accomplished through the channel spinner in the Morpher modifier. In this example, the generic head model has a Morpher modifier attached and the smirk morph target applied to Channel #1 of the Morpher modifier. In Figures 7.6, 7.7, and 7.8, the amount spinner of the channel containing the smirk morph target has been set to 0%, 50%, and 100%, respectively.

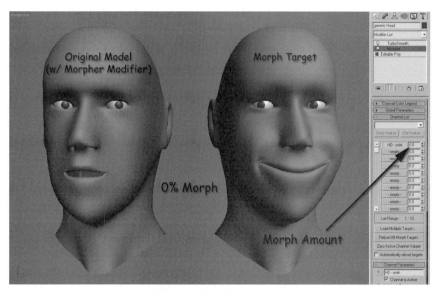

FIGURE 7.6   A morph target added, but the influence amount still set at 0%.

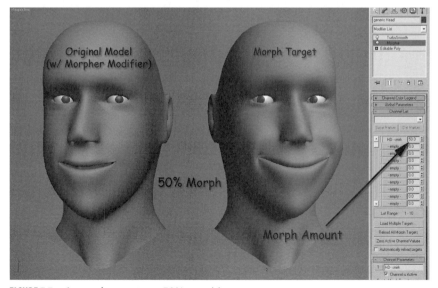

FIGURE 7.7   A morph target at a 50% transition.

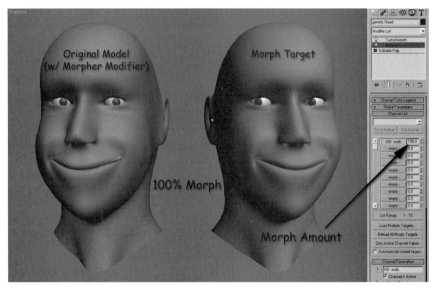

FIGURE 7.8 The morph target has 100% influence, and the original model has changed shape completely.

Obviously, the morph amounts can be animated, just as any other spinner control in 3ds Max can be. By using multiple morph targets and animated influence amounts, your character will be chatting away in no time.

There is much more to learn about the Morpher modifier in 3ds Max. It's a powerful tool with many parameters, although an in-depth look at the other parameters is outside the scope of this book.

USING LINKED XFORMS FOR FACIAL ANIMATION

Morph targets are a great way to animate facial features, especially when the animation includes lip synching. However, there are times when you'd just like to animate a portion of a model without setting up morph targets. For that, there is the Linked XForm.

A Linked XForm is a modifier that is applied to a mesh object and more specifically, a subobject selection, such as a group of vertices, edges, or polygons. The subobject selection is then linked to an external control, such as a dummy or Point Helper. By animating the control object, you can affect just a portion of the model.

The Linked XForm Control Object

The Linked XForm starts with a control object. The control object can be any other object in 3ds Max, although most animators prefer a Point Helper or a dummy object. For this example, we will use a Point Helper because they have adjustable parameters and they do not render. It's a great idea to position the helper object at a place relative to the model that can easily be found. In this case, the control object is a Point Helper and it has been positioned so that it is aligned to the center of the eyes vertically and pivots to maximum X value horizontally, as shown in Figure 7.9. By aligning to specific positions, the Point Helper can be returned to a neutral state easily.

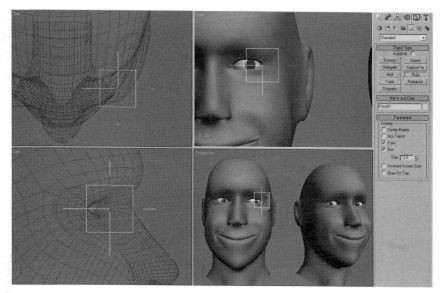

FIGURE 7.9   A Point Helper is used as a control object for the Linked XForm.

Using an Edit Poly Modifier with the Linked XForm

Before the model can be controlled, we need to be able to access the subobjects of the mesh. New to version 7 and improved in version 8 of 3ds Max is the Edit Poly modifier. We will use an Edit Poly modifier so that specific vertices can be selected and linked to the Linked XForm control object. If you're using a version of 3ds Max earlier than version 7, you can use the Edit Mesh modifier, although the Edit Poly modifier is preferred. By using an Edit Poly modifier to select the vertices to be controlled, one can easily dispose of any erroneous animation by removing the Edit Poly modifier from the mesh object, returning the model to its original state. That's the whole purpose behind the Modifier motif that is the essence of 3ds Max. In addition, numerous Edit Poly and Linked XForm modifiers can be applied, giving the animator much more control over the model. As an example, Woody from the *Toy Story* films had over 100 facial controls for everything from hair to eyelids to lips to cheek muscles.

Add an Edit Poly modifier after the Morpher modifier. Activate vertex subobject mode and select the vertices to be controlled. In this case, the vertices around the cheek have been selected as shown in Figure 7.10.

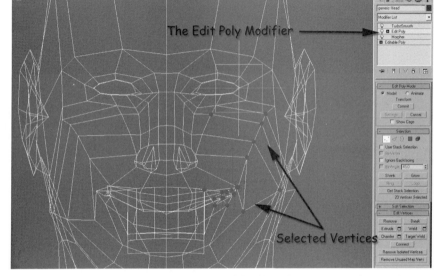

FIGURE 7.10   After applying the Edit Poly modifier, select the vertices in the cheek area.

Applying the Linked XForm

Prior to applying the Linked XForm, keep the subobject selection active. After the vertices to be controlled have been selected, a Linked XForm modifier is added to the mesh object from the Modifier List, as shown in Figure 7.11.

Once the XForm modifier has been applied, a Control object must be chosen. Click the Pick Control Object button on the Linked XForm modifier as shown in Figure 7.12 to activate the selection tool, and then click on the Point Helper created earlier to make it the controlling object. The Control Object parameters will then display the name of the Point Helper, indicating it is the controlling object, as shown in Figure 7.13. The Linked XForm functionality is now in place and ready to perform.

Animating with a Linked XForm

Now that the Linked XForm control is in place, the character's left cheek can be manipulated independently of any other part of the mesh. Animation of the cheek is achieved by animating the Point Helper to which it is linked. The Point Helper is animated like any other object in 3ds Max, and all 3ds Max animation tools can be applied to the Point Helper. As

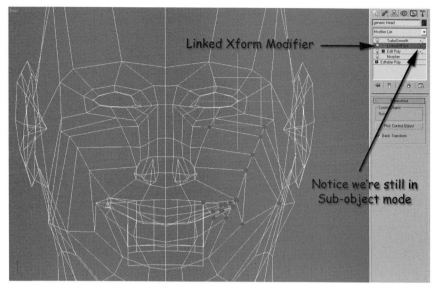

FIGURE 7.11   Adding the Linked XForm modifier. Be sure to keep the Edit Poly modifier subobject selection active.

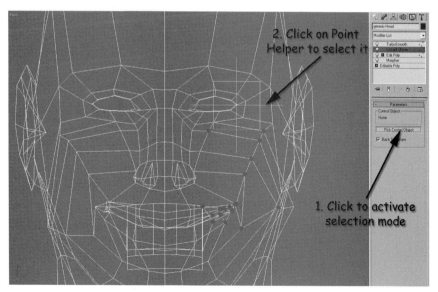

FIGURE 7.12   After applying the Linked XForm modifier, click the Pick Control Object button and then select the Point Helper to make it the control object.

can be seen in Figure 7.14, the cheek has been raised by moving the Point Helper, not the vertices of the mesh.

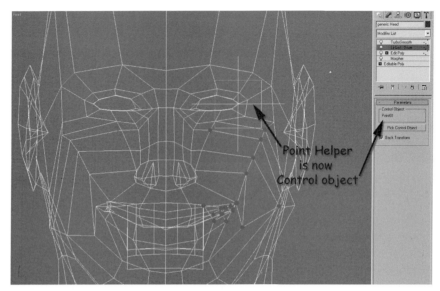

FIGURE 7.13 After selecting the Point Helper, its name will be displayed as the control object within the Linked XForm's parameters.

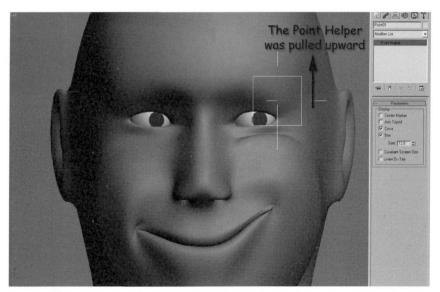

FIGURE 7.14 By animating the Point Helper, the cheek muscles can be animated independently of the rest of the model.

Special care must be taken when animating a portion of the model with a Linked XForm to avoid double translation. Using the Linked XForm's Back Transform option will help alleviate the double transform problem.

Using Physique for Facial Animation

For subtleties in animation, especially facial features, the Physique modifier is highly diversified. The Physique modifier combines the technology of bones, Spline IK, and Linked XForms to create a unique method for facial animation. While Physique can be used to animate entire characters, in this section, we'll discuss how it can be used to animate the lips of a character.

Physique starts as a bone manipulation tool using envelopes. The envelopes are used to influence the amount and the extent of control that is exerted on a mesh surface. Envelopes look like elongated capsules surrounding a portion of a mesh object, as shown in Figure 7.15.

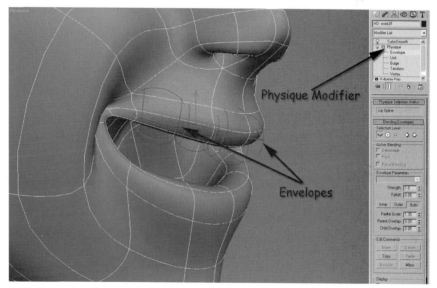

FIGURE 7.15   Envelopes of the Physique modifier.

The Physique Control Structure

What's unique about the Physique modifier is that it doesn't control an object directly. Physique is a bridge between a control object and the mesh object needing to be animated. To control a mesh, Physique can use a standard bones structure, floating bones, any object hierarchy, or a spline to control a mesh. For this example, we are going to use a spline, as this will give the lips more elasticity.

Start with a mesh object in a neutral pose. In this case, the mouth of the model has been opened to make it easier to determine how Physique controls the mesh. Since our control object is going to be a spline, use an NGon to create a spline around the mouth, as shown in Figure 7.16.

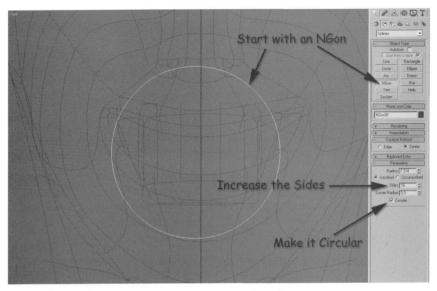

FIGURE 7.16 An NGon is used to create the controlling spline.

After creating the NGon, position the NGon near the mouth, as shown in Figure 7.17. The spline should be centered to the mouth in the front view as well as in a side view. Positioning of the spline must be done

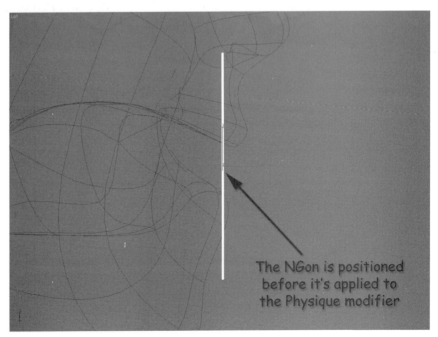

FIGURE 7.17 Center the NGon before converting it.

prior to being used as part of the Physique modifier to avoid inappropriate animation. Moving the spline after being implemented by Physique will cause your mesh to animate or distort.

To use the spline effectively, we need to have control over its vertices. To do this, convert it to an Editable Spline. This can be done by right-clicking and choosing Convert to Editable Spline from the Quad menu, as shown in Figure 7.18.

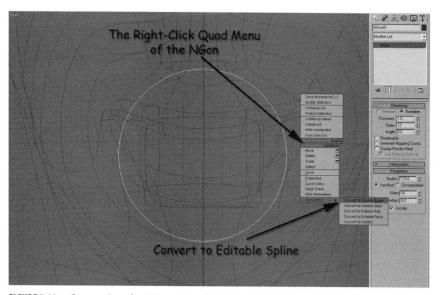

FIGURE 7.18   Converting the NGon to an Editable Spline.

Converting the Spline

Once the NGon has been converted, its vertices are now accessible as with any other Editable Spline object. In vertex mode, position the side vertices at the corners of the mouth, as shown in Figure 7.19. Notice the handles that appear around the vertices. The default configuration for a circular NGon is Bezier type vertices. For this example, the vertices will be converted to Smooth vertex types.

To convert all the vertices to Smooth, drag a marquis selection around the entire spline while in Vertex Sub-Object mode, and choose Smooth from the right-click menu, as shown in Figure 7.20. Notice that the Bezier handles have disappeared.

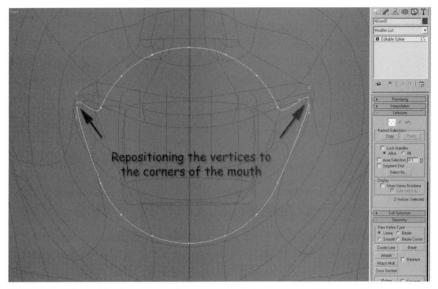

FIGURE 7.19 Repositioning the vertices to control the corners of the mouth.

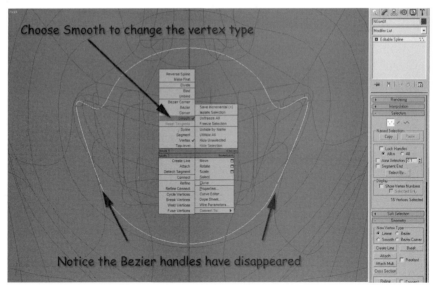

FIGURE 7.20 Converting the vertices to Smooth.

Once the spline's vertices have been converted, position the vertices along the inner position of the lips. When positioning the vertices, imagine the spline as a thick tube, and position the vertices so they are within the lips, not on the surface of the lips, as shown in Figure 7.21.

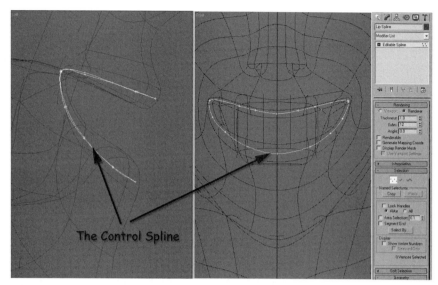

FIGURE 7.21   Position the spline as if it was a tube, to not position the control vertices on the edges of the mesh.

Adding the Control Spline to the Physique Modifier

Now that the control structure is in place, the Physique modifier needs to be added to the mesh to be animated. In this case, it's the head model. Select the head model and choose Physique from the Modifier panel to add the Physique modifier to the head mesh. After the Physique modifier has been added, click the Floating Bones rollout to display its parameters, as shown in Figure 7.22. This is where the control structure is added.

Since Physique is just the control bridge, we need to add animation controls that will ultimately control the mesh. This is where the NGon we created and converted earlier comes in. Within the Physique modifier, click the Add button in the Floating Bones rollout. Then, click on the NGon/Editable Spline created earlier to add it to the list of floating bones. The NGon was renamed to Lip Spline for this example. Figure 7.23 shows the Physique modifier after the control spline has been added to the Floating Bones rollout.

Manipulating Envelopes

After the control spline has been added to the Physique modifier, the envelopes need to be adjusted to properly control the mesh. Click the + sign next to the Physique modifier to open its Sub-Object properties. Highlight the Envelope item from the list in the Modify panel. Drag a marquis around the area that encompasses the spline to select all of the envelopes created in association with the spline object. The envelopes are part of the

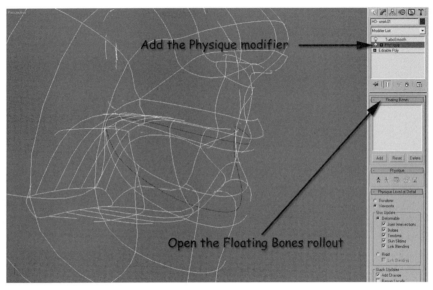

FIGURE 7.22   Adding and configuring the Physique modifier.

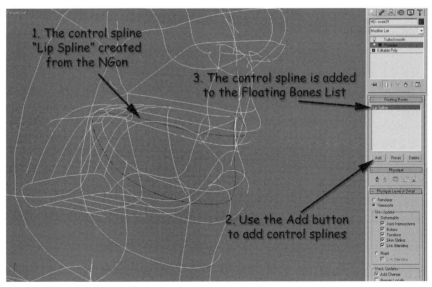

FIGURE 7.23   Adding the control spline to the Physique modifier.

Physique modifier for the head model, but they are positioned along the vertices of the controlling spline, as shown in Figure 7.24.

Once the spline has been added to the Floating Bones list, the envelopes can be adjusted for better control of the mesh surface. Use the Envelope Parameters to change the size and strength of each envelope individually or

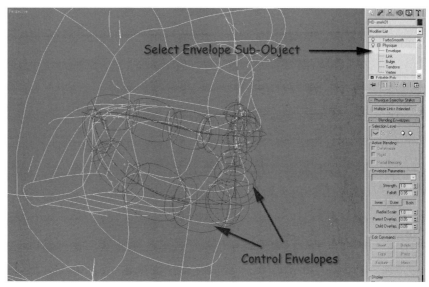

FIGURE 7.24   The control envelopes.

as a group. Adjusting the Radial Scale parameter changes the envelope size. This is crucial when dealing with a dense mesh or lots of envelopes or controls. Adjust the envelopes to encompass the vertices that need to be controlled with the Lip Spline control object. As the envelopes are adjusted, the vertices they affect are shown in bright green in the viewport. Figure 7.25 shows an example of envelopes where the size has been adjusted.

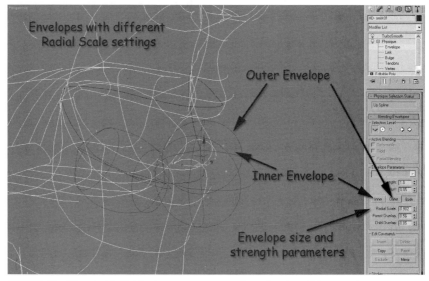

FIGURE 7.25   Use the Radial Scale parameter to adjust the size of the envelope.

When adjusting the envelopes of a Physique control structure, remember that the envelope's control is based on the mesh object below the Physique modifier in the Modifier stack. Therefore, if TurboSmooth or MeshSmooth is used above the Physique modifier, adjust the envelopes with the smoothing modifiers turned off for more accurate vertex control. Adding a TurboSmooth or MeshSmooth modifier before the Physique modifier is not recommended, as it will slow the system and will not improve vertex control.

Manipulating the Mesh with Physique

Now that the control structure is in place and the envelopes adjusted, the mesh can be controlled, simply by animating the vertices of the control structure. Although Physique is applied to the mesh needing to be controlled, the animation actually occurs with the control object. In this case, the control object is the NGon created earlier called Lip Spline. By animating the vertices of the Lip Spline, the lips can be controlled independently of the rest of the face. As shown in Figure 7.26, the vertices of the Lip Spline have been manipulated and the lips of the mesh object have followed.

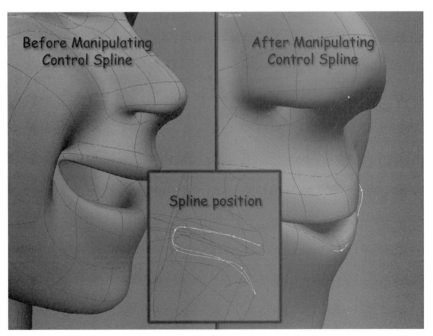

FIGURE 7.26   Animating the lips using Physique and a control spline.

ANIMATING THE TONGUE WITH SPLINE IK

Being that a tongue has very fluid movement in a restricted space, Spline IK is a great solution when animating a tongue is required. The best part about Spline IK is that it can control a large number of bones with a few control points.

Simple Is Best

When using Spline IK in any situation, the simplest solution is often the best. By using the least number of control points, a smoother animated mesh can be achieved. Regardless of how many vertices the mesh model contains or how many bones on the associated chain, Spline IK can use minimal control points to manipulate the mesh. In the tongue example, a tongue has been created with enough vertices to provide smooth movement of the mesh without binding, as shown in Figure 7.27.

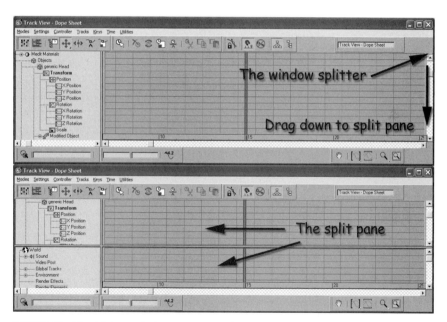

FIGURE 7.27   The high-resolution tongue mesh.

Create the Spline

Once the mesh model has been created, a control spline needs to be drawn. The control spline should match the model in length and curvature to provide the most accurate control. When creating the control spline, use the least number of vertices possible for the desired control. In Figure 7.28, the control spline has been drawn with four vertices and matches the curvature of the tongue. The vertices have also been set to smooth. The vertex size has been enhanced for better visibility in this image. Your actual vertex size may vary.

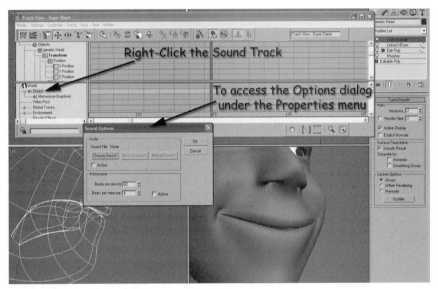

FIGURE 7.28   A spline with four vertices has been drawn along the length of the tongue.

Create the Bones

For a Spline IK solver to work, a bones structure needs to be in place. For the tongue, four bones were used, although the number of bones does not have to equal the number of vertices on the control spline. The spline is meant to simplify the control of the bones, so using fewer spline vertices is preferable. Figure 7.29 shows a simple four-bone chain for the tongue.

Add the Spline IK Solver to the Bone Chain

Now that the spline has been drawn, a Spline IK solver must be added to the bone chain. With the root bone selected, click on the Animation menu, and then choose Spline IK solver from the IK Solvers submenu, as shown in Figure 7.30.

FIGURE 7.29   A four-bone chain (and end bone) is used to control the tongue.

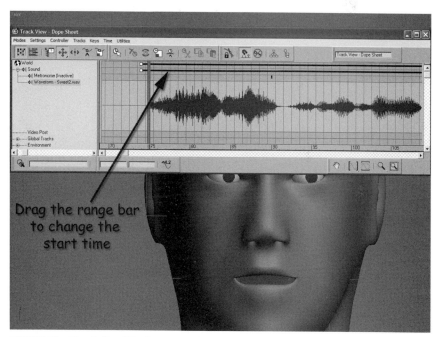

FIGURE 7.30   The Spline IK solver menu item.

After choosing the Spline IK solver, the cursor has a dotted line to it. The status line at the base of the 3ds Max interface will indicate that a joint needs to be chosen to complete the IK chain. Simply click on the end bone of the chain to complete the chain. The IK solver will now solve movement of the entire bone hierarchy. An end effector has been created at the base of the end bone, as shown in Figure 7.31.

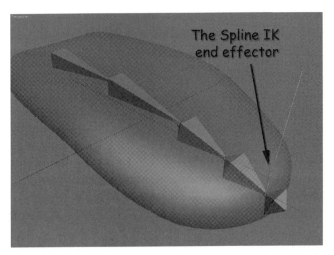

FIGURE 7.31   An end effector is created when the end joint is selected.

Choosing a Spline

After choosing the end joint to complete the IK chain, the operation is still not complete. A spline must be chosen before the IK solver is complete. Simply click on the spline created earlier to complete the process. You will notice that 3ds Max creates dummy objects for each of the vertices in the spline, as shown in Figure 7.32.

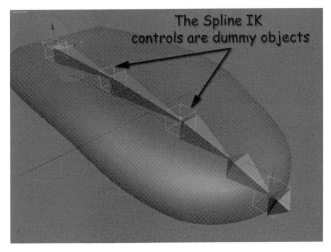

FIGURE 7.32   The Spline IK controls are dummy objects created automatically when choosing a Spline IK solver.

Apply the Skin Modifier to the Tongue

After choosing the spline and completing the setup for the Spline IK solver, a Skin Modifier needs to be applied to the tongue so the bones structure can control the mesh object. After the Skin Modifier has been applied to the tongue, add the bones created earlier through the Skin Modifier's Add Bones button (see Figure 7.33). After adjusting the envelopes of the skin modifier, the tongue can easily be controlled by the dummy objects created by the Spline IK solver, as shown in Figure 7.34.

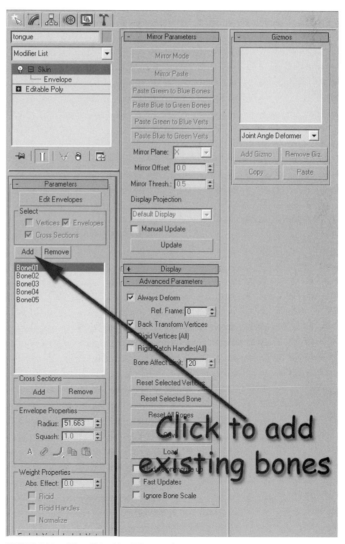

FIGURE 7.33   The Skin Modifier and its parameters.

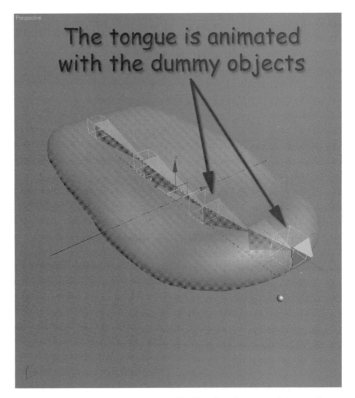

FIGURE 7.34 The tongue is controlled by the dummy objects after the skin modifier has been applied.

The Skin Modifier has several other parameters that are beyond the scope of this book. For more information on the Skin Modifier or controlling envelopes, consult the 3ds Max documentation.

LIP SYNCHING TO A VOICEOVER TRACK IN 3DS MAX

You've learned several ways to animate facial features in 3ds Max. If you want to synch up animation with a voiceover track, it's best to add it to your scene prior to animating, so you can animate to the sounds and phonemes of the voiceover track. This section was added to the end of the chapter for improved lesson flow.

Importing a Sound

Sound is added to 3ds Max through the Track View editor. From the Graph Editors menu, select Track View Dope Sheet. Just above the scroll bar on the right side of the Dope Sheet window is a small horizontal divider. Click and drag the divider down to split the window into two windows, as shown in Figure 7.35.

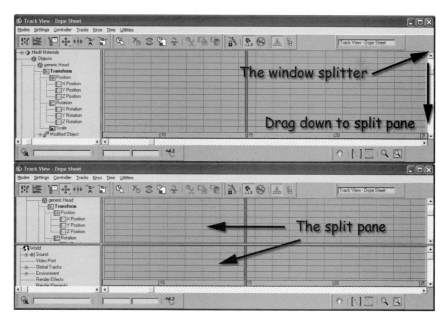

FIGURE 7.35   The Track View editor with a split pane.

In the Track View window, drag in the left side of the lower pane to reveal the Sound Track. Right-click the Sound Track and choose Properties from the Quad menu, as shown in Figure 7.36.

Once the Sound Options dialog is presented, click the Choose Sound button for a standard Windows File Open dialog. Navigate to the directory where the sound file is stored, and double-click the file to import it. Click OK in the Sound Options dialog to add the sound file to the Track View editor. 3ds Max can import .wav and .avi files for the soundtrack.

After importing the sound, you will see the sound file's waveform in the lower pane of the Track View editor and the name of the file in the left lower pane, as shown in Figure 7.37.

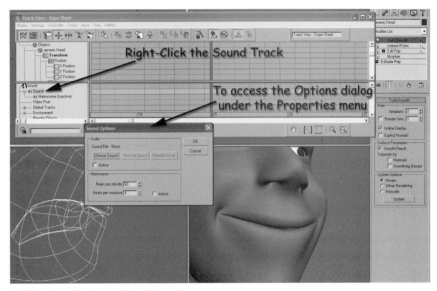

FIGURE 7.36   The Sound Track Quad menu.

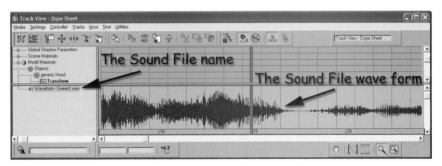

FIGURE 7.37   The waveform of a sound file that's been imported into Track View.

After the sound is added to Track View, use the range bar to align the sound with the proper position in time. For example, if the speaking portion of the animation starts at frame 75, move the range bar so the sound begins at frame 75, as shown in Figure 7.38.

Now that the audio file has been imported into 3ds Max, you can begin using the methods described in this chapter to begin lip synching to the voiceover track. It's important to note that having a timing sheet and phoneme list makes the entire process easier, by setting the major phonemes prior to adjusting for the subtle sounds.

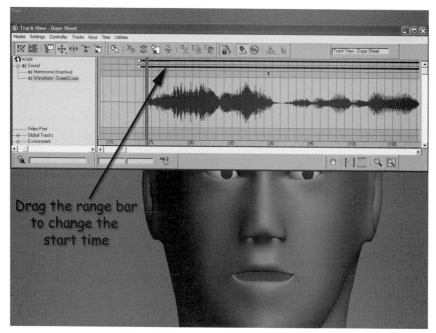

FIGURE 7.38   Use the range bar to adjust when the sound begins.

Conclusion

There are several methods for animating facial features for expressions or lip synching. Regardless of the type of facial animation you intend to create, planning is involved. Choose your method of animation based on what type of animation needs to be performed. In some cases, bones will be the answer, while in others, morph targets or Linked XForms. Regardless of the method, facial features need to be analyzed for the most believable results. The most important tool for facial animation isn't the software or the computer. The most important tool for facial animation is a mirror. Speak the lines with sincerity into a mirror (or videotape yourself) so you have the best reference for how the facial muscles are affected with each expression.

FACIAL ANIMATION
WITH MAYA

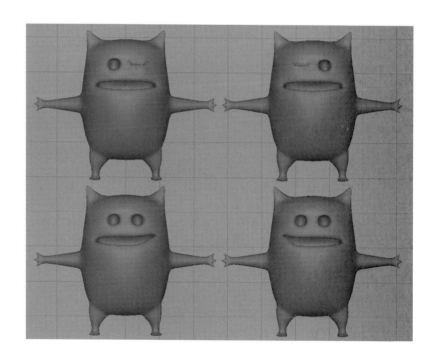

This chapter deals with the different working methods and solutions for facial animation in Maya. Like most other challenges within Maya, there are a myriad of ways to get the results you want. The differing methods have varying amounts of setup and control. We'll start with the use of blend shapes—probably the most popular method of facial deformation. We'll also cover the use of joints, clusters, and lattices and how they relate to facial setup. Finally, we'll set up an IK tongue, and go over importing audio so you can begin lip synch. This chapter assumes a basic knowledge of the software.

There are several methods for accomplishing facial animation in Maya. In this chapter, we explore the following methodologies:

- Joints
- Clusters
- Lattices
- Animating a tongue with IK
- Importing audio for lip sync

PICKING THE CONTROLS YOU WISH TO CREATE

When setting up your characters, the first thing to consider is how you want to animate. Do you want a quick setup solution that might give you less control but let you start animating sooner, or do you want maximum control so if you want to tweak the tiniest part of the face it is all ready to do so? It's a time trade-off—the longer the setup, the more control; but then again, you're setting up characters rather than animating. The different methods will have varying amounts of the setup time to results ratio. We'll start with blend shapes, one of the most immediate methods of facial deformation.

USING BLEND SHAPES FOR MORPHING

Blend shapes are easily the most popular method for facial deformation within Maya. They are relatively easy to produce, and the setup time is based on how quickly you can model the desired poses. Blend shapes create a morph between two differing pieces of geometry. The working method is to start with a base head and a modified target head in the end pose (or partial pose). After you set up the base model and the first target, Maya provides a slider that lets you dial in the degree to which the base head is modified by the target.

To create the target shape, start by duplicating the base head with the default options by selecting Edit > Duplicate, as shown in Figure 8.1.

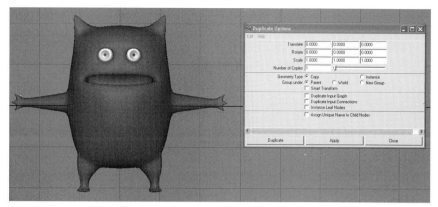

FIGURE 8.1   Duplicating the base head with default options.

On the duplicate target head, modify the topology as you wish in Sub-Object mode. The blend shape deforms by comparing how the vertices or CVs have moved. When you're ready to set up the blend shape controls, select the target modified head, and then shift-select the base head. In the Animation menu, select Deform > Create Blend Shape > Options. With the default options, select Create, as shown in Figure 8.2.

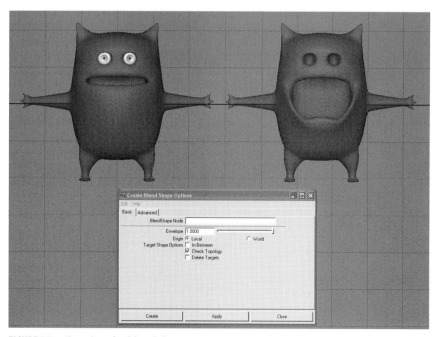

FIGURE 8.2   Creating the blend shape.

To bring up the Blend Shape Editor window, select Window > Animation Editors > Blend Shape, as shown in Figure 8.3. By moving the slider, you'll see the base head change, moving toward the target shape you just created.

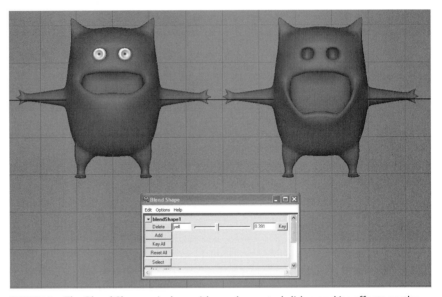

FIGURE 8.3   The Blend Shape window with newly created slider, and its effects on the base head at the left.

Blend shapes are not limited solely to a move between the base and one target shape—you can combine targets to get a wide range of results. For instance, if you had a large "mouth open" shape, and a large "smile" shape, you can dial in the two of them, to produce a third shape when animating. If you create a variety of target shapes, the number of shape combinations that can be dialed in grows exponentially. The method of creation is the same as before—just Shift-select each of the target shapes and the base head last before creating the blend shape deformation in Deform > Create Blend Shape, as shown in Figure 8.4.

Adding More Control with More Blend Shapes

The number of blend shapes you create is limited only by your imagination, but usually for successful animation you'll want to break down the face into several different areas to give you greater flexibility and more final poses when animating. The main areas are the mouth, the eyes, and

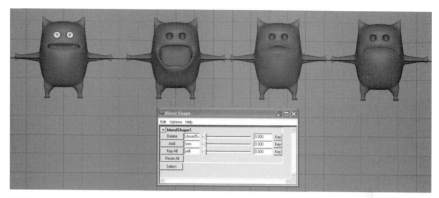

FIGURE 8.4   Multiple blend shapes are easily created with the same method.

the brows. Other areas to consider are the cheeks, ears, or whatever else you might want to move later. Again, depending on how much control you want, your setup could take much more time. You could model the mouth as a single object, or you could model half of the face in one series of shapes, and the other half in another series. Usually, though, the mouth is less critical to have asymmetry in comparison to the other areas. For the eyes, for instance, you want to have independent control. If, say, you want to have the eyes blink with a one-frame offset, you would need to have a closed left eye shape, and a closed right eye shape. If you didn't have this asymmetry, the eyes would have to close and open together. Similarly, if you wanted to have the brows have a quizzical look with one brow up and one down, there are two ways to approach this. You could model this shape as one target, or, if you had a "left brow up" and "right brown down" control, you could combine the two. Most animators want the freedom to hit all of the poses they can think of, so the asymmetry is important to keep in mind, and probably a good use of time to put the extra effort into the needed shapes (see Figure 8.5).

Usually for modeling the face, you want to at least have the following sets of shapes:

Mouth: Open, Closed, Smile, Frown, and all of the phonemes you want (a, e, c, m, b, v, etc.)
Eyes: Open, Closed, Wide (left and right versions of both)
Brows: Mad, Shocked, Sad (left and right versions of both)

Remember, you'd most likely want a left and right version for at least the eyes and the brows, and for the mouth as well. Poses like smile and frown would be divided into a left and right side, giving you that many more options when animating. This is the bare bones list of what you could get by with (see Figure 8.6).

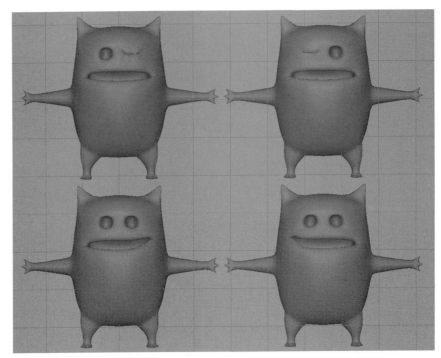

FIGURE 8.5 By using separate shape targets for the left and right side of the face, the animator has much more flexibility when it comes time to animate.

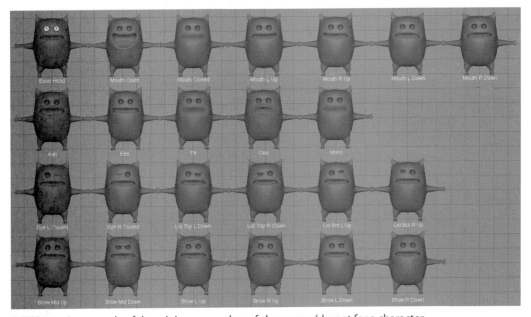

FIGURE 8.6 An example of the minimum number of shapes you'd want for a character.

Additionally, you might want to consider shapes such as cheeks puffing out, and any other targets you might want to hit, such as a huge surprised mouth if that's called for in your story. Say there's also a moment where a character tugs at his ear—you'd want to make a target for the pulled down shape as well. It's not uncommon to end with a legion of shapes, that when all connected, give you a huge range of emotional possibilities (see Figure 8.7).

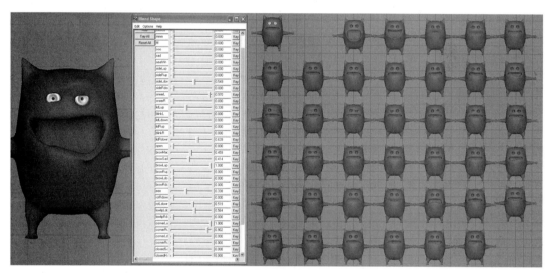

FIGURE 8.7   You may end up with tons of target shapes to get the eventual performance range you desire.

Corrective Blend Shapes

Blend shapes can also be corrective in nature, used not just to hit the poses you want, but to fix errors as well. Say you have an open eye blend shape, and because of the nature of the eyeball, the lid penetrates the eyeball as the vertices move up to the open position (Figure 8.8).

You can create another blend in the mid position where you adjust the vertices to avoid this penetration. You can even create this new shape using the blend shape window itself. Dial in the lid down halfway with the slider, and then duplicate the base head, with the default options. You'll get a new mesh "frozen" in the dialed-in combination (see Figure 8.9).

Take this new shape, Shift-click the original base head, and create a new blend shape (Deform > Create Blend Shape). In the Blend Shape editor window, dial the original blend back to 0, and the newly created blend up to 1, as shown in Figure 8.10.

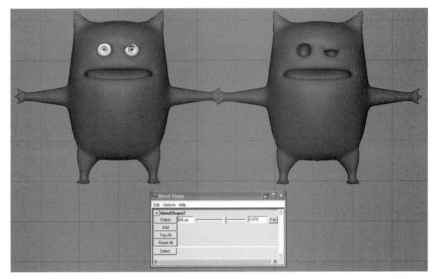

FIGURE 8.8 Our blend shape of the left lid down penetrates the eye when dialed halfway.

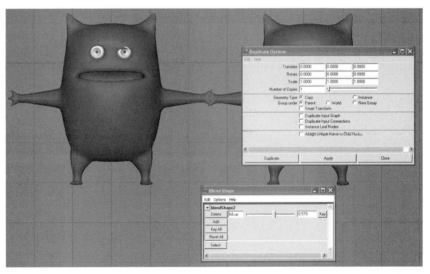

FIGURE 8.9 Duplicate a copy of the base head, with the blend shape dialed in to where the error occurs.

Now, with the blend shape dialed in to 1, we can see the effects of the blend in real time on the base head. You can then adjust the vertices to correct the lid penetration, and you have a new shape you can combine back into the blend shape editor (see Figure 8.11).

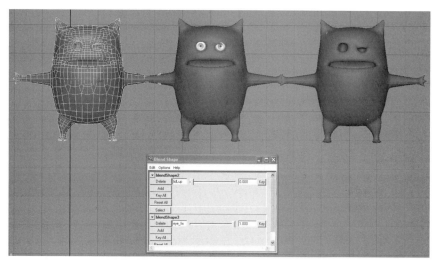

FIGURE 8.10   The new shape that will be the fix is dialed to 1 to see its effect, and is ready to be modified.

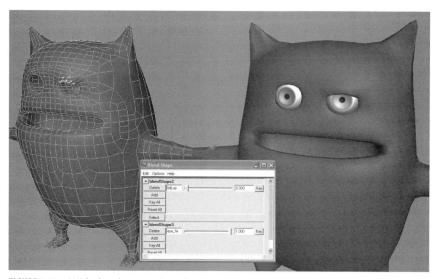

FIGURE 8.11   With the shape we're adjusting dialed in, we can modify the vertices of the target head (left) and see their effect immediately on the base head (right). This gives us real-time feedback to see our adjustments.

Using Corrective Blend Shapes

Now that we have this corrected blend shape, wouldn't it be cool if we could have it be dialed in automatically as the lid closed? Well, Maya allows us this option. Similarly to how we set up the blend before, we're going to select the fixed shape, Shift-select the original lid closed shape, and then Shift-select the base head. Bring up the Create Blend Shape Options window (Deform > Create Blend Shape > Options). In the window, click on the checkbox next to In-Between to turn it on. Click on Create to create the blend shape, and then open the Blend Shape window. Dial in the newly created shape, and you'll see the lid will close, and now the corrective target shape is hit midway (see Figure 8.12).

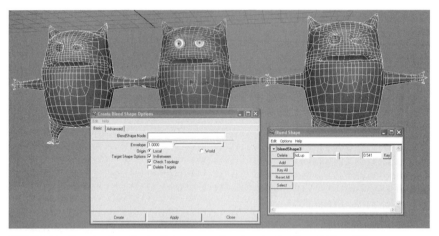

FIGURE 8.12   By selecting the In-Between option box in the Create Blend Shape Options window, (left) we end up with a slider (right) that dials through two shapes.

Maya allows you to hit multiple targets in a blend shape. This method can be used on the mouth, brows, and anywhere else you might need to. You could even use this tool to create a cycle for a tail swishing back and forth, where you hit each of the poses (target shapes) in order dialing one slider. Blend shapes are a powerful tool.

Progressive Blend Shapes

Blend shapes don't have to be large sculpts of parts of the face; they can also be small incremental adjustments that work together. Instead of having a shape that is "mouth smile" for instance, you could break down the mouth into several different areas to reach the same result. You could have the corners of the mouth be separate shapes, as well as the middle of the lips, halfway from the corner of the mouth to the middle, and so forth. Thus, you have tiny controls that work together to get the same result. Of course, this method takes much more setup and a sophisticated solution to make working with all these pieces production friendly. A great example of this is Jason Osipa's popular face setup he demonstrates in his book *Stop Staring: Facial Modeling and Animation Done Right.*

You may have noticed that Maya's Blend Shape window interface doesn't give you many display options. All those sliders next to each other can be a pretty messy way to animate, but one simple fix can make it easier. In the Blend Shape window, select Options > Orientation > Horizontal. The window will shift from a vertical to horizontal orientation, and you can suddenly see many more of the controls onscreen at once (see Figures 8.13 and 8.14).

FIGURE 8.13   By selecting Options > Orientation > Horizontal in the window, we can see many more of the sliders at once.

Maya gives you a few more options for modifying your blend shape set. In Deform > Edit Blend Shape you will find the options to Add, Remove, or Swap, which give you the ability to change which shapes are in the blend shape node. In addition, you can go back and modify the target shapes as long as you keep them in the scene, which gives you the ability to make small tweaks after you see how all of the different targets work together. Often times, though, people delete the targets once they get farther down the character setup path so they have a lighter rig. Since Maya keeps the data of how the shape changed, the original targets can be removed, and the blend shape will still work. If you accidentally delete a target shape you wanted to modify, you can always recreate it by dialing in the target shape's slider in the Blend Shape window, and duplicating the base head in its modified state. You can then add it back into the blend shape.

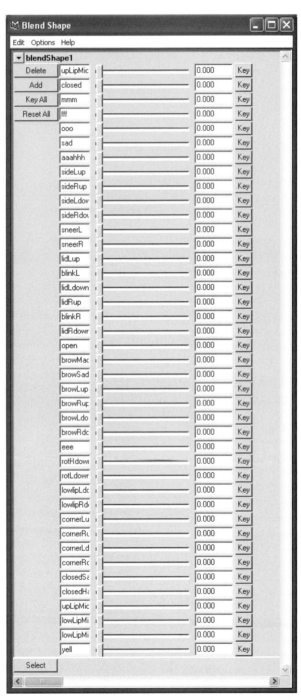

FIGURE 8.14   The default Blend Shape window uses vertical orientation, which makes it very difficult to see all of the blends.

WORKING WITH JOINTS FOR FACIAL ANIMATION

Another way to set up facial animation within Maya is with joints, which can be used in facial setup in several ways. Often, a jawbone is put in so that regardless of the other tools used to modify the face, you have the option of manipulating the jaw area with a bone control. You might have a face driven by blend shapes, but that jawbone can give you that extra extreme shape you might want to hit. Joints can also be laid out to represent the muscles of the face. Using bones snapped to the face geometry and setting an IK chain at the end, you can create a series of controls at key points, such as around the perimeter of the mouth, or at several points on each eyebrow. These can attempt to give a more realistic control of the face, since they are somewhat simulating the path of the muscles.

If cartoony flexibility is desired instead of reality, bones can help there also. Bones are a good solution for ears, hair, or even a character's head if you wish to have it deform during the performance (see Figure 8.15).

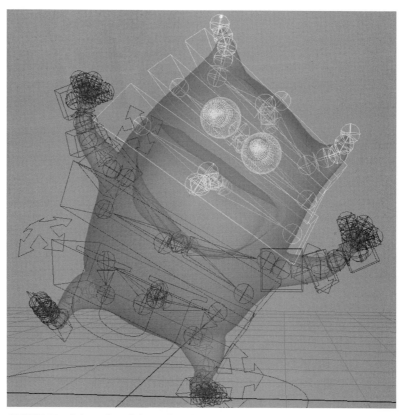

FIGURE 8.15   Joints placed through a character's head and ears can give that extra deformation you might want in nonrealistic characters.

Joints can also be a good solution for eyelids. By placing joints from the center of the eye to an eyelid, and some careful skin weighting, the rotational nature of the FK joint will cause the lid to wrap around the eye as it closes. Using several joints can allow for shapes such as angry or sad on the lids for extra expressiveness (see Figure 8.16).

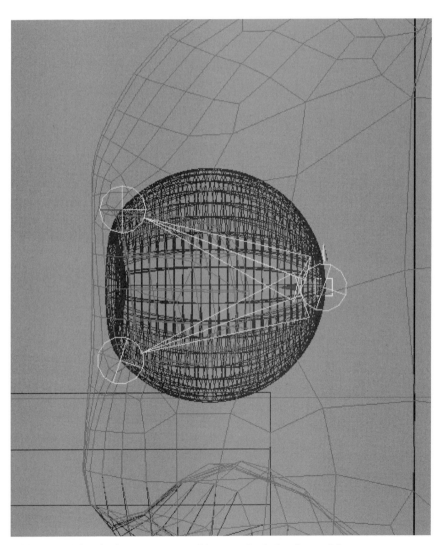

FIGURE 8.16 Joints in the eyes can provide a good solution for eyelids.

USING CLUSTERS FOR MODIFYING SHAPES

Clusters are a simple way to create a quick control to manipulate an area of the face, and can be used as a late addition to another setup method, or as a larger part. Clusters are a set of vertices, lattice points, or CVs, and are easily created and can be animated. Say there was a part of the upper lip that you wanted to pull up for a snarl expression. It's easy to set up. First, select the vertices or CVs you want to move. Then, select Animation > Deform > Create Cluster > Options. With the options at the default setting, select Create. The resulting "C" that shows up in the viewport can be manipulated to change the face. It can be connected to the rig so you have the tweaking ability during animation that clusters can provide (see Figure 8.17).

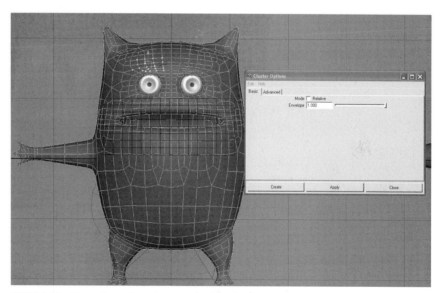

FIGURE 8.17　The selected vertices on the face for the cluster, and the Cluster Options dialog box.

Clusters can also be used in the creation of blend shapes, as a tool to more easily get to the final shape. You can create a cluster on the base head, modify it to get the shape you want, and then duplicate the base head to get your new target shape similar to what you see in Figure 8.18. The base head can then easily be returned to its normal state by deleting the cluster. You can also keep the cluster, and kick out a bunch of different shapes by manipulating the cluster and duplicating them off. It's a great time saver.

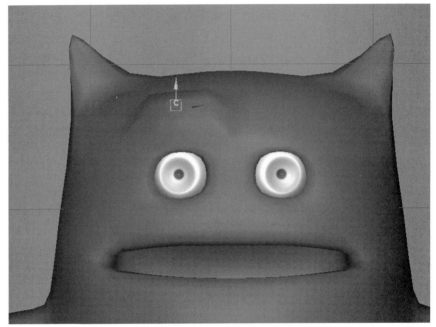

FIGURE 8.18   The newly created cluster and the resulting area it can modify.

USING LATTICES FOR FACIAL DEFORMATION

Lattices can be useful for several applications for facial animation in Maya. Similar to the use of clusters to create blend shapes, so too can lattices be used in this manner. Rather than tweaking the individual vertices or CVs of a face, a lattice gives us an easier method for altering these sometimes highly detailed areas. For instance, you could grab all of the points around a character's mouth. With these points selected, go to Animation > Deform > Create Lattice > Options. In the Lattice Options box, the Divisions will tell how much detail you'll have across the X-, Y-, and Z-axis of the lattice. Click Create to have your lattice appear (see Figure 8.19).

The lattice will show up as a box with a grid across it. To modify the lattice points, right-click over the lattice and select Lattice Point. You can then move the lattice points around to see how you can modify the mesh underneath. It's a much quicker method to alter the geometry than going in to each individual vertex. You can use the methods we discussed previously to modify the lattice on the base head, and duplicate off a copy to create target shapes for blend shape production (see Figure 8.20).

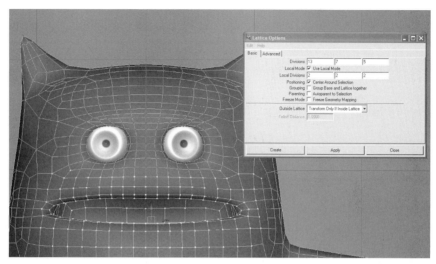

FIGURE 8.19   With the vertices of the mouth selected, the Lattice Options dialog box lets us choose how much detail will go into the lattice.

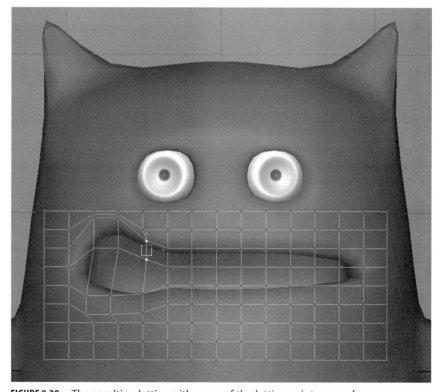

FIGURE 8.20   The resulting lattice with some of the lattice points moved.

Using Lattices for Secondary Animation

Lattices can also be used to create animatable controls and automated secondary animation. Often used to fix things such as forearm twist, shoulder areas, and other parts on the body, on the face lattices could be used to create a character with giant jowls or floppy ears, for instance. We'd select the vertices we want to deform, and create a lattice. Then, the lattice points can be driven by bones, spring controllers, or other solutions. These would take much longer to explain than we have time for here, but you should be aware of the power of the lattice. Keep in mind when setting up this solution, as well as with clusters, that the deformation order of your input and how it's connected on your rig are important, as to not end up with double translation and other caveats.

TONGUE CONTROL WITH SPLINE IK

Spline IK is a great way to give control to animate a tongue. We'll start with the basic tongue geometry, and put a series of joints in it from the base of the tongue to the tip, with the default options selected. In this case, we're putting in four main joints plus the end joint. We can do a smooth bind to the joints with the default options through Animation > Skin > Bind Skin > Smooth Bind (see Figures 8.21 and 8.22).

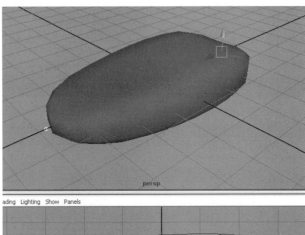

FIGURE 8.21   The basic tongue with the joints running through it.

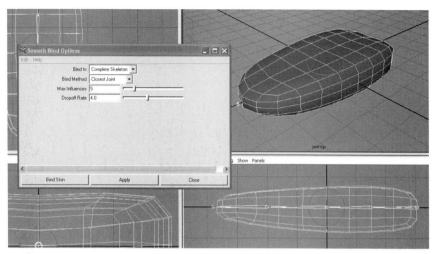

FIGURE 8.22   Binding the tongue with Smooth Bind at the default settings.

You'll see now that you could animate the tongue if you wanted to using the FK bones that are running through it. That might be a little slow, though, so we're going to use Spline IK to make it a quicker process. We'll next select the Spline IK creation tool through Skeleton > IK Spline Handle Tool > Options. With the default options, click on the joint at the base of the tongue, and the end joint at the tip. That creates our Spline IK (see Figure 8.23).

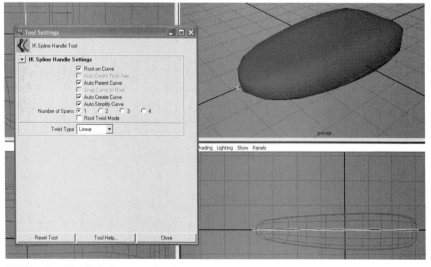

FIGURE 8.23   The IK Spline creation box.

There's not really much to move with the resulting curve that's drawn or the IK handle. We're going to set up some controls using clusters that will help us to easily control the Spline IK and thus the tongue.

First, working in the side view, hide the joints by selecting Show > Joints. Then, we're going to hide the tongue geometry through the same Show menu (we're using polygons, so we'll hide those). With nothing in the viewport but the spline curve and the IK handle, we're going to right-click and select Control Vertex. Grab a vertex and move it, and you'll see the curve bends with the translation of the vertex (CV), as we'd expect. Grab the first CV at the base of tongue. With it selected, we're going to create a cluster through Deform > Create Cluster > Cluster Options. In the Options window, next to Mode, click on Relative in the checkbox. You'll see the cluster appear in the window. Continue creating clusters on each of the remaining three CVs. For the last one, you'll probably have to "Select by component type joints only," as the last CV sits right on top of the IK handle (see Figure 8.24).

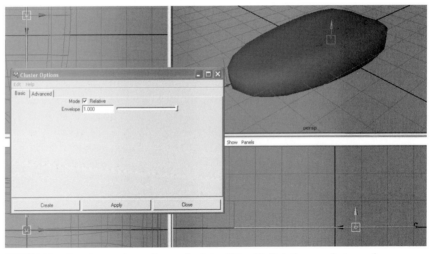

FIGURE 8.24   Creating a cluster for each of the CVs with Relative mode turned on.

Unhide the tongue geometry, grab a cluster, and move it around. You'll see that quickly we've created a tongue that can move in almost any way you can imagine. When you eventually put the tongue in a mouth and rig setup, take care in the way you connect the tongue, bones, and clusters to the rig so you get the results you want (see Figure 8.25).

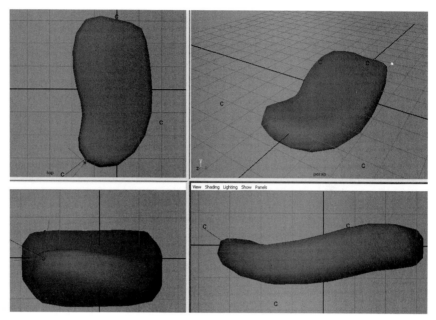

FIGURE 8.25   The final tongue, driven by Spline IK, can move almost any way you want.

WORKING WITH AUDIO IN MAYA

Bringing audio files into Maya is straightforward. Go to File > Import, and select your sound file in the dialog pop-up. Then, go to the timeline at the bottom of the screen. Right-click and hold on the timeline, and where it says "Sound," move the mouse over the arrow to the right. Move over the box next to the name of your desired sound file, and release the mouse button.

The Attribute Editor window for your sound file will open. It doesn't have much information, but the one important area to note is the Offset box in the Audio Attributes area. This is where you can adjust the start time of the audio in the timeline. The offset amount is based on frames. If you enter "10" in the box, the audio will start at frame 10. Use the Offset box to start the audio clip at the desired frame number.

Also in this dialog is the box "audio:" with the name of the file next to it. You can rename the audio file (as it is referenced in Maya, not the actual file itself) in this dialog box as well. You might want to abbreviate the filename, for instance, if the name is awkwardly long in the timeline (see Figure 8.26).

FIGURE 8.26 The sound Attribute Editor window.

For practical purposes, Maya can only have one sound file loaded in the timeline at a given time. (We'll get into the Trax Editor, which attempts to offer multiple sounds.) To get around this, you can load in different sounds to the timeline by right-clicking in the timeline, as before, and selecting a different imported sound from the list. The offsets are sound file specific, so you can have them drop into the timeline at different points along the timeline.

The Trax Editor allows additional limited options for working with audio. You can import audio through the File > Import dialog box, which mirrors the normal Import method. The Trax Editor then shows multiple audio tracks. At this point, you can drag the tracks left or right to adjust their starting point in the timeline. You can also double-click the waveform on the track to rename the audio within Maya (see Figure 8.27).

With the audio in the Trax Editor, you now have another option in the main Maya timeline. If you return to the Sound selection box by right-clicking on the timeline, you'll see the option of "Use Trax Sounds," which we ignored before. If you select this option and play the timeline, you will see that it will play one sound, but stop the first audio file and cut to the second at its start frame. Combined with the fact that now the audio is represented by a straight line, not a waveform, this option quickly falls out of favor. Usually, if you want to hear multiple, overlapping audio clips, it's recommended to edit them together in a sound application before bringing them in to Maya.

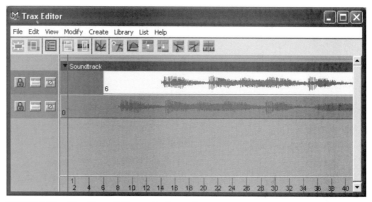

FIGURE 8.27   The Trax Editor window allows importing audio and the ability to move tracks to different start frames.

Adjusting the Height of the Timeline

Sometimes when animating, seeing the waveform in the timeline is helpful, and Maya allows you to scale the timeline to more easily see it. Go to the Preferences dialog box through either Window > Settings/Preferences > Preferences, or with the Preferences icon in the bottom-right corner of the screen.

In the Preferences dialog box, click on Timeline in the Categories section. Under the Timeline options on the right, you can see where it says "Height" and the options "1x," "2x," and "4x." Selecting these options will scale the timeline, and you can see the waveform more easily (see Figures 8.28 and 8.29).

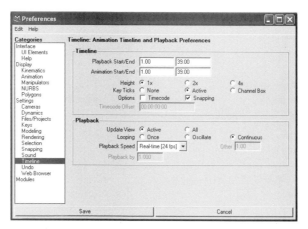

FIGURE 8.28   The Preferences > Timeline dialog where you can change the height of the audio in the timeline display.

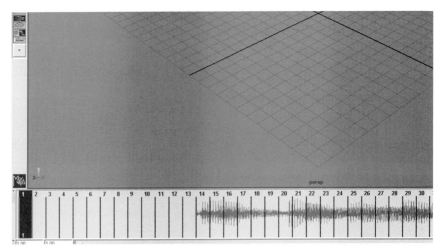

FIGURE 8.29   The Maya timeline showing the audio waveform at a height of 4x.

Deleting Audio

Getting rid of audio in Maya isn't readily apparent, but there are a few easy methods. First, if you simply don't want to hear the audio anymore, you can select the Off option in the Sound menu when you right-click on the timeline. To delete audio files out of Maya, you can do so by selecting the name and using the "delete" key in the Outliner. In addition, within the Trax Editor, you can click on the track and press the Delete key. The selected sound is then removed from the scene.

CONCLUSION

In this chapter, we touched on some of the main methods and tools available for facial setup and animation within Maya. Like most of the workflow in Maya, there are many ways to get the solutions you want. These exercises should give you a head start in finding the best solution for your needs.

TYPICAL HUMAN EXPRESSION WEIGHTED MORPH TARGETS

This appendix is a visual reference of key facial poses that, when used as weighted morph targets, enable many transitional poses. Keep in mind that while these poses can all be used at 100% weight, many of them when used at less than 100% weight can give a character subtle facial expressions that make for more interesting viewing.

BROWS ANGRY

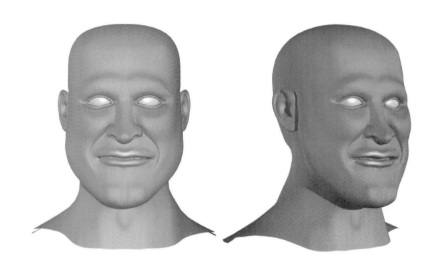

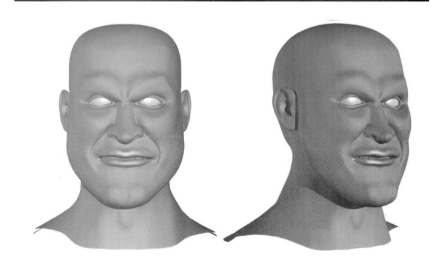

Distinguishing Features

The brows are pulled down and together at the inside corners. This target is used primarily for expressions of pain or effort.

BROWS ARCHED

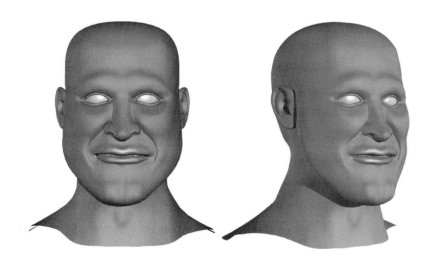

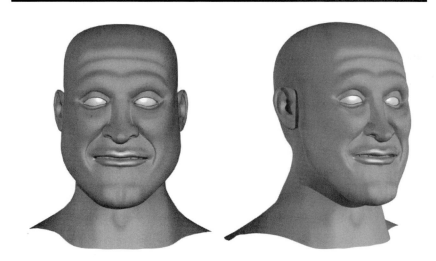

Distinguishing Features

The brows are raised straight up, creating deep furrows in the forehead. This target is used for expressions such as surprise, terror, and shock.

BROWS COMPRESSED

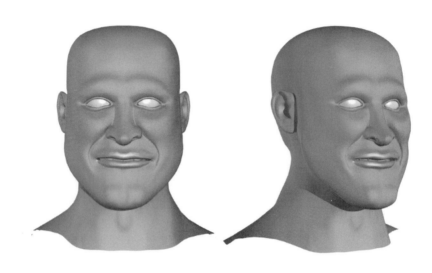

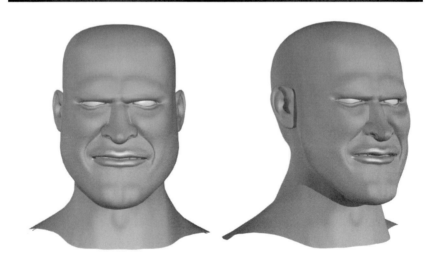

Distinguishing Features

The brows are drawn straight down, partially obscuring the eyes. This is used for expressions such as concentration, crying, anger, and to soften the raised and angry brow targets.

BROWS MIDDLE UP

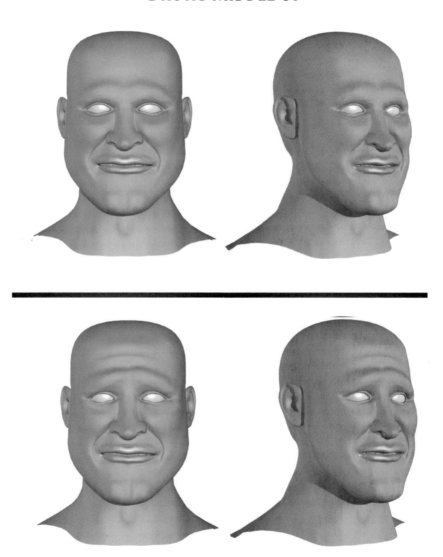

Distinguishing Features

The brows are drawn up in the middle. This target is used for expressions of sadness.

EYES LEFT DOWN

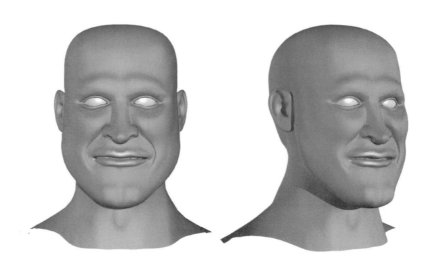

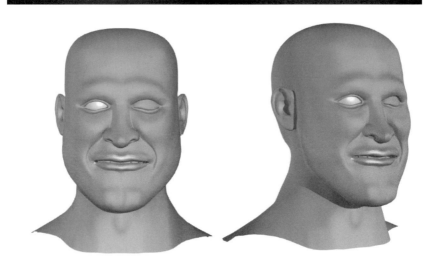

Distinguishing Features

The left eye is closed. By creating separate closing targets for the left and right, winking and asymmetrical squinting are possible.

EYES RIGHT DOWN

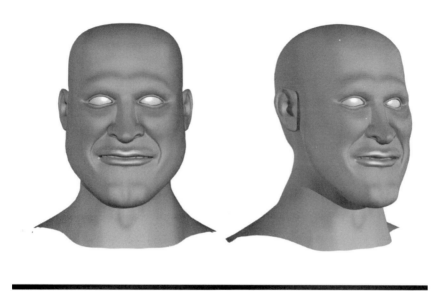

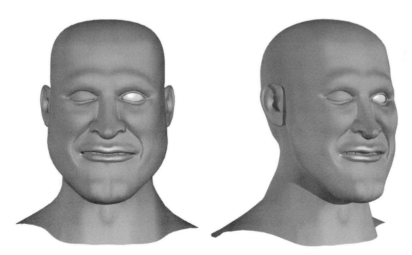

Distinguishing Features

The right eye is closed. By creating separate closing targets for the left and right, winking and asymmetrical squinting are possible.

EYES WIDE

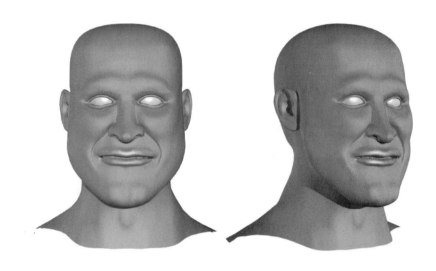

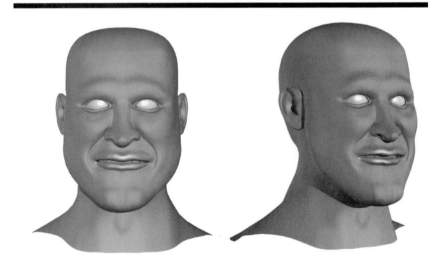

Distinguishing Features

The eyelids are drawn farther up than normal. Useful for such poses as terror, fear, and enthusiasm.

MOUTH CLOSED

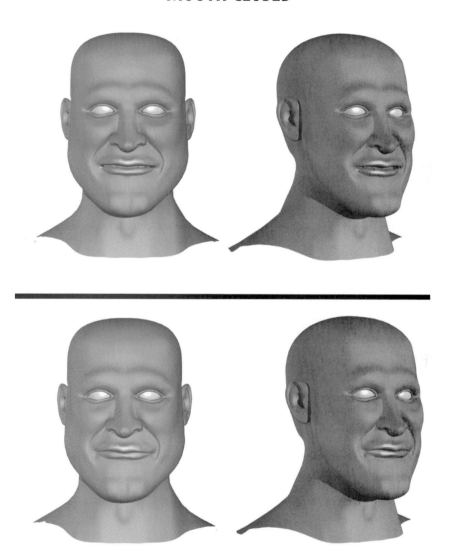

Distinguishing Features

The mouth is closed in a relaxed, somewhat neutral pose. This is useful for calm expressions, and for toning down other open and closed mouth targets.

MOUTH CRYING

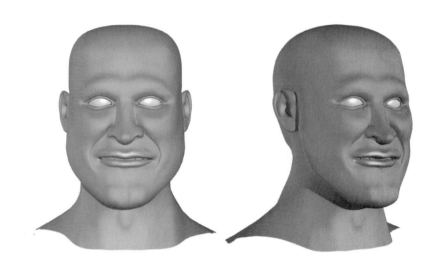

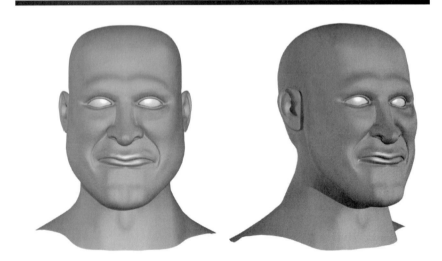

Distinguishing Features

This is a crying target with the mouth closed. The eyelids have not been modified. Useful for subdued crying expressions.

MOUTH CRY OPEN

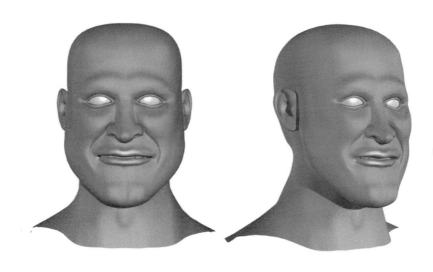

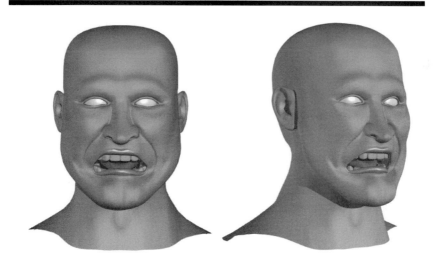

Distinguishing Features

This is an extreme crying mouth target. No eyelid movement in this pose. The mouth is open, and the corners are drawn down and back, causing the cheeks to bulge under the zygomatic bone.

MOUTH DISGUST

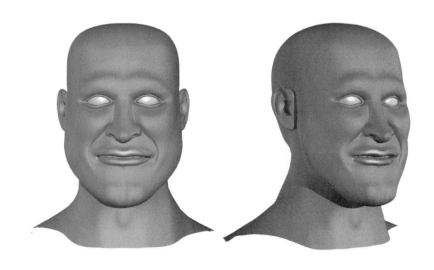

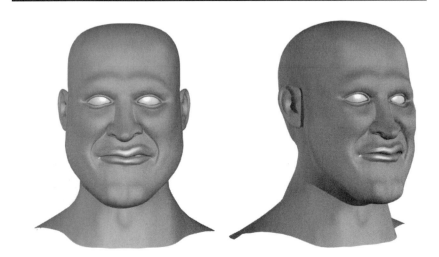

Distinguishing Features

One side of the upper lip is drawn upward, creating a bulge in the cheek and a crease around the nose on that side of the face. This is a useful target for expressions of disgust, or a snarl.

MOUTH FRIGHTENED

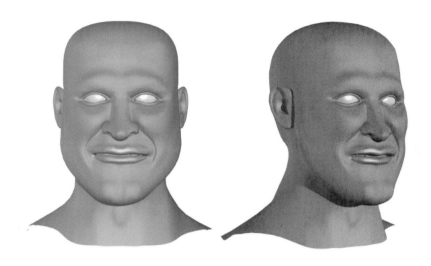

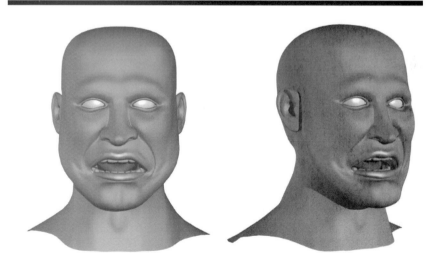

Distinguishing Features

The corners of the mouth are drawn back with the lower lip almost straight across. It's useful for expressions of fear. It can also be used to create an expression of exertion, at less than 100% weight with the teeth together.

MOUTH LAUGHTER

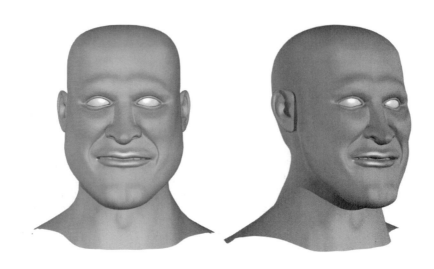

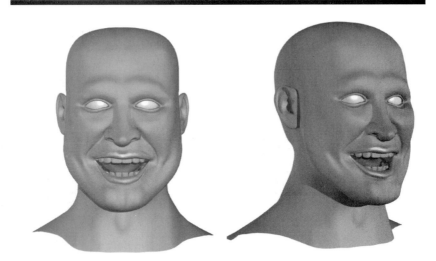

Distinguishing Features

The mouth is opened and the corners are drawn up and back toward the ears, tightening the lips against the teeth. The cheeks bulge under the zygomatic bone.

MOUTH PURSE

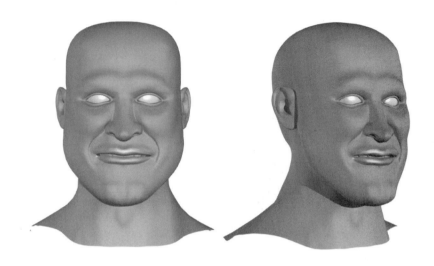

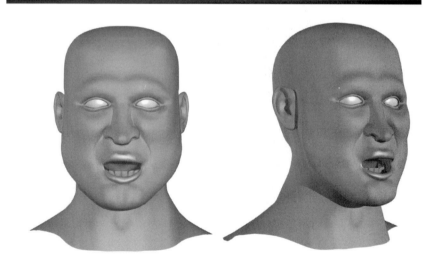

Distinguishing Features

The lips are compressed horizontally and drawn away from the teeth. This is useful for modifying expressions that need the lips drawn out somewhat, such as a false smile or a smirk.

MOUTH REPULSION

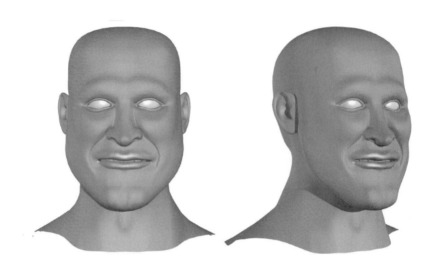

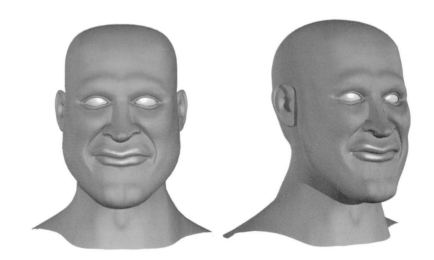

Distinguishing Features

The upper lip is curled into a sneer. Similar to disgust, but the lip is drawn up on both sides, which causes bulging in the cheeks.

MOUTH SMILE CLOSED

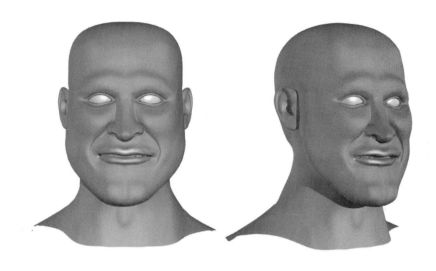

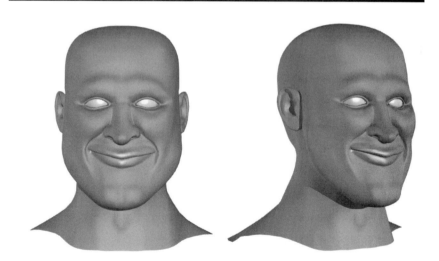

Distinguishing Features

The mouth is closed and the corners are drawn up and back toward the ear. The cheeks bulge under the zygomatic bone and dimples may appear (animated separately), depending on how chubby your character is.

MOUTH SUPPRESSED SADNESS

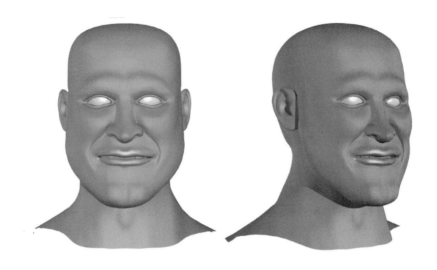

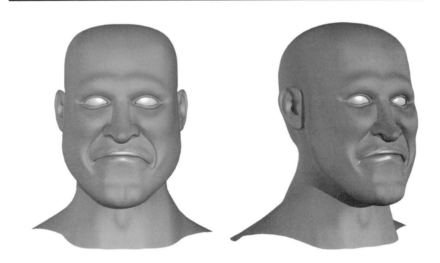

Distinguishing Features

The mouth is closed and the corners are dramatically curled downward. It's useful for expressions such as crying, sadness, and facial shrugs (with less than 100% weight).

MOUTH SURPRISE

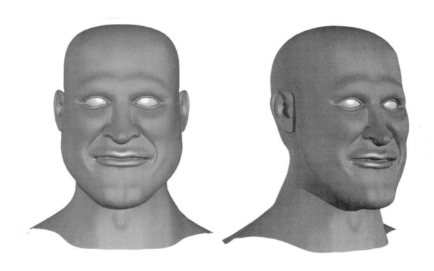

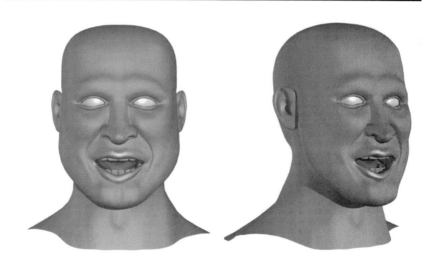

Distinguishing Features

The mouth is opened and somewhat relaxed, with the tips of the upper and lower teeth revealed.

MOUTH TERROR

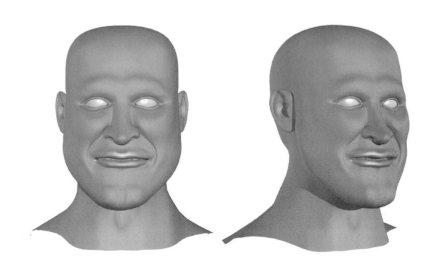

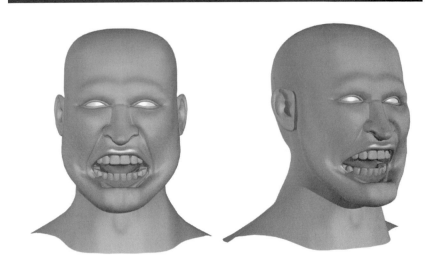

Distinguishing Features

The mouth is opened as wide as possible, with the corners drawn down and back toward the ears. This is a necessary target for extreme forms of terror or aggression, and yawning.

MOUTH YAWN

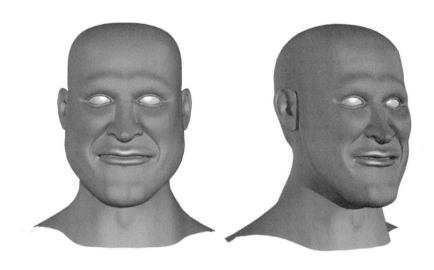

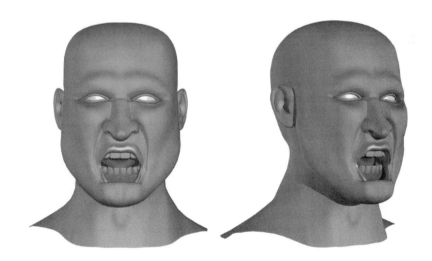

Distinguishing Features

The mouth is opened very wide, but the corners are drawn neither up nor down. This target is useful for modifying other targets that need a wide-open mouth, such as yawns.

JAW CLOSED

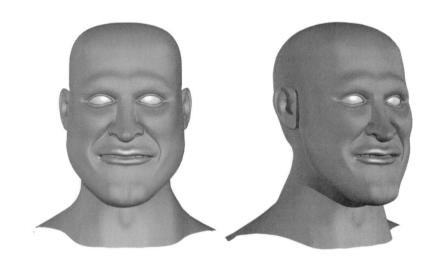

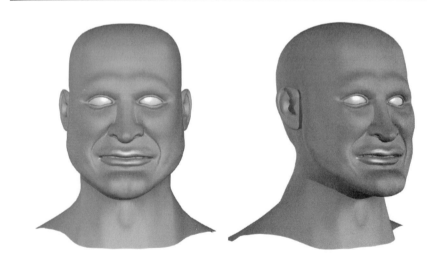

JAW OPEN

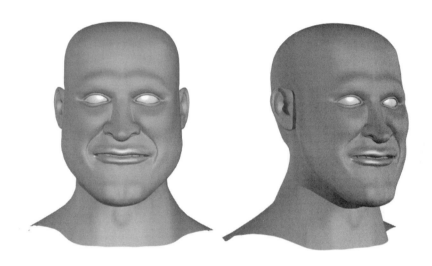

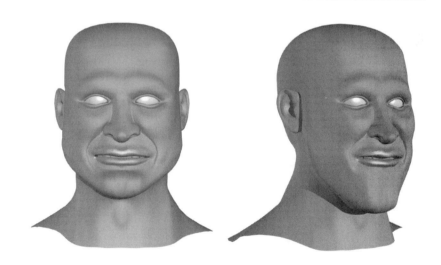

JAW FORWARD

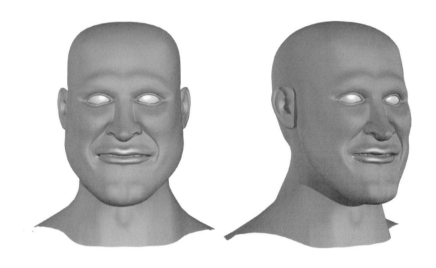

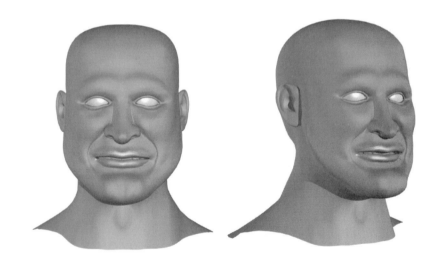

JAW LEFT

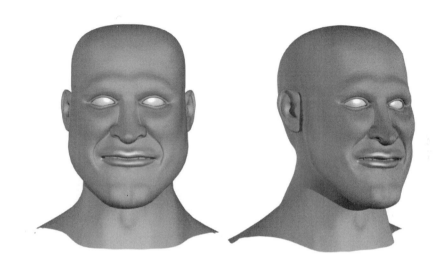

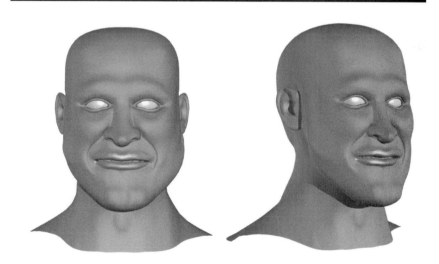

Jaw Right

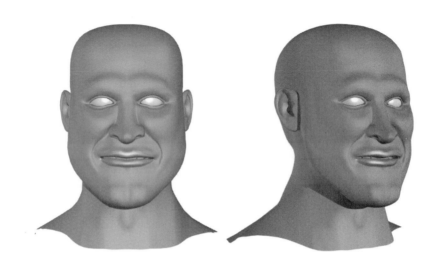

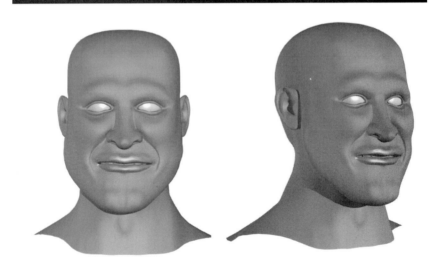

B

TYPICAL HUMAN VISUAL PHONEMES

This appendix is a visual reference of the visual phonemes. In each pose, the head is shown from the front and a three-quarter view. Additionally, a cross sectional view of the mouth is shown to illustrate the tongue position.

TARGET #1 PHONEME: IY

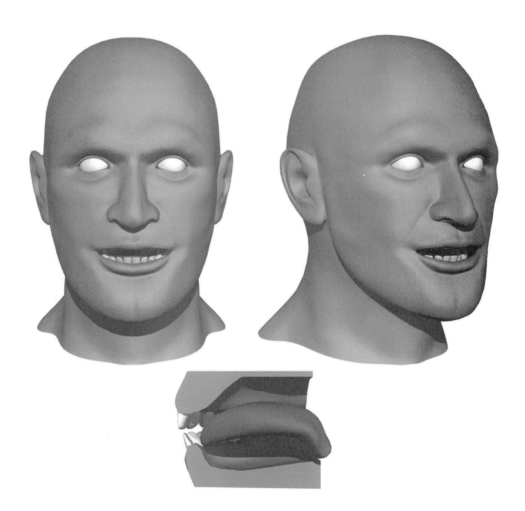

Distinguishing Features

The corners of mouth are pulled sideways and back over the teeth, partially revealing the teeth. The tongue floats in the middle of the mouth cavity.

TARGET #2 PHONEMES:
IH/ EY/ EH/ AE/ AH/ AY/ AW/ AN/ H

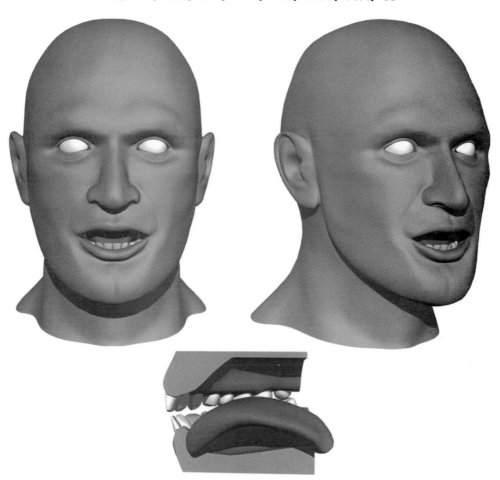

Distinguishing Features

The mouth is opened with the corners relaxed, revealing only the lower teeth. The back of the tongue hovers and the tip is curled slightly against the lower teeth.

TARGET #3 PHONEMES: AA/ AO

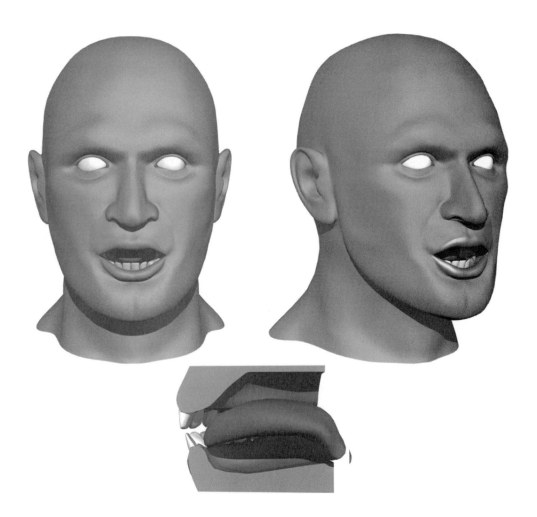

Distinguishing Features

The mouth gapes open, showing only the bottom teeth. The tongue floats in the center of the mouth cavity.

TARGET #4 PHONEMES: OW/ UW/ AX/ OY/ YU/

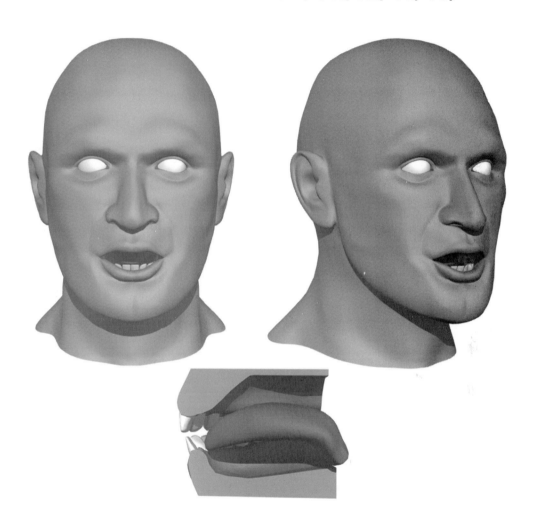

Distinguishing Features

The mouth is rounded with little or no teeth showing. The tongue floats in the middle of the mouth cavity.

TARGET #5 PHONEMES: UH/ER

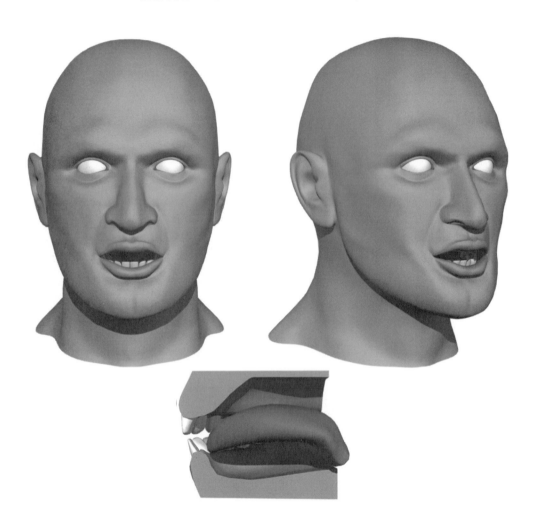

Distinguishing Features

The mouth is rounded and drawn away from the teeth, which are hidden. The tongue floats in the middle of the mouth cavity.

TARGET #6 PHONEME: Y

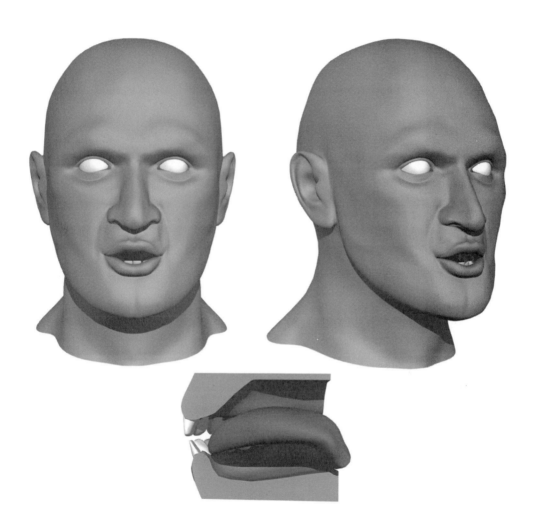

Distinguishing Features

The mouth is rounded with no teeth showing. The base of the tongue is pressed against the hard palate.

TARGET #7 PHONEMES: L/ T/ D

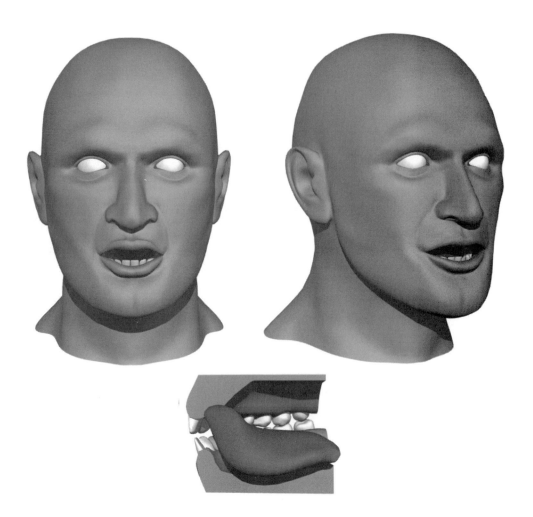

Distinguishing Features

The mouth is open slightly, revealing the tips of the upper and lower teeth. The tip of the tongue is pressed against the hard palate.

TARGET #8 PHONEME: R

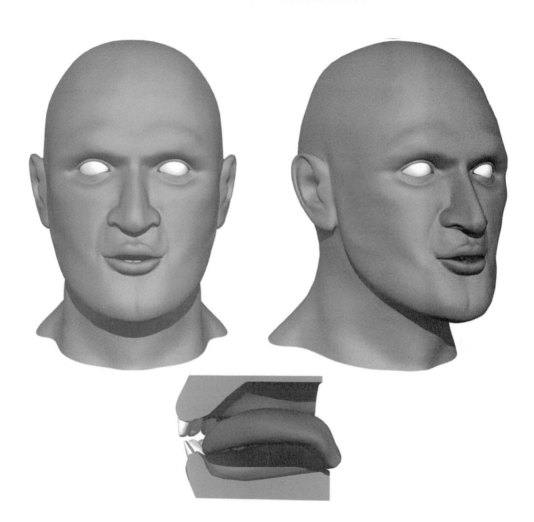

Distinguishing Features

The mouth is opened with the lips slightly pursed, hiding the teeth. The tongue floats in the middle of the mouth cavity.

TARGET #9 PHONEMES: M/ P/ B

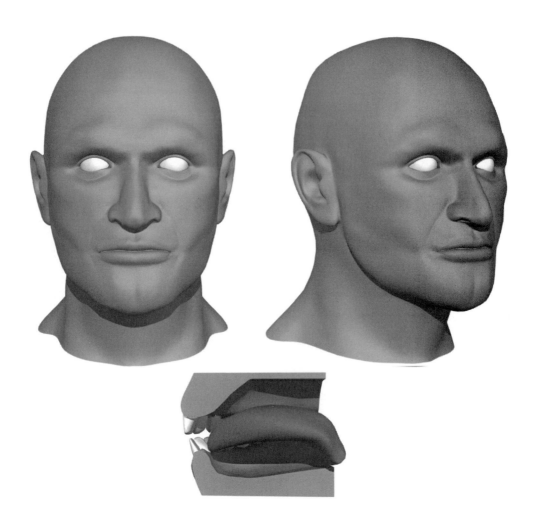

Distinguishing Features

The mouth is closed in a straight line.

TARGET #10 PHONEME: N

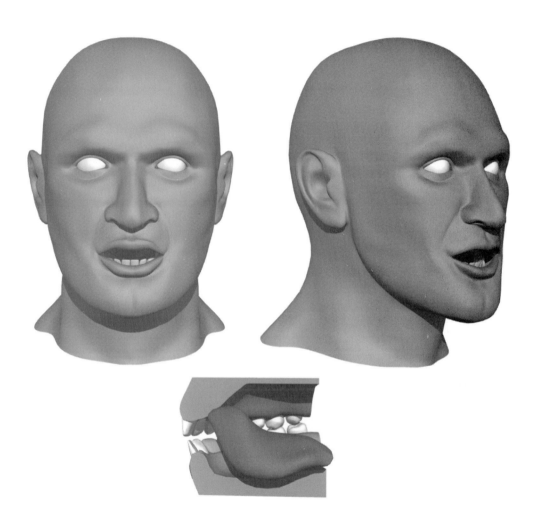

Distinguishing Features

The mouth is opened slightly, revealing the tips of the upper and lower teeth. The front portion of the tongue is pressed against the hard palate.

Target #11 Phonemes: F/V

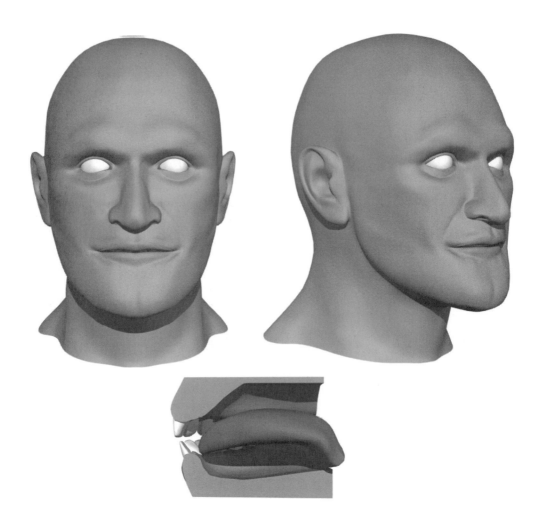

Distinguishing Features

The mouth is opened very slightly, with the lower lip curled and pressed against the upper teeth. The tongue floats in the center of the mouth cavity.

TARGET #12 PHONEMES: TH/ DH

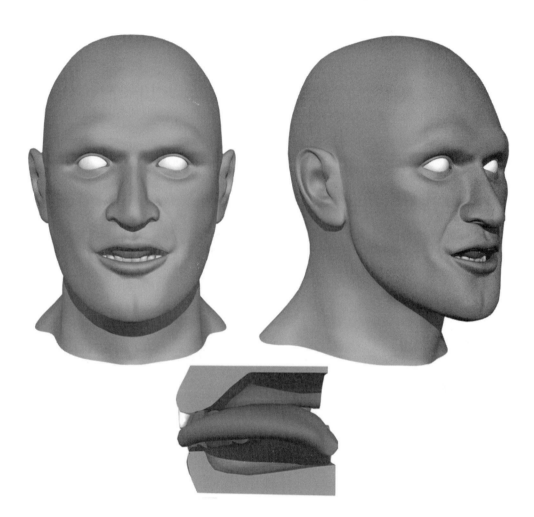

Distinguishing Features

The mouth is slightly opened (more than the F/V phoneme) and the tip of the tongue is placed between the upper and lower teeth.

TARGET #13 PHONEMES: S/ Z

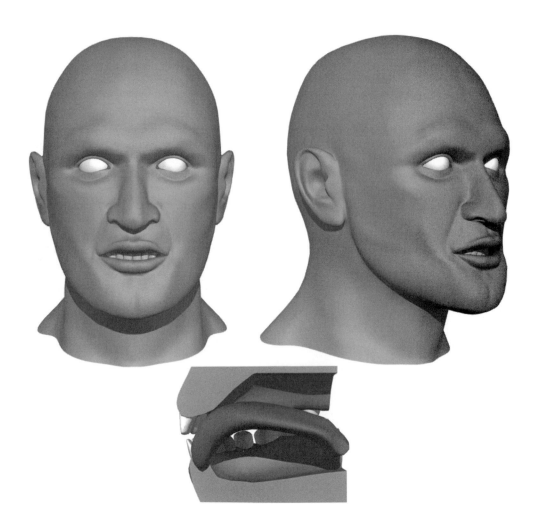

Distinguishing Features

The lips are parted, baring clenched teeth. The tip of the tongue is pressed against the lower teeth.

TARGET #14 PHONEMES: SH/ ZH/ CH

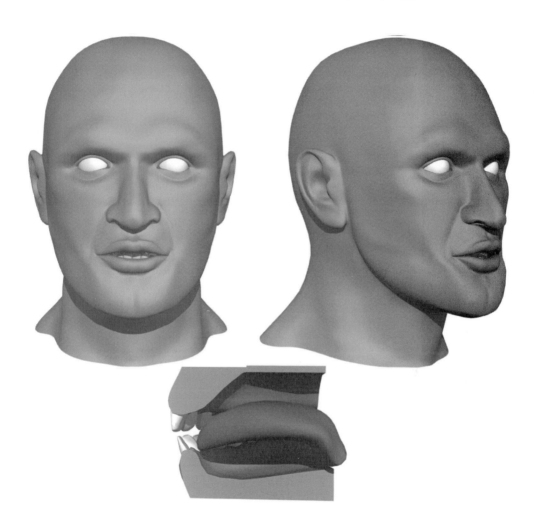

Distinguishing Features

The lips are parted, revealing clenched teeth. The tip of the tongue floats in the center of the mouth cavity.

TARGET #15 PHONEME: G

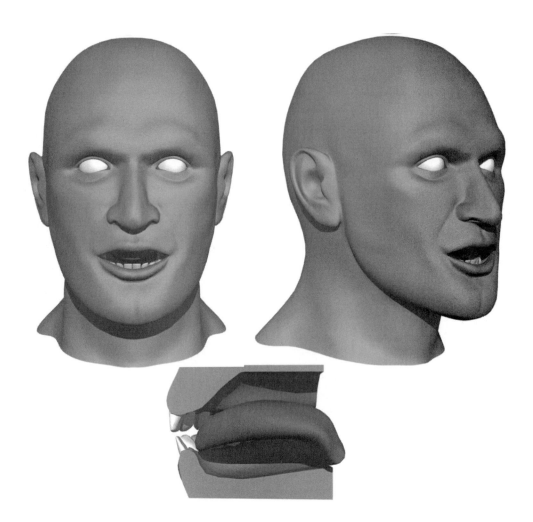

Distinguishing Features

The mouth is opened, revealing the tips of the upper and lower teeth. The back of the tongue presses against the soft palate.

TARGET #16 PHONEME: J

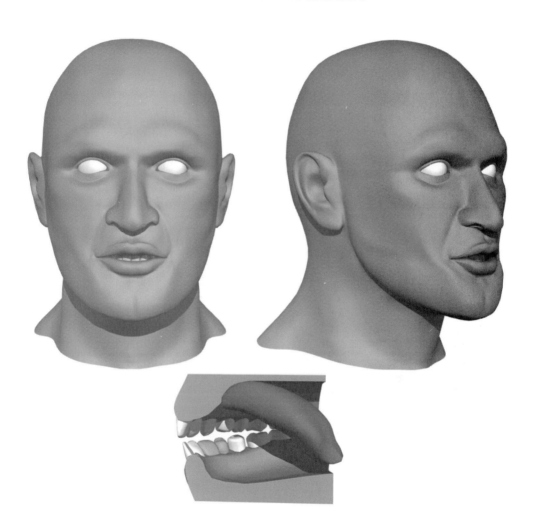

Distinguishing Features

The lips are parted, revealing clenched teeth. The tongue is pressed against the hard palate.

TYPICAL CARTOON EXPRESSION WEIGHTED MORPH TARGETS

In this appendix, morph targets for cartoon-style characters are shown. Typically, with cartoon characters, the expressions are more exaggerated than those of realistic characters. This guide illustrates most of the expressions also listed in Appendix A, "Typical Human Expression Weighted Morph Targets," but for cartoon characters.

BROWS ANGER

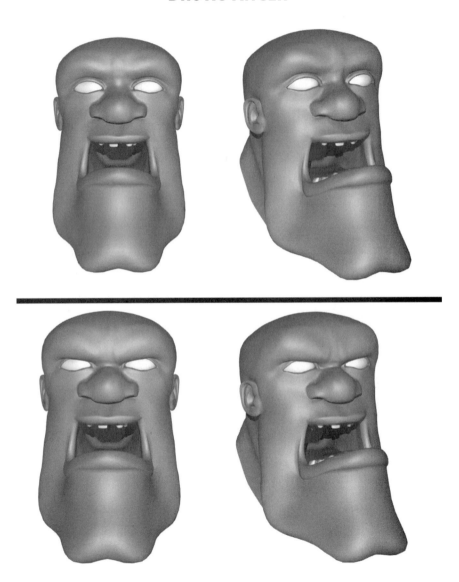

Distinguishing Features

The brows are pulled down and together at the inside corners. This target is used primarily for expressions of anger, pain, or effort.

BROWS LEFT RAISED

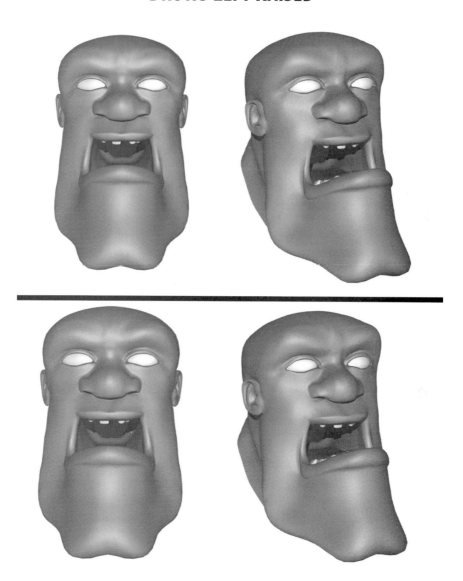

Distinguishing Features

The left brow is arched. By giving separate morph targets to the right and left eyebrows, you can raise one or both, making for more expressive eyebrows.

BROWS RAISED RIGHT

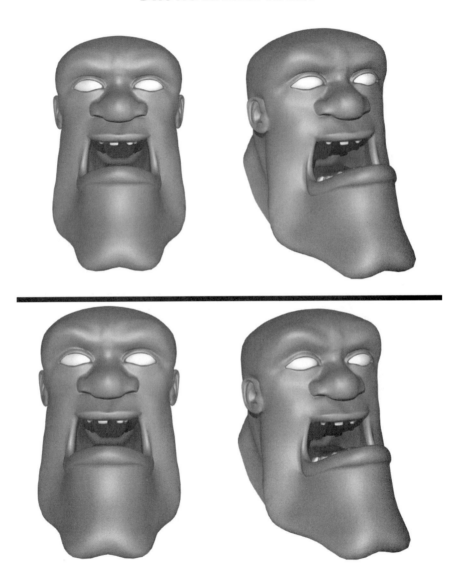

Distinguishing Features

The right brow is arched. By giving separate morph targets to the right and left eyebrows, you can raise one or both, making more expressions possible.

BROWS LOWERED

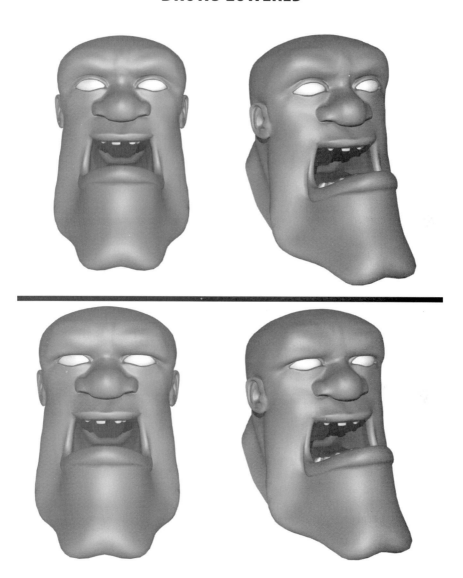

Distinguishing Features

The brows are drawn straight down, partially obscuring the eyes. This is useful for expressions such as effort and concentration, and for modifying other brow targets.

BROWS MIDDLE RAISED

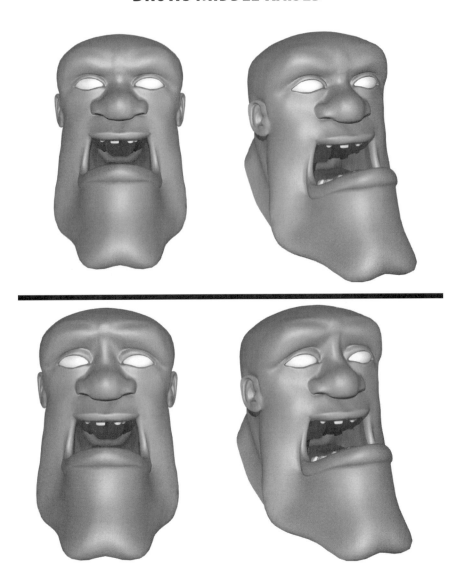

Distinguishing Features

The brows are drawn together and the inner portion is pulled upward. This is used for expressions such as sadness, questioning smiles, and facial shrugs.

BROWS AFRAID

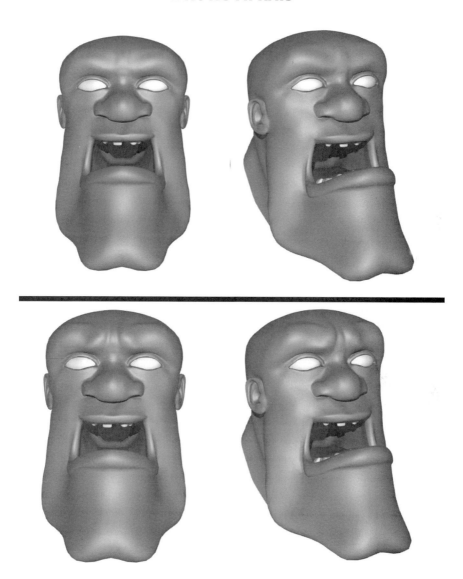

Distinguishing Features

The brows are drawn together in the center and create creases that are more pronounced than the Brows Middle Raised target. This is used primarily for expressions of fear.

EYES LEFT DOWN

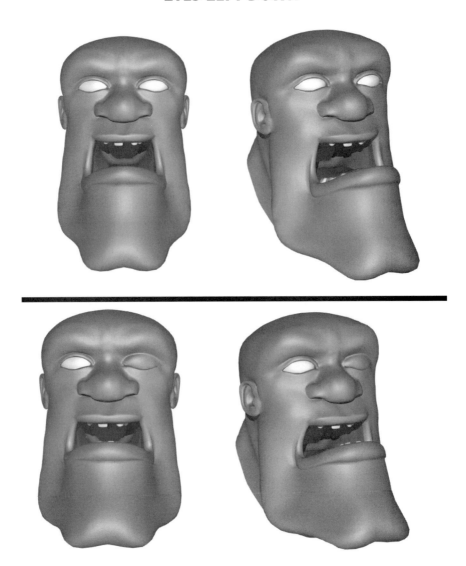

Distinguishing Features

The left eye is closed. Giving separate morph targets to the left and right eyelids allows us to pose the eyes asymmetrically.

EYES RIGHT DOWN

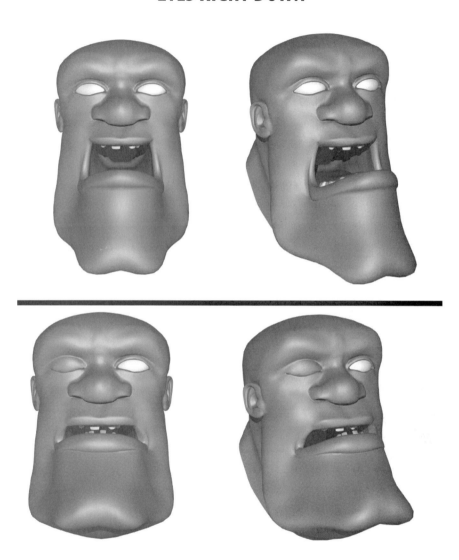

Distinguishing Features

The right eye is closed. Giving separate morph targets to the left and right eyelids allows us to pose the eyes asymmetrically.

MOUTH CLOSED

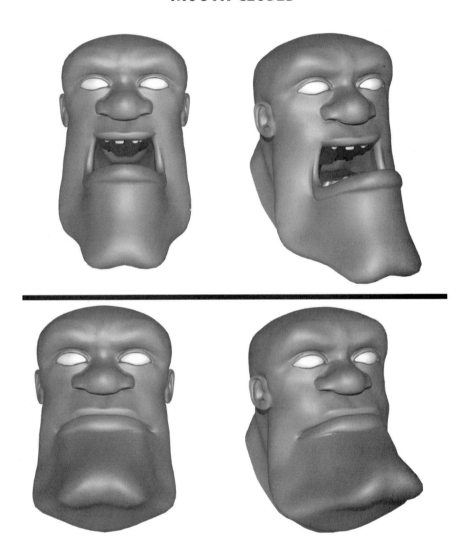

Distinguishing Features

The mouth is closed and relaxed. This can be used as the resting pose for a character, though in the case of our cartoon, the natural pose is with the mouth hanging open.

MOUTH CRY CLOSED

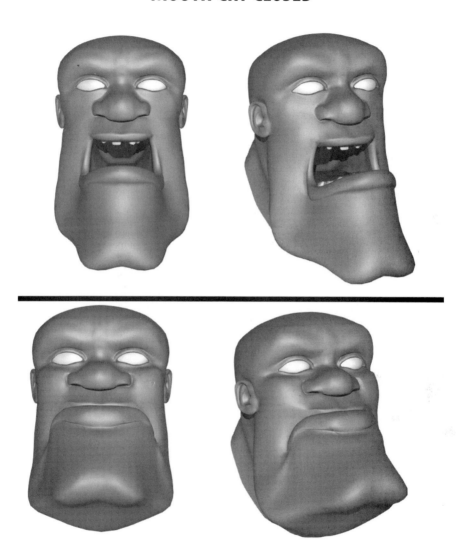

Distinguishing Features

The mouth is closed and the corners of the mouth turn down dramatically. The lower lip sticks out in a pout and the cheeks bulge under the zygomatic bone.

MOUTH CRY OPEN

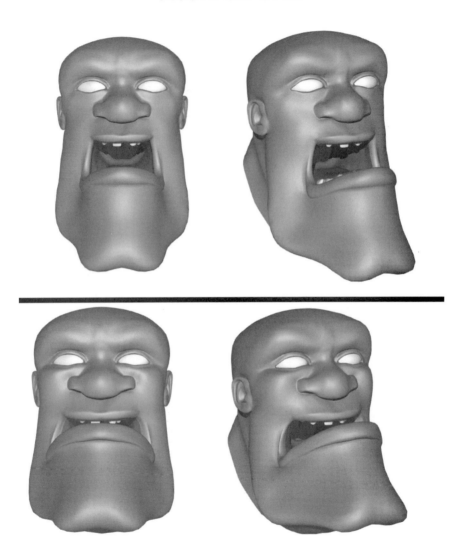

Distinguishing Features

The mouth is open and the lower corners are pulled back and down. The cheeks bulge under the zygomatic bone.

MOUTH DISGUST

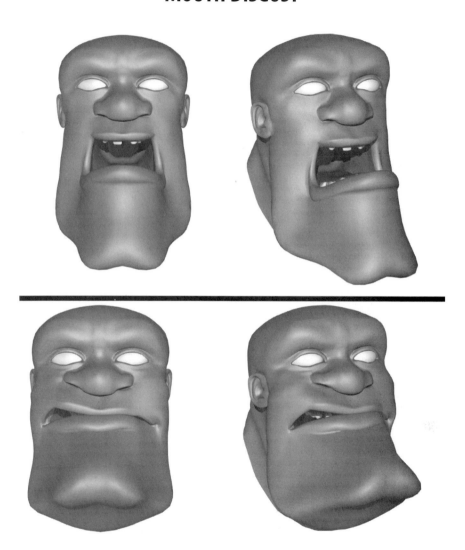

Distinguishing Features

The mouth is closed and one side of the upper lip is drawn upward in a sneer. This is useful for expressions such as disdain or hatred.

MOUTH FRIGHTENED

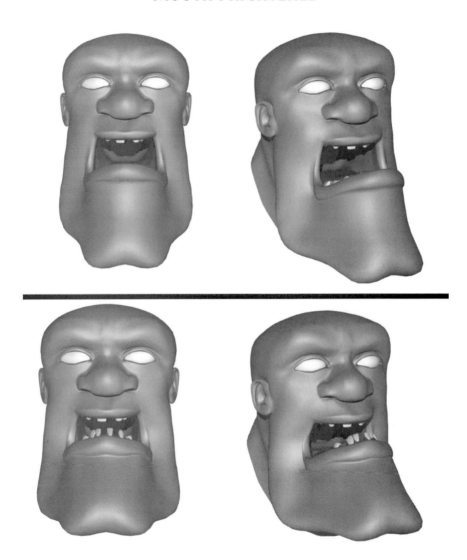

Distinguishing Features

The mouth is open and the lower corner of the mouth is pulled back. The cheeks don't bulge under the zygomatic bone.

MOUTH FROWN

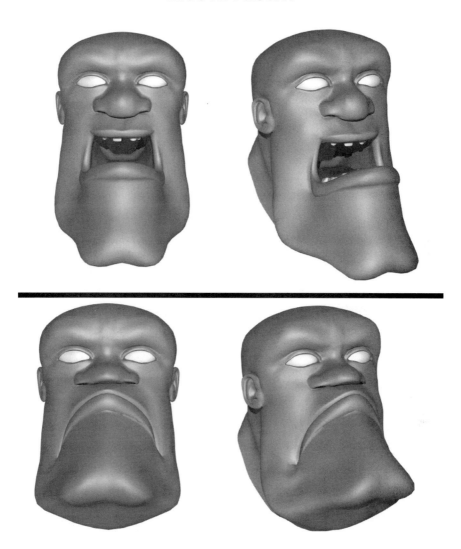

Distinguishing Features

The corners of the mouth are pulled down and the middle drawn up toward the nose. This is useful for all sorts of unhappy expressions, though it is not as dramatic as the crying or suppressed sadness targets. One reason for this is that the cheeks do not bulge under the zygomatic, arch so the character appears more upset than sad.

MOUTH LAUGHTER

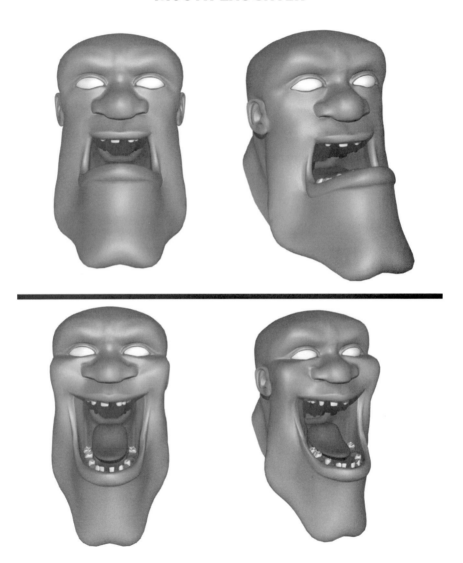

Distinguishing Features

The jaw is dropped open and the mouth is open very wide, with the corners pulled up high. By creating an extreme pose, you allow yourself the flexibility of generating a wide range of laughter, from subdued, to crazed.

MOUTH REPULSION

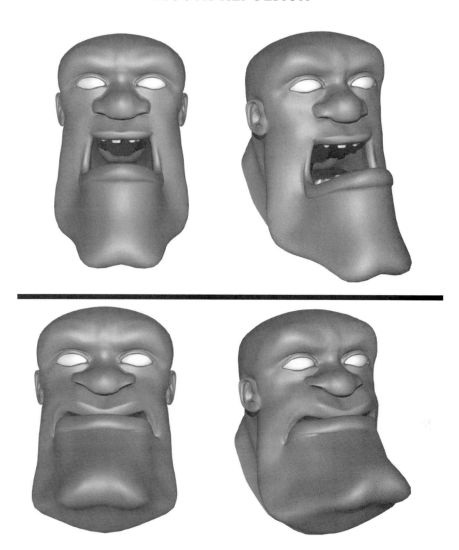

Distinguishing Features

The mouth is closed and both sides of the upper lip are drawn upward in a sneer. This target is useful for expressions such as disdain or physical repulsion. In a cartoony character such as Knuckles, the sneer may be so extreme that the upper teeth and gums appear.

MOUTH SMILE

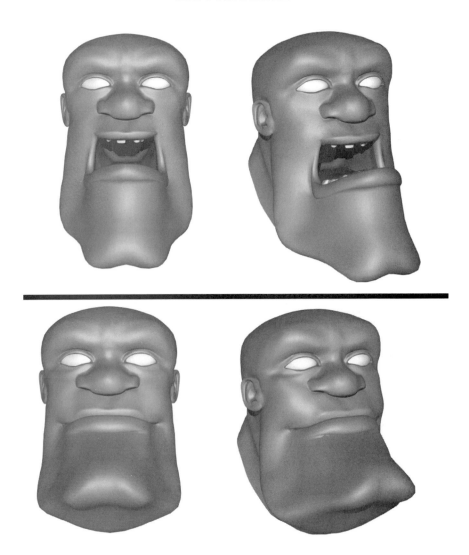

Distinguishing Features

The mouth is closed, stretched horizontally and back toward the ears, and the corners of the mouth are curled into a smile. The cheeks bulge somewhat under the zygomatic bone.

MOUTH SMILE OPEN

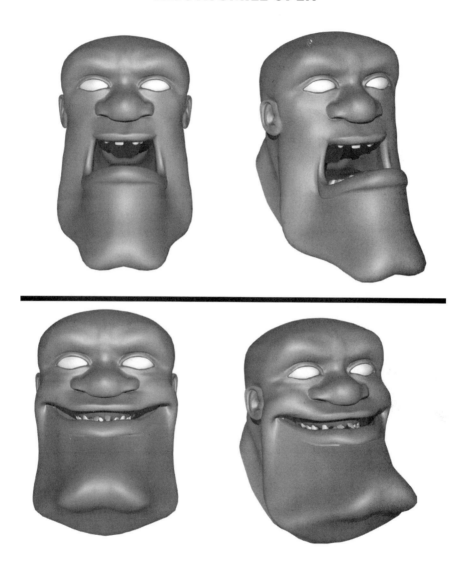

Distinguishing Features

The mouth is open with the corners pulled up and back toward the ears.

MOUTH SUPPRESSED SADNESS

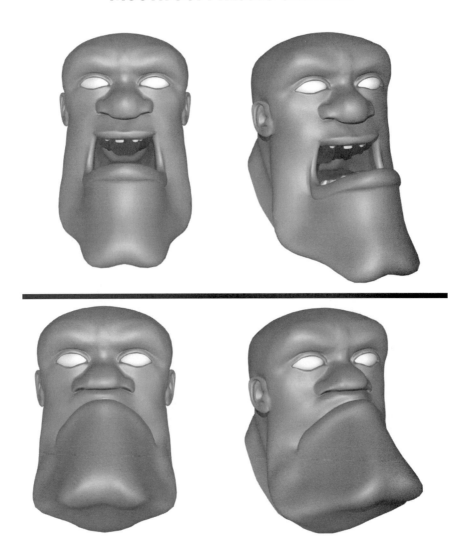

Distinguishing Features

The mouth is closed and the corners are pulled into a frown. The lower lip is curled inward, blending into the chin as it bulges out at the base. This target is useful for building expressions such as facial shrugs and poses where the character is close to bursting into tears.

MOUTH SURPRISE

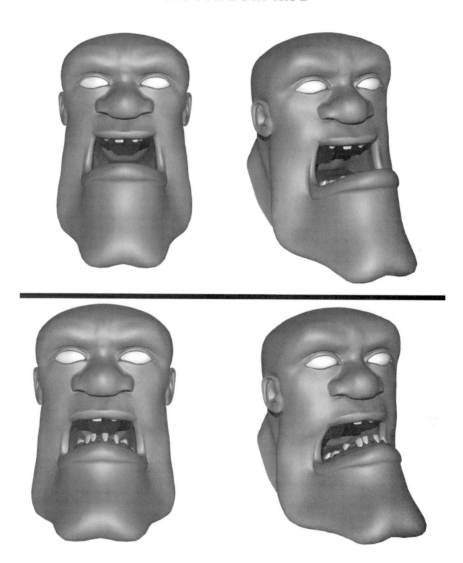

Distinguishing Features

The jaw is dropped and the mouth is opened and pulled back. The lower lip is pulled down, revealing the lower teeth and possibly the gums.

MOUTH YAWN

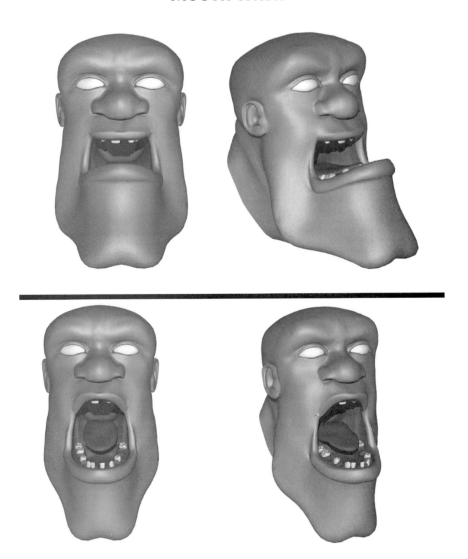

Distinguishing Features

The mouth is opened to its fullest extent. Unlike fear or laughter, the corners of the mouth are drawn neither up nor down.

MOUTH MISERABLE

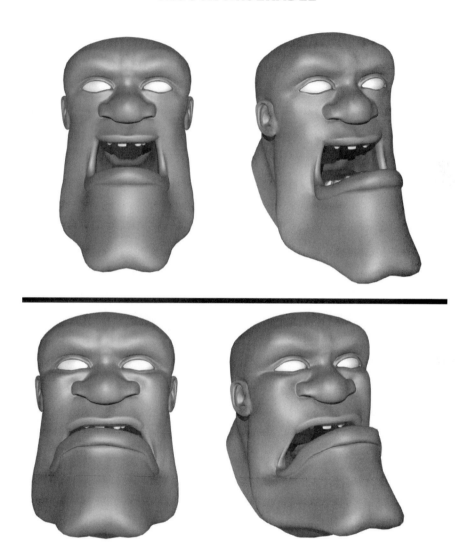

Distinguishing Features

The mouth is open and the lower corners are drawn back and rippled.

MOUTH CLOSED RAGE

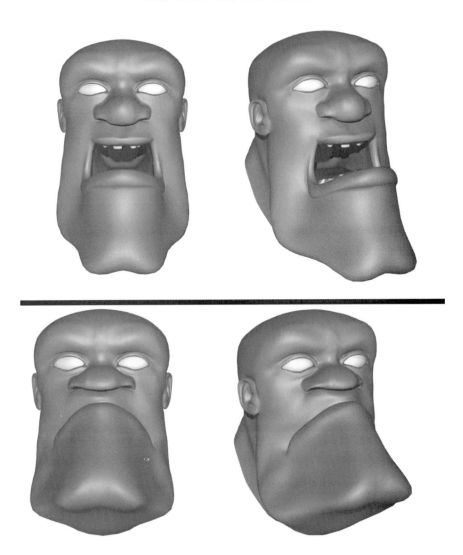

Distinguishing Features

The mouth is closed and drawn into a frown. The nostrils are lifted and flared and the cheeks bulge under the zygomatic bone.

TYPICAL CARTOON VISUAL PHONEMES

This appendix lists the visual phonemes as they apply to cartoon characters.

TARGET #1 PHONEMES: M/ B/ P

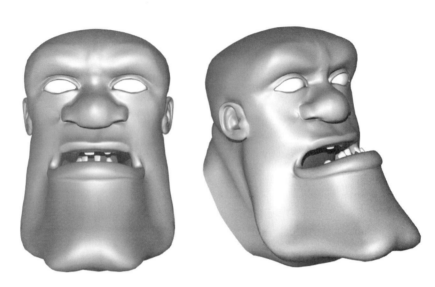

TARGET #2 PHONEMES: N/ L/ D T

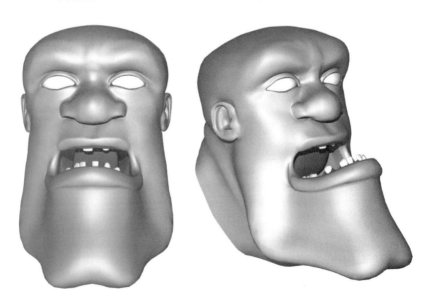

TARGET #3 PHONEMES: F/V

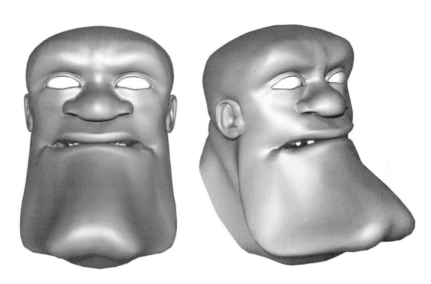

TARGET #4 PHONEMES: TH/DH

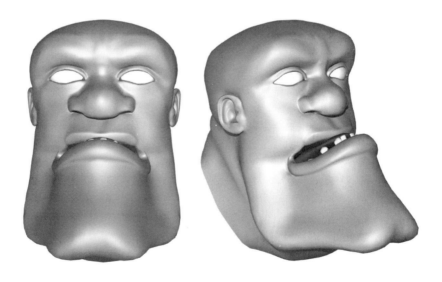

TARGET #5 PHONEMES: K, G

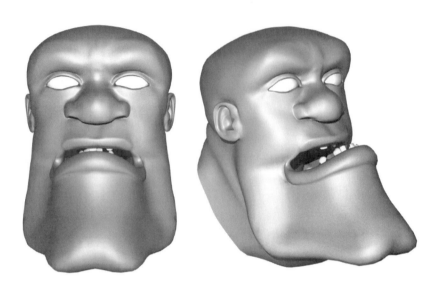

TARGET #6 PHONEMES: SH/ ZH/ CH/ J

TARGET #7 PHONEMES: Y/ OY/ YU/ W/ UH/ ER

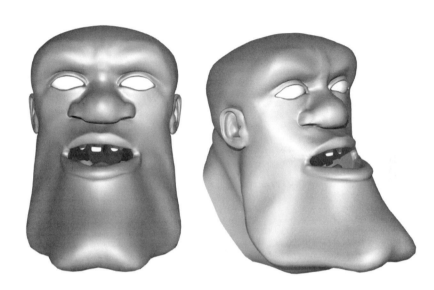

TARGET #8 PHONEMES:
IH/ EY/ EH/ AH/ AY/ AW/ AE/ AN/ H/ S/ Z/ R

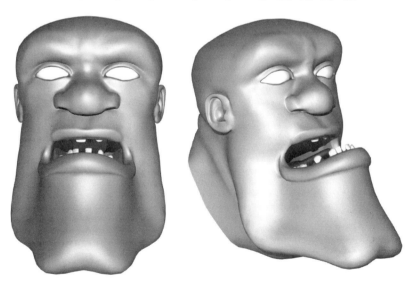

TARGET #9 PHONEMES: AA/ AO/ OW/ UW/ AX

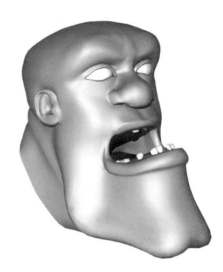

TARGET #10 PHONEMES: IY

FACIAL EXPRESSION EXAMPLES

T his appendix contains a large variety of facial expressions using a realistic human character and a Living Toon cartoon character as examples. The description and the morph target percentage tables can give you a head start on morphing your own character. The "Distinguishing Features" bulleted lists contain verbal descriptions of the expressions broken down into four sections:

Brows: Includes the forehead and eyebrows.

Eyes: The eyelids.

Mouth: The cheeks, nose, and mouth.

Jaw: The rotation and translation of the jaw.

The tables following each bulleted list provide the weighted morph targets listed in Appendices A and C that were used to construct the expression. An explanation of how expressions are built using multiple weighted morph targets is given in Chapter 6, "Weighted Morphing Animation."

ON THE CD

Modeling templates for creating human facial expressions are included in the Appendix E folder on the companion CD-ROM. The templates include a front and side render of the head, which can be used as background templates in your modeling program. While your head may be different from this particular human head, the proportions should be similar. The templates are meant to give you an approximate idea of how the face changes with each expression.

HUMAN SMILE WITH OPEN MOUTH

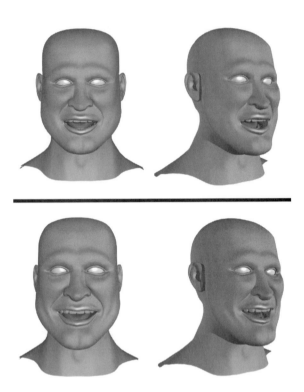

Distinguishing Features

Brows: The brow is relaxed.

Eyes: The eyelids are relaxed, although they may be slightly lowered. The eyeballs are alert, focusing steadily on whatever is making the character smile.

Mouth: The mouth is widened in front and pulled back toward the ears. Dimples may appear, and the cheek creases running from the nose to the mouth deepen. In addition, the upper cheek bulges out slightly.

Jaw: The teeth are slightly parted, showing the upper teeth.

MORPH TARGET GROUP	MORPH TARGET	PERCENTAGE
Brows	• NONE	N/A
Eyes	• Left Eyelid Down	5
	• Right Eyelid Down	5
Mouth	• Laughter	
	• Smile Closed	70
Jaw	• NONE	N/A

CARTOON SMILE WITH OPEN MOUTH

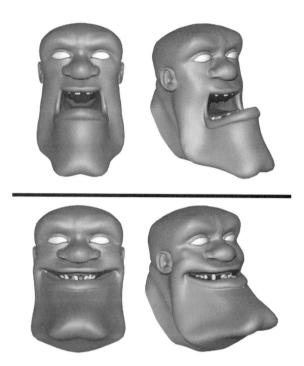

Distinguishing Features

Brows: The brow is relaxed.

Eyes: The eyelids are relaxed, although they may be slightly lowered. The eyeballs are alert, focusing steadily on whatever is making the character smile.

Mouth: The mouth is widened in front and pulled back toward the ears. Dimples may appear, and the cheek creases running from the nose to the mouth deepen. In addition, the upper cheek bulges out slightly.

Jaw: The teeth are slightly parted, showing the upper teeth.

MORPH TARGET GROUP	MORPH TARGET	PERCENTAGE
Brows	• NONE	N/A
Eyes	• Left Eyelid Down	10
	• Right Eyelid Down	10
Mouth	• Smile	15
	• Smile Open	100

HUMAN SMILE WITH MOUTH CLOSED

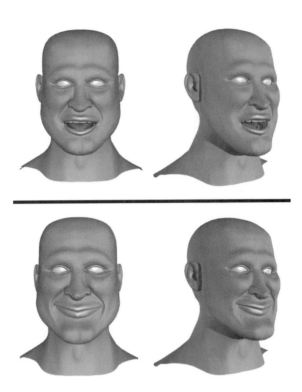

Distinguishing Features

Brows: The brow is relaxed

Eyes: The eyelids are relaxed or lowered slightly.

Mouth: The mouth is widened and the corners pulled back toward the ears, tightening the mouth against the teeth. Dimples may show, although less pronounced than on the Smile with Open Mouth.

Jaw: The jaw is closed.

MORPH TARGET GROUP	MORPH TARGET	PERCENTAGE
Brows	• NONE	N/A
Eyes	• Left Eyelid Down	5
	• Right Eyelid Down	5
Mouth	• Smile Closed	70
	• Suppressed Sadness	60
Jaw	• Jaw Closed	75

CARTOON SMILE WITH MOUTH CLOSED

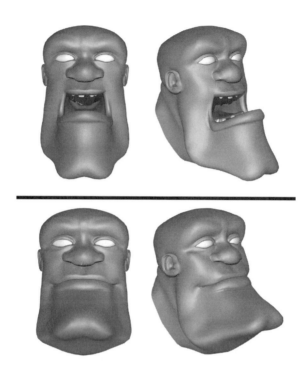

Distinguishing Features

Brows: The brow is relaxed.

Eyes: The lids are opened or lowered slightly.

Mouth: The mouth is widened and the corners pulled back toward the ears, tightening the mouth against the teeth. Dimples may show, although less pronounced than on the Smile with Open Mouth.

Jaw: The jaw is closed.

MORPH TARGET GROUP	MORPH TARGET	PERCENTAGE
Brows	• NONE	N/A
Eyes	• Left Eyelid Down	10
	• Right Eyelid Down	10
Mouth	• Smile	100

HUMAN SAD SMILE

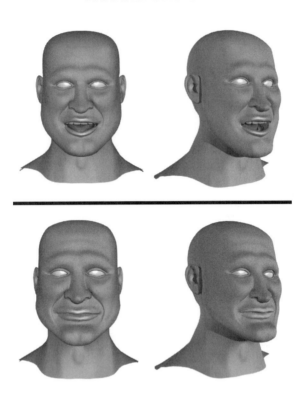

Distinguishing Features

Brows: The inner portion of the brows is lifted slightly.

Eyes: The lids might be slightly lowered.

Mouth: The mouth is widened and pulled back toward the ears, tightening it against the teeth. The appearance is virtually the same as the Smile with Mouth Closed. The cheeks may or may not bunch up under the eyes, depending on how much effort the character is putting into the appearance of happiness.

Jaw: The jaw is closed.

MORPH TARGET GROUP	MORPH TARGET	PERCENTAGE
Brows	• Brows Middle Up	35
Eyes	• Eye Left Down	20
	• Eye Right Down	20
Mouth	• Smile Closed	40
	• Suppressed Sadness	30
Jaw	• Jaw Closed	100

CARTOON SAD SMILE

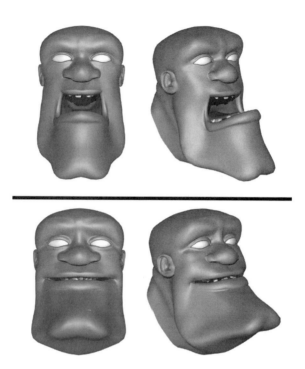

Distinguishing Features

Brows: The inner portion of the brows is lifted slightly.

Eyes: The lids might be slightly lowered.

Mouth: The mouth is widened and pulled back toward the ears, tightening it against the teeth. The cheeks may or may not bunch up under the eyes, depending on how much effort the character is putting into the appearance of happiness. The character's intention is to betray its sadness. The weakness of the smile and the eyebrows give it away.

Jaw: The jaw closed or slightly opened.

MORPH TARGET GROUP	MORPH TARGET	PERCENTAGE
Brows	• Brows Middle Raised	70
Eyes	• Left Eyelid Down	10
	• Right Eyelid Down	10
Mouth	• Smile	70
	• Smile Open	90

HUMAN ENTHUSIASTIC SMILE

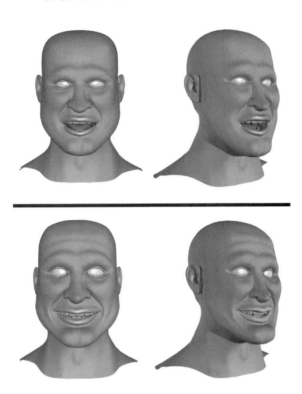

Distinguishing Features

Brows: The brows are lifted straight up, causing wrinkles on the forehead.

Eyes: The upper lid is opened wide. It's even possible that some white will show above the iris.

Mouth: The mouth is widened and pulled back toward the ears, pulling it tight against the teeth. The cheeks bunch up under the eyes.

Jaw: The jaw can be closed or slightly open.

MORPH TARGET GROUP	MORPH TARGET	PERCENTAGE
Brows	• Brows Arched	50
Eyes	• Eyes Wide	100
Mouth	• Mouth Laughter	80
	• Smile Closed	100
Jaw	• Jaw Closed	70

CARTOON ENTHUSIASTIC SMILE

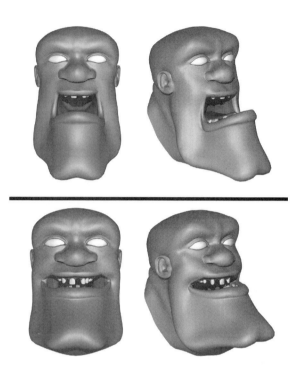

Distinguishing Features

Brows: The brows are arched, as if saying, "I'm open to anything!"

Eyes: The eyes are open fully. If possible, they can open even wider than normal, possibly even showing some white above the iris.

Mouth: The mouth is widened and pulled back toward the ears, pulling it tight against the teeth. The cheeks bunch up under the eyes.

Jaw: The jaw can be closed or slightly open.

MORPH TARGET GROUP	MORPH TARGET	PERCENTAGE
Brows	• Left Raised	20
	• Right Raised	20
Eyes	• NONE	N/A
Mouth	• Smile Open	75
	• Laughter	10

HUMAN CHARMING SMILE

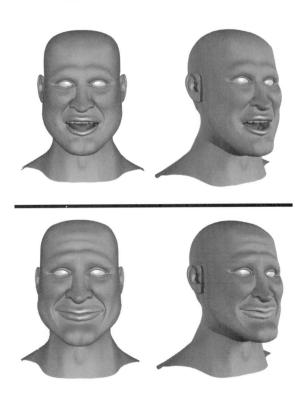

Distinguishing Features

Brows: The brows are lifted in the center in a manner similar to most sad and crying expressions. Deep furrows appear on the forehead.

Eyes: The eyes may fully open, or the lids may be lowered slightly.

Mouth: The mouth is widened and pulled back toward the ears, tightening it against the teeth. The cheeks bulge under the eyes.

Jaw: The jaw is closed.

MORPH TARGET GROUP	MORPH TARGET	PERCENTAGE
Brows	• Brows Middle Up	80
Eyes	• Eye Left Down	10
	• Eye Right Down	10
Mouth	• Smile Closed	75
Jaw	• Jaw Closed	85

CARTOON CHARMING SMILE

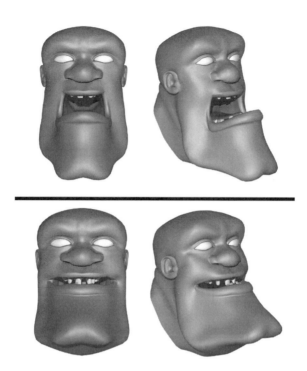

Distinguishing Features

Brows: The brows are lifted in the center, in effect posing the question "Do you like?" or "Is it okay?"

Eyes: The eye is fully open. The upper eyelid may be lowered slightly.

Mouth: The mouth is widened and pulled back toward the ears, tightening it against the teeth. The cheeks bunch up under the eyes.

Jaw: The jaw is closed.

MORPH TARGET GROUP	MORPH TARGET	PERCENTAGE
Brows	• Middle Raised	40
Eyes	• Eye Left Down	10
	• Eye Right Down	10
Mouth	• Smile	100

HUMAN DEVIOUS SMILE

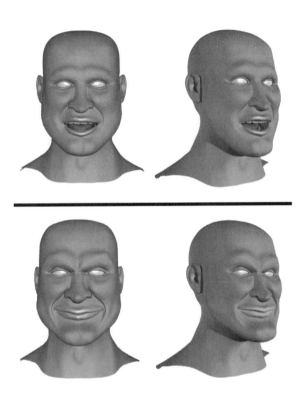

Distinguishing Features

Brows: The eyebrows are pulled down over the eye, almost as if in anger.

Eyes: The eyes are narrowed.

Mouth: The mouth is widened and pulled back toward the ears, pulling it tight against the teeth.

Jaw: The jaw is closed.

MORPH TARGET GROUP	MORPH TARGET	PERCENTAGE
Brows	• Brow Angry	90
Eyes	• Eye Left Down	25
	• Eye Right Down	25
Mouth	• Smile Closed	75
Jaw	• Jaw Closed	75

CARTOON DEVIOUS SMILE

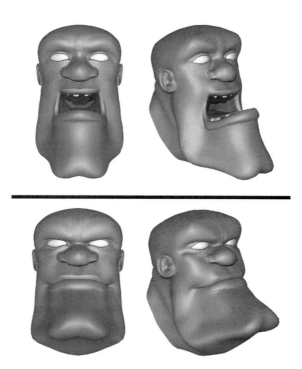

Distinguishing Features

Brows: The eyebrows are pulled down over the eye, almost as if in anger.

Eyes: The eyes are narrowed.

Mouth: The mouth is widened and pulled back toward the ears, pulling it tight against the teeth.

Jaw: The jaw is closed.

MORPH TARGET GROUP	MORPH TARGET	PERCENTAGE
Brows	• Brows Anger	100
Eyes	• Eye Left Down	10
	• Eye Right Down	10
Mouth	• Smile	100

HUMAN DRUNK SMILE

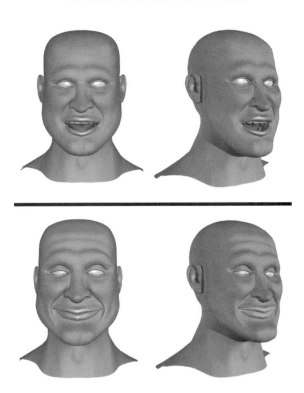

Distinguishing Features

Brows: The brows are lifted in a fruitless attempt to lift the eyelids.

Eyes: The upper lid is lowered almost to the halfway point in an attempt to focus the eye.

Mouth: The lips are widened, pulled back toward the ears, and tightened against the teeth.

Jaw: The jaw is closed.

MORPH TARGET GROUP	MORPH TARGET	PERCENTAGE
Brows	• Brows Arched	70
Eyes	• Eye Left Down	30
	• Eye Right Down	30
Mouth	• Smile Closed	100
Jaw	• Jaw Closed	85

CARTOON DRUNK SMILE

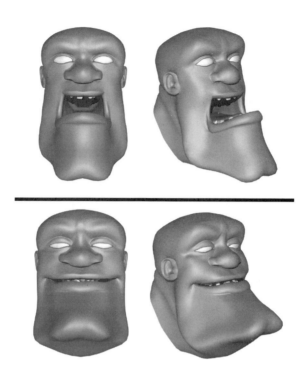

Distinguishing Features

Brows: The brows are lifted in a fruitless attempt to lift the eyelids.

Eyes: The upper lid is lowered almost to the halfway point in an attempt to focus the eye.

Mouth: The lips are widened, pulled back toward the ears, and tightened against the teeth.

Jaw: The jaw is closed.

MORPH TARGET GROUP	MORPH TARGET	PERCENTAGE
Brows	• Middle Raised	60
	• Right Raised	70
	• Left Raised	70
Eyes	• Eye Left Down	40
	• Eye Right Down	40
Mouth	• Smile	100
	• Smile open	100

HUMAN LAUGHTER

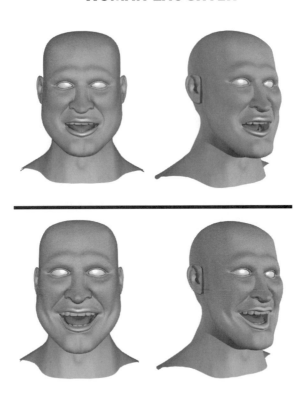

Distinguishing Features

Brows: The brows are relaxed.

Eyes: The lids are lowered slightly.

Mouth: The mouth is opened, widened, and pulled back toward the ears. The top lip is straightened out, revealing the upper teeth.

Jaw: The jaw is opened.

MORPH TARGET GROUP	MORPH TARGET	PERCENTAGE
Brows	• NONE	N/A
Eyes	• Eye Left Down	15
	• Eye Right Down	15
Mouth	• Laughter	100
Jaw	• Jaw Open	45

Cartoon Laughter

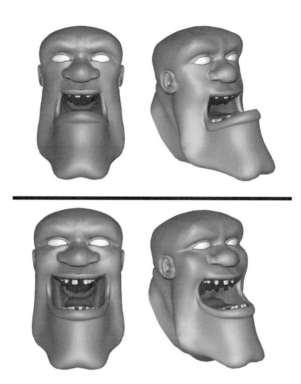

Distinguishing Features

Brows: The brows are relaxed.

Eyes: The upper eyelids are pushed down slightly by the pressure of the upper lid.

Mouth: The mouth is opened, widened, and pulled back toward the ears. The top lip is straightened out, revealing the upper teeth.

Jaw: The jaw is opened.

MORPH TARGET GROUP	MORPH TARGET	PERCENTAGE
Brows	• Brows Lowered	50
Eyes	• Eye Left Down	10
	• Eye Right Down	10
Mouth	• Laughter	80
	• Smile Open	70

HUMAN LOUD LAUGHTER

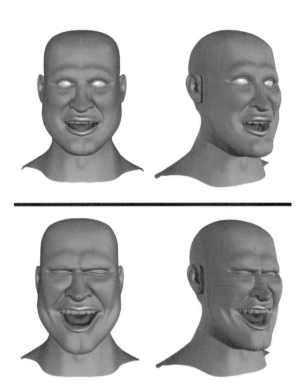

Distinguishing Features

Brows: The brows are lowered. In extreme laughter, they may be raised to their full extent.

Eyes: The lids are clamped shut. In extreme laughter, they might be opened very wide as if in terror.

Mouth: The mouth is opened, widened, and pulled back toward the ears. The top lip is straightened out, revealing the upper teeth. The cheeks bulge under the eyes. In the extreme positions mentioned under Brows and Eyes, the mouth is the only element that keeps the expression from fully appearing as terror.

Jaw: The jaw is opened.

MORPH TARGET GROUP	MORPH TARGET	PERCENTAGE
Brows	• Brows Compressed	100
Eyes	• Eye Left Down	100
	• Eye Right Down	100
Mouth	• Laughter	120
Jaw	• Jaw Open	100

CARTOON LOUD LAUGHTER

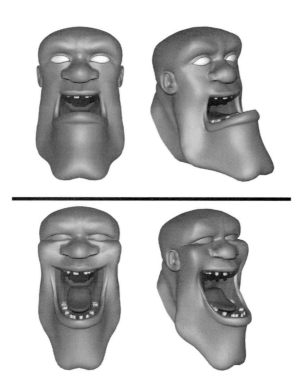

Distinguishing Features

Brows: The brows are relaxed.

Eyes: The eyes are closed tight.

Mouth: The mouth is opened wide with raised corners, revealing the upper teeth.

Jaw: The jaw is opened wide.

MORPH TARGET GROUP	MORPH TARGET	PERCENTAGE
Brows	• Brows Lowered	100
Eyes	• Eye Left Down	100
	• Eye Right Down	100
Mouth	• Laughter	100

HUMAN PHONY SMILE

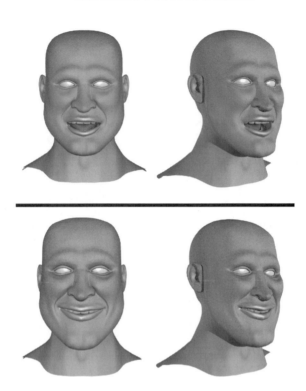

Distinguishing Features

Brows: The eyebrows are relaxed or slightly raised. If the character is attempting to appear endearing, the brows may be drawn up in the center.

Eyes: Eyes are open fully or narrowed very slightly.

Mouth: The mouth is opened slightly, widened, pulled back toward the ears, and tightened against the teeth. The cheeks don't bulge under the eyes as much as they do in a sincere smile.

Jaw: The jaw is slightly opened.

MORPH TARGET GROUP	MORPH TARGET	PERCENTAGE
Brows	• NONE	N/A
Eyes	• Eye Left Down	15
	• Eye Right Down	15
Mouth	• Laughter	60
	• Smile Closed	75
Jaw	• Jaw Open	10

CARTOON PHONY SMILE

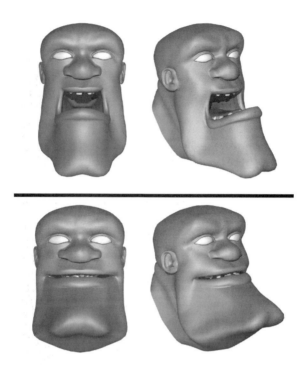

Distinguishing Features

Brows: The eyebrows are relaxed or slightly raised.

Eyes: Eyes are narrowed very slightly.

Mouth: The mouth is opened, widened, pulled back toward the ears, and tightened against the teeth. The cheeks don't bulge under the eyes as much as they do in a sincere smile.

Jaw: The jaw is slightly opened.

MORPH TARGET GROUP	MORPH TARGET	PERCENTAGE
Brows	• Brows Lowered	25
Eyes	• NONE	N/A
Mouth	• Smile Open	100
	• Closed	100

Human Phony Laughter

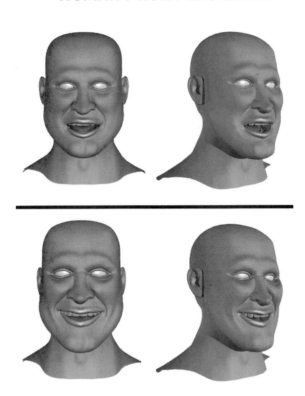

Distinguishing Features

Brows: The eyebrows are relaxed or slightly raised.

Eyes: Eyes are narrowed slightly.

Mouth: The mouth is opened, widened, pulled back toward the ears, and tightened against the teeth. The cheeks are bulged out only slightly and dimples appear.

Jaw: The jaw is opened about halfway.

MORPH TARGET GROUP	MORPH TARGET	PERCENTAGE
Brows	• NONE	N/A
Eyes	• Eye Left Down	15
	• Eye Right Down	15
Mouth	• Laughter	100
	• Smile Closed	100
Jaw	• Jaw Open	10

Cartoon Phony Laughter

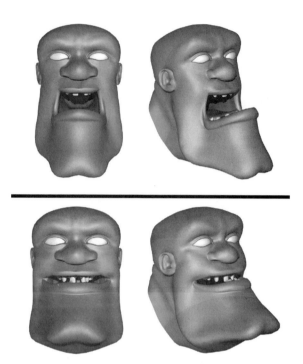

Distinguishing Features

Brows: The eyebrows are relaxed or slightly raised.

Eyes: Eyes are narrowed slightly.

Mouth: The mouth is opened, widened, pulled back toward the ears, and tightened against the teeth. The cheeks are bulged out only slightly and dimples appear.

Jaw: The jaw is opened about halfway.

MORPH TARGET GROUP	MORPH TARGET	PERCENTAGE
Brows	• NONE	N/A
Eyes	• NONE	N/A
Mouth	• Smile	70
	• Smile Open	90

HUMAN CRYING WITH A CLOSED MOUTH

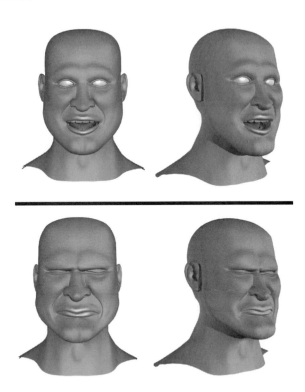

Distinguishing Features

Brows: The eyebrows are lowered, almost as if in anger.

Eyes: The eyes are clenched shut. If they do open, it's done with considerable effort.

Mouth: The mouth is clenched shut and in animation may tremble. The cheeks bunch up and dimples may appear on the chin.

Jaw: The jaw can be shut tight or open slightly. It might also quiver.

MORPH TARGET GROUP	MORPH TARGET	PERCENTAGE
Brows	• Brows Compressed	120
Eyes	• Eye Left Down	100
	• Eye Right Down	100
Mouth	• Crying	100
Jaw	• Jaw Closed	100

CARTOON CRYING WITH A CLOSED MOUTH

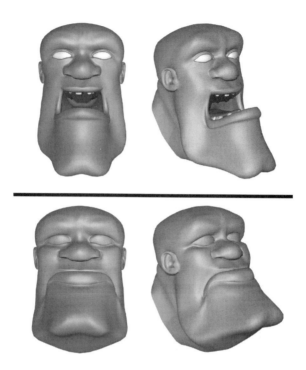

Distinguishing Features

Brows: The eyebrows are lowered, almost as if in anger.

Eyes: The eyes are clenched shut. If they do open, it's done with considerable effort.

Mouth: The mouth is clenched shut and in animation may tremble. The cheeks bunch up and dimples may appear on the chin.

Jaw: The jaw can be shut tight or open slightly. It might also quiver.

MORPH TARGET GROUP	MORPH TARGET	PERCENTAGE
Brows	• Brows Lowered	100
	• Brows Middle Raised	100
Eyes	• Eye Left Down	100
	• Eye Right Down	100
Mouth	• Cry Closed	100

HUMAN CRYING WITH MOUTH OPEN

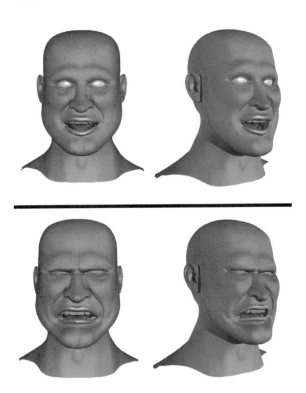

Distinguishing Features

Brows: The eyebrows are lowered.

Eyes: The eyes are clenched shut. If they do open, it's done with considerable effort.

Mouth: The mouth opened, and the lower corners pulled back. The cheeks bunch up under the eyes.

Jaw: The jaw is held stiffly open.

MORPH TARGET GROUP	MORPH TARGET	PERCENTAGE
Brows	• Brow Compressed	100
Eyes	• Eye Left Down	100
	• Eye Right Down	100
Mouth	• Cry Open	65
Jaw	• Jaw Closed	35

CARTOON CRYING WITH MOUTH OPEN

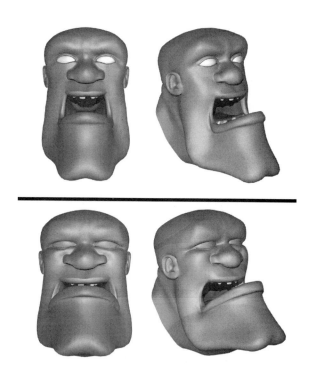

Distinguishing Features

Brows: The eyebrows are lowered.

Eyes: The eyes are clenched shut. If they do open, it's done with considerable effort.

Mouth: The mouth is open with the lower corners pulled back. The cheeks bunch up under the eyes.

Jaw: The jaw is open.

MORPH TARGET GROUP	MORPH TARGET	PERCENTAGE
Brows	• Brows Lowered	100
Eyes	• Eye Left Down	100
	• Eye Right Down	100
Mouth	• Cry Open	100

HUMAN NEARLY CRYING

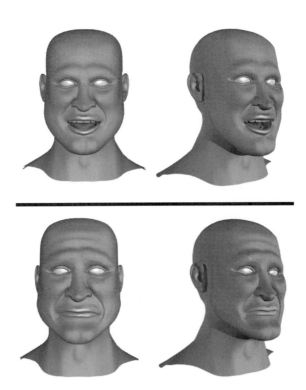

Distinguishing Features

Brows: The eyebrows are lowered, almost as if in anger.

Eyes: The eyes are clenched.

Mouth: The mouth is clenched shut and in animation may tremble. The cheeks bunch up and dimples may appear on the chin.

Jaw: The jaw can be shut tight or open slightly. It might also quiver.

MORPH TARGET GROUP	MORPH TARGET	PERCENTAGE
Brows	• Brows Arched	35
	• Brows Middle Up	100
Eyes	• Eye Left Down	15
	• Eye Right Down	15
Mouth	• Crying	80
	• Suppressed Sadness	80
Jaw	• Jaw Closed	90

CARTOON NEARLY CRYING

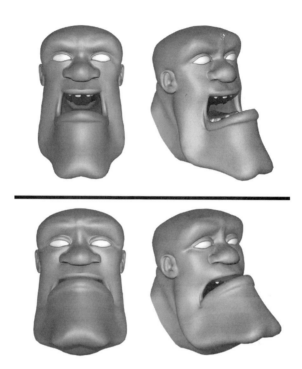

Distinguishing Features

Brows: The eyebrows are lowered, almost as if in anger.

Eyes: The eyes are clenched shut. If they do open, it's done with considerable effort.

Mouth: The mouth is clenched shut and in animation may tremble. The cheeks bunch up and dimples may appear on the chin.

Jaw: The jaw can be shut tight or open slightly. It might also quiver.

MORPH TARGET GROUP	MORPH TARGET	PERCENTAGE
Brows	• Brows Middle Raised	80
Eyes	• Eye Left Down	15
	• Eye Right Down	15
Mouth	• Cry Closed	70
	• Cry Open	100
	• Suppressed Sadness	100

HUMAN MISERABLE

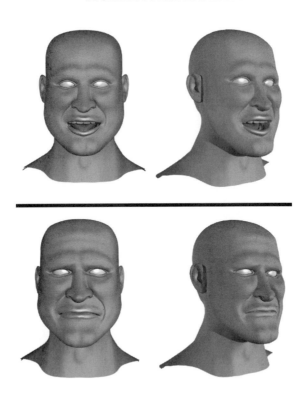

Distinguishing Features

Brows: The inner brows are bent upward and pinched together.

Eyes: The eyelids are lowered slightly.

Mouth: The mouth is slightly pouted, and the corners may be drawn down.

Jaw: The jaw is shut.

MORPH TARGET GROUP	MORPH TARGET	PERCENTAGE
Brows	• Brows Middle Up	90
	• Brows Compressed	100
Eyes	• Eye Left Down	100
	• Eye Right Down	100
Mouth	• Suppressed Sadness	40
Jaw	• Jaw Closed	90

CARTOON MISERABLE

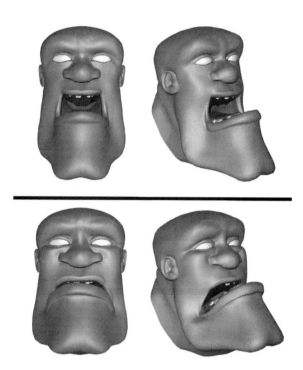

Distinguishing Features

Brows: The inner brows are bent upward and pinched together.

Eyes: The lids are relaxed or lowered and tightened slightly.

Mouth: The mouth is open and the corners of the mouth are drawn back and rippled. The lower lip might curl out

Jaw: The jaw hangs open.

MORPH TARGET GROUP	MORPH TARGET	PERCENTAGE
Brows	• Brows Lowered	50
	• Brows Middle Raised	100
Eyes	• Eye Left Down	15
	• Eye Right Down	15
Mouth	• Miserable	50

Human Worried

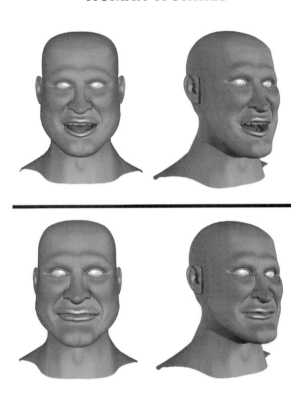

Distinguishing Features

Brows: The eyebrows may be relaxed or drawn up slightly as if sad.

Eyes: The eyes are open with a worried pose. Most action is taking place in the mind so the eyes are focused on nothing in particular.

Mouth: The mouth may be relaxed or squeezed together somewhat depending on the severity of the pose.

Jaw: The jaw is closed.

MORPH TARGET GROUP	MORPH TARGET	PERCENTAGE
Brows	• Brows Middle Up	75
Eyes	• NONE	N/A
Mouth	• Suppressed Sadness	50
Jaw	• Jaw Closed	70

CARTOON WORRIED

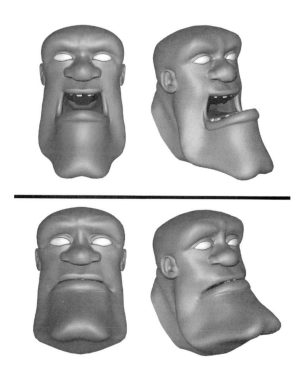

Distinguishing Features

Brows: The eyebrows may be relaxed or drawn up slightly as if sad.

Eyes: The eyes are open, with a worried pose. Most action is taking place in the mind, so the eyes are focused on nothing in particular.

Mouth: The mouth may be relaxed or squeezed together somewhat depending on the severity of the pose.

Jaw: The jaw is closed or hangs open. The mind is likely too concerned with other matters to keep the jaw shut.

MORPH TARGET GROUP	MORPH TARGET	PERCENTAGE
Brows	• Brows Middle Raised	75
Eyes	• NONE	N/A
Mouth	• Mouth Closed	75

HUMAN AFRAID

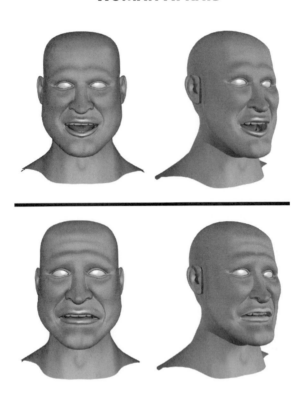

Distinguishing Features

Brows: The brows are lifted straight up and possibly drawn together in the middle.

Eyes: The eyes are open, and in animation, they might dart about.

Mouth: The mouth is relaxed or might be parted slightly with no strain or tightening.

Jaw: The jaw is open slightly.

MORPH TARGET GROUP	MORPH TARGET	PERCENTAGE
Brows	• Brows Middle Up	75
Eyes	• NONE	N/A
Mouth	• Frightened	70
Jaw	• Suppressed Sadness	55

CARTOON AFRAID

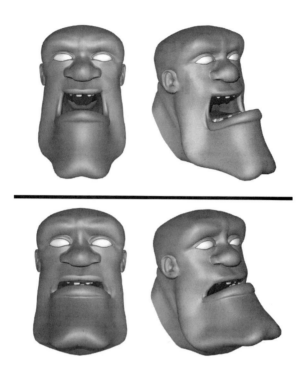

Distinguishing Features

Brows: The brows are lifted straight up and possibly drawn together in the middle.

Eyes: The eyes are open, and in animation, they might dart about.

Mouth: The mouth is relaxed or might be parted slightly with no strain or tightening.

Jaw: The jaw is open slightly.

MORPH TARGET GROUP	MORPH TARGET	PERCENTAGE
Brows	• Brows Middle Raised	70
Eyes	• NONE	N/A
Mouth	• Closed	65

HUMAN VERY FRIGHTENED

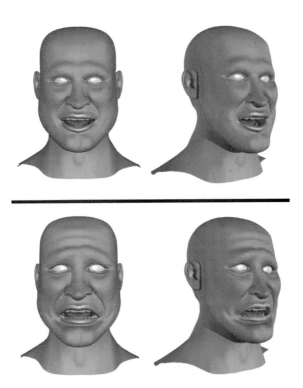

Distinguishing Features

Brows: The brows are lifted and drawn together in the middle slightly.

Eyes: The lids are open wide and the eyes stare straight ahead.

Mouth: The mouth is opened and the lower lip stretched horizontally, revealing the bottom teeth but not the upper.

Jaw: The jaw is dropped to about the halfway position.

MORPH TARGET GROUP	MORPH TARGET	PERCENTAGE
Brows	• Brows Middle Up	100
Eyes	• Eyes Wide	120
Mouth	• Cry Open	50
	• Frightened	100
Jaw	• Jaw Closed	15

CARTOON VERY FRIGHTENED

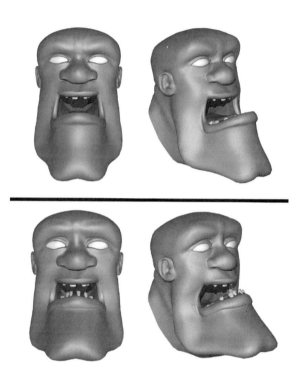

Distinguishing Features

Brows: The brows are lifted and drawn together in the middle slightly.

Eyes: The lids are open wide and the eyes stare straight ahead.

Mouth: The mouth is opened and the lower lip stretched horizontally, revealing the bottom teeth but not the upper.

Jaw: The jaw is dropped to about the halfway position.

MORPH TARGET GROUP	MORPH TARGET	PERCENTAGE
Brows	• Brows Middle Raised	70
Eyes	• NONE	N/A
Mouth	• Frightened	100

HUMAN TERROR

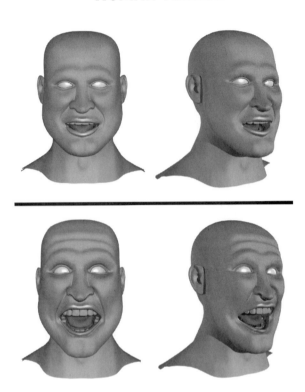

Distinguishing Features

Brows: The brows are raised as high as they will go, causing deep furrows in the forehead.

Eyes: The eyes are opened as wide as possible.

Mouth: The mouth is opened as wide as possible. The cheeks are stretched taut and pulled in toward the teeth somewhat.

Jaw: The jaw is opened to its full extent.

MORPH TARGET GROUP	MORPH TARGET	PERCENTAGE
Brows	• Brows Arched	100
	• Brows Middle Up	100
Eyes	• Eyes Wide	100
Mouth	• Yawn	100
Jaw	• Jaw Open	120

CARTOON TERROR

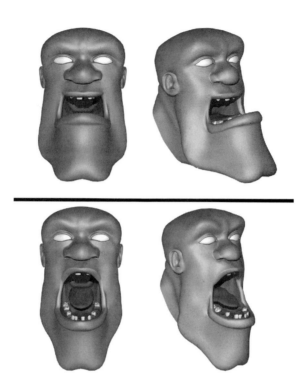

Distinguishing Features

Brows: The brows are raised as high as they will go, causing deep furrows in the forehead.

Eyes: The eyes are opened as wide as possible.

Mouth: The mouth is opened as wide as possible. The cheeks are stretched taut and pulled in toward the teeth somewhat.

Jaw: The jaw is opened to its full extent.

MORPH TARGET GROUP	MORPH TARGET	PERCENTAGE
Brows	• Brows Right Raised	100
	• Brows Left Raised	100
Eyes	• Eye Left Down	100
	• Eye Right Down	100
Mouth	• Yawn	100

HUMAN STERN

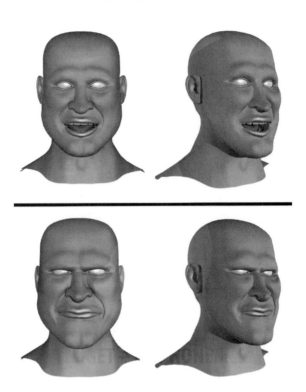

Distinguishing Features

Brows: The brows are lowered.

Eyes: The lids are lowered somewhat.

Mouth: The mouth is closed and the lips may be compressed together.

Jaw: The jaw is closed.

MORPH TARGET GROUP	MORPH TARGET	PERCENTAGE
Brows	• Brows Compressed	80
Eyes	• NONE	N/A
Mouth	• Mouth Closed	100
	• Mouth Frightened	100
Jaw	• Jaw Closed	100

CARTOON STERN

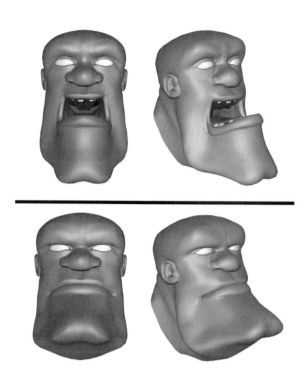

Distinguishing Features

Brows: The brows are lowered.

Eyes: The lids are lowered somewhat.

Mouth: The mouth is closed and the lips may be pressed together.

Jaw: The jaw is closed.

MORPH TARGET GROUP	MORPH TARGET	PERCENTAGE
Brows	• Brows Anger	100
Eyes	• Eye Left Down	15
	• Eye Right Down	
Mouth	• Closed	100

HUMAN ENRAGED WITH MOUTH CLOSED

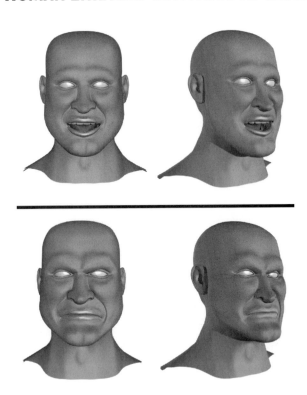

Distinguishing Features

Brows: The brows are down and drawn together in the center.

Eyes: The eyes are open wide, but may be partially obscured by the brows.

Mouth: The mouth is tightly compressed, and the corners may be drawn down slightly at the corners.

Jaw: The jaw is shut.

MORPH TARGET GROUP	MORPH TARGET	PERCENTAGE
Brows	• Brows Angry	100
	• Brows Compressed	50
Eyes	• Eye Left Down	20
	• Eye Right Down	20
Mouth	• Suppressed Sadness	60
Jaw	• Jaw Closed	100

CARTOON ENRAGED WITH MOUTH CLOSED

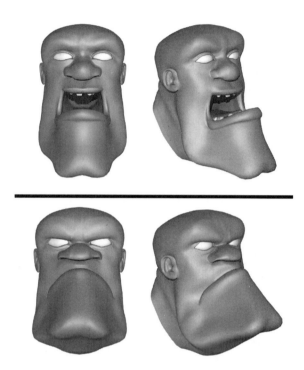

Distinguishing Features

Brows: The brows are down and together in the center.

Eyes: The eyes are open wide, but may be partially obscured by the brows.

Mouth: The mouth is tightly compressed, and the corners are drawn down.

Jaw: The jaw is shut.

MORPH TARGET GROUP	MORPH TARGET	PERCENTAGE
Brows	• Brows Anger	100
Eyes	• NONE	N/A
Mouth	• Suppressed Sadness	100

HUMAN SHOUT

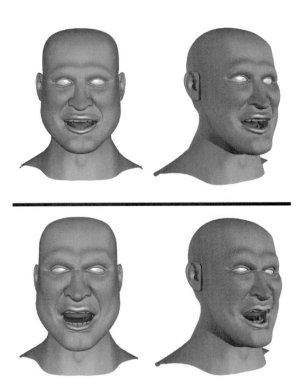

Distinguishing Features

Brows: The brows move from relaxed to raised straight up. As shouting continues, the brows might be lowered slowly.

Eyes: The eyes are either relaxed or open wide.

Mouth: The mouth is opened wide, with both upper and lower teeth showing.

Jaw: The jaw pumps open and closed, possibly to its full extent depending on the vigor of the shouting.

MORPH TARGET GROUP	MORPH TARGET	PERCENTAGE
Brows	• Brows Angry	62
Eyes	• Eye Left Down	20
	• Eye Right Down	20
Mouth	• Laughter	100
	• Surprise	120
	• Yawn	70
Jaw	• Jaw Open	60

CARTOON SHOUT

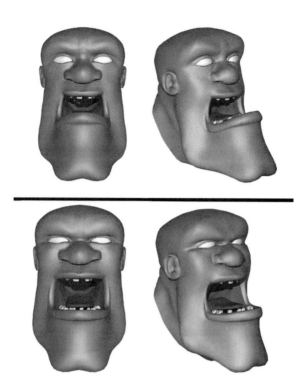

Distinguishing Features

Brows: The brows move from relaxed to raised straight up. As shouting continues, the brows might be lowered slowly.

Eyes: The eyes are either relaxed or open wide.

Mouth: The mouth is opened wide, with both upper and lower teeth showing.

Jaw: The jaw pumps open and closed, possibly to its full extent depending on the vigor of the shouting.

MORPH TARGET GROUP	MORPH TARGET	PERCENTAGE
Brows	• Brows Anger	90
Eyes	• Eye Left Down	20
	• Eye Right Down	20
Mouth	• Cry Open	100
	• Laughter	85
	• Yawn	80

HUMAN ENRAGED SHOUT

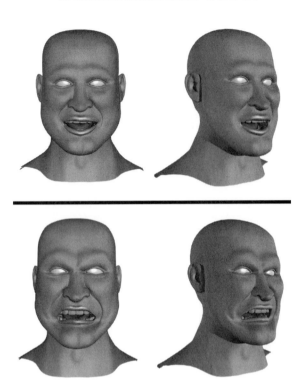

Distinguishing Features

Brows: The brows are lowered in anger.

Eyes: The eyes are opened wide.

Mouth: The mouth is opened, pulled down and back toward the ears, and tightened against the skull. The upper lip is raised, revealing the teeth.

Jaw: The jaw is opened about one-fifth of its limit. During animation, it doesn't pump nearly as much as a normal shout, as the muscles seem to be locked in place.

MORPH TARGET GROUP	MORPH TARGET	PERCENTAGE
Brows	• Brows Angry	70
Eyes	• Eye Left Down	10
	• Eye Right Down	10
Mouth	• NONE	N/A
Jaw	• Jaw Closed	20

CARTOON ENRAGED SHOUT

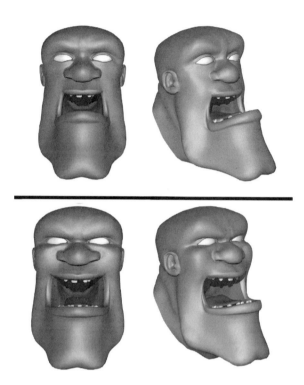

Distinguishing Features

Brows: The brows are lowered in anger.

Eyes: The eyes are opened wide.

Mouth: The mouth is opened, pulled back toward the ears, and tightened against the skull. The upper lip is raised, revealing the teeth.

Jaw: The jaw is opened wide. During animation, it doesn't pump nearly as much as a normal shout, as the muscles seem to be locked in place.

MORPH TARGET GROUP	MORPH TARGET	PERCENTAGE
Brows	• Brows Anger	90
Eyes	• NONE	N/A
Mouth	• Cry Open	100
	• Laughter	62

HUMAN EXERTION

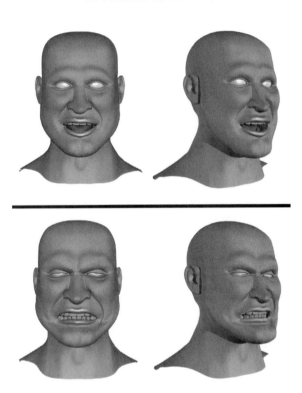

Distinguishing Features

Brows: The brows can be relaxed or lowered as if in anger, depending on the level of exertion. In animation, the eyebrows can move into almost any position, as long as the mouth and jaw are correct.

Eyes: The eyes are clamped shut.

Mouth: The mouth is opened and pulled tightly against the teeth.

Jaw: The jaw is opened just so that the upper and lower teeth meet at the tips.

MORPH TARGET GROUP	MORPH TARGET	PERCENTAGE
Brows	• Brows Angry	70
Eyes	• Eye Left Down	10
	• Eye Right Down	10
Mouth	• Cry Open	80
Jaw	• Jaw Closed	20

CARTOON EXERTION

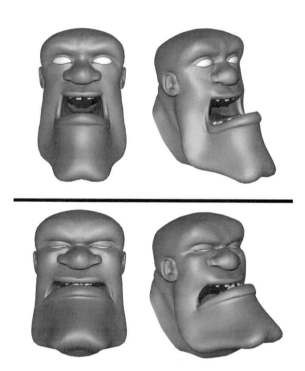

Distinguishing Features

Brows: The brows can be relaxed or lowered as if in anger, depending on the level of exertion. In animation, the eyebrows can move into almost any position, as long as the mouth and jaw are correct.

Eyes: The eyes are clamped shut.

Mouth: The mouth is opened and pulled tightly against the teeth.

Jaw: The jaw is opened just so that the upper and lower teeth meet at the tips.

MORPH TARGET GROUP	MORPH TARGET	PERCENTAGE
Brows	• Brows Anger	90
Eyes	• Eye Left Down	100
	• Eye Right Down	100
Mouth	• Cry Open	100
	• Surprise	100
	• Disgust	100

HUMAN PAIN

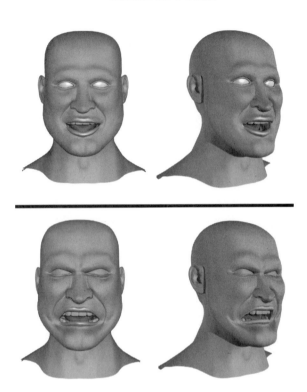

Distinguishing Features

Brows: The brows can be relaxed or lowered as if in anger, depending on the level of pain. Although pain and exertion are similar in appearance, during animation the brows will remain pressing down in pain.

Eyes: The eyes are clamped shut.

Mouth: The mouth is opened and pulled tightly against the teeth.

Jaw: The jaw is opened just so that the upper and lower teeth meet at the tips.

MORPH TARGET GROUP	MORPH TARGET	PERCENTAGE
Brows	• Brows Angry	100
	• Brows Compressed	70
Eyes	• Eye Left Down	100
	• Eye Right Down	100
Mouth	• Cry Open	90
Jaw	• Jaw Closed	15

CARTOON PAIN

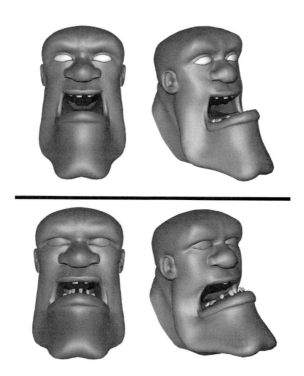

Distinguishing Features

Brows: The brows can be relaxed or lowered as if in anger, depending on the level of pain. Although pain and exertion are similar in appearance, during animation the brows will remain pressing down in pain.

Eyes: The eyes are clamped shut.

Mouth: The mouth is opened and pulled tightly against the teeth. The lower corner can be pulled down and back.

Jaw: The jaw is opened.

MORPH TARGET GROUP	MORPH TARGET	PERCENTAGE
Brows	• Brows Lowered	80
Eyes	• Eye Left Down	100
	• Eye Right Down	100
Mouth	• Surprise	100

HUMAN PAIN 2

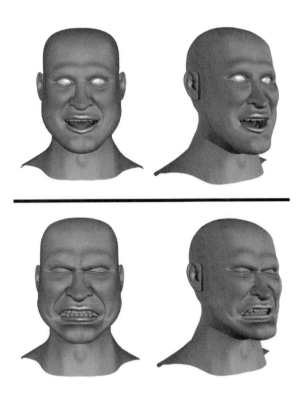

Distinguishing Features

Brows: The brows can be relaxed or lowered as if in anger.

Eyes: The eyes are open or squinting. It's even possible that one eye will be tightly shut while the other strains to open a crack.

Mouth: The mouth is closed, with the upper lip raised in a sneer. The upper lip may remain in contact with the lower lip, or may be lifted a bit to show some of the teeth.

Jaw: The jaw is closed.

MORPH TARGET GROUP	MORPH TARGET	PERCENTAGE
Brows	• Brows Angry	75
	• Brows Compressed	90
Eyes	• Eye Left Down	50
	• Eye Right Down	50
Mouth	• Repulsion	100
Jaw	• Closed	70

CARTOON PAIN 2

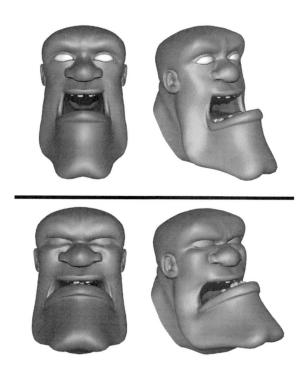

Distinguishing Features

Brows: The brows can be relaxed or lowered as if in anger.

Eyes: The eyes are open or squinting. It's even possible that one eye will be tightly shut while the other strains to open a crack.

Mouth: The mouth is closed, with the upper lip raised in a sneer. The lower corner of the mouth is pulled down and back.

Jaw: The jaw is closed.

MORPH TARGET GROUP	MORPH TARGET	PERCENTAGE
Brows	• Brows Anger	90
Eyes	• Eye Left Down	100
	• Eye Right Down	100
Mouth	• Cry Open	150
	• Surprise	100

HUMAN DISGUST

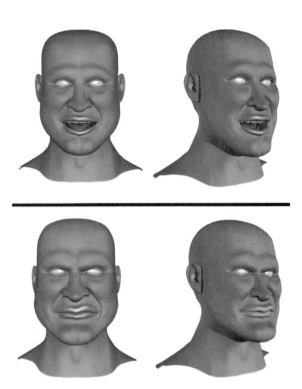

Distinguishing Features

Brows: The brows are relaxed.

Eyes: The eyes are open and relaxed.

Mouth: The mouth is closed, with one-half of the upper lip pulled upward and outward in a sneer.

Jaw: The jaw is closed.

MORPH TARGET GROUP	MORPH TARGET	PERCENTAGE
Brows	• Brows Angry	80
	• Brows Compressed	70
Eyes	• Eye Left Down	20
	• Eye Right Down	20
Mouth	• Disgust	90
Jaw	• Jaw Closed	70

CARTOON DISGUST

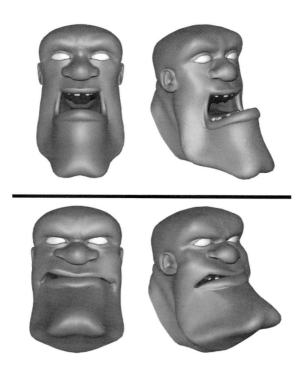

Distinguishing Features

Brows: The brows are relaxed.

Eyes: The eyes are open and relaxed.

Mouth: The mouth is closed, with one-half of the upper lip pulled upward and outward in a sneer.

Jaw: The jaw is closed.

MORPH TARGET GROUP	MORPH TARGET	PERCENTAGE
Brows	• Brows Anger	90
Eyes	• NONE	N/A
Mouth	• Disgust	100

HUMAN DISDAIN

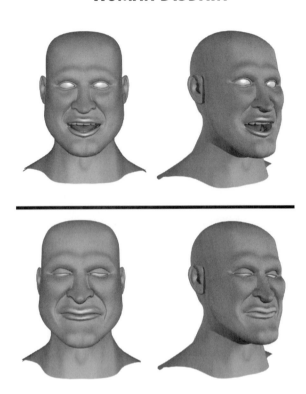

Distinguishing Features

Brows: The brows are relaxed.

Eyes: The lids are open or lowered, and the eye may look down or sideways.

Mouth: The mouth is closed, with the upper lip raised in a sneer.

Jaw: The jaw is closed.

MORPH TARGET GROUP	MORPH TARGET	PERCENTAGE
Brows	• Brows Angry	40
Eyes	• Eye Left Down	60
	• Eye Right Down	60
Mouth	• Repulsion	70
Jaw	• Jaw Closed	60

CARTOON DISDAIN

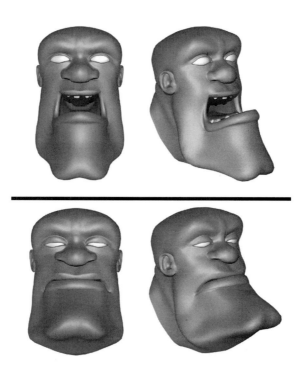

Distinguishing Features

Brows: The brows are relaxed.

Eyes: The lids are open or lowered, and the eye may look down or sideways.

Mouth: The mouth is closed, with the upper lip raised in a sneer.

Jaw: The jaw is closed.

MORPH TARGET GROUP	MORPH TARGET	PERCENTAGE
Brows	• Brows Left Raised	20
	• Brows Right Raised	20
Eyes	• Eye Left Down	50
	• Eye Right Down	50
Mouth	• Closed	100
	• Repulsion	100

HUMAN EVIL LAUGHTER

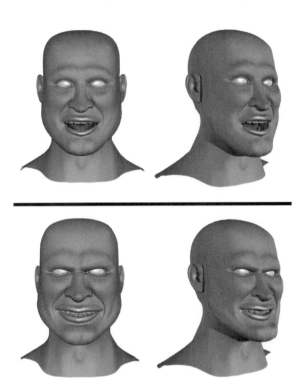

Distinguishing Features

Brows: Brows are drawn down as if in anger.

Eyes: The eyes are relaxed.

Mouth: The mouth is open, with the corners pulled back toward the ears, stretching it against the skull.

Jaw: The jaw is closed.

MORPH TARGET GROUP	MORPH TARGET	PERCENTAGE
Brows	• Brows Angry	70
	• Brows Compressed	100
Eyes	• NONE	N/A
Mouth	• Laughter	60
	• Smile Closed	70
Jaw	• Jaw Closed	80

CARTOON EVIL LAUGHTER

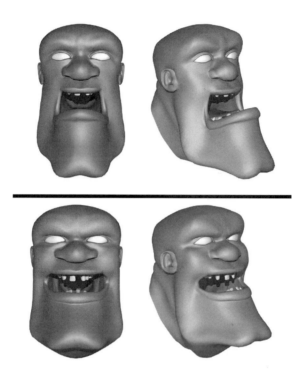

Distinguishing Features

Brows: The brows are lowered as if in anger.

Eyes: The eyes are open wide.

Mouth: The mouth is widened and pulled back toward the ears.

Jaw: The jaw is held stiffly open.

MORPH TARGET GROUP	MORPH TARGET	PERCENTAGE
Brows	• Brows Anger	80
Eyes	• NONE	N/A
Mouth	• Laughter	90
	• Smile	100
	• Smile Open	100

HUMAN INTENSE CONCENTRATION

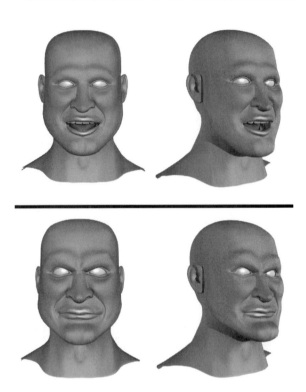

Distinguishing Features

Brows: The brows are lowered somewhat almost as if angered.

Eyes: The eyes are opened wider than normal.

Mouth: The mouth is relaxed.

Jaw: The jaw is closed.

MORPH TARGET GROUP	MORPH TARGET	PERCENTAGE
Brows	• Brows Angry	80
Eyes	• Eyes Wide	100
Mouth	• Mouth Closed	100
Jaw	• Jaw Closed	100

CARTOON INTENSE CONCENTRATION

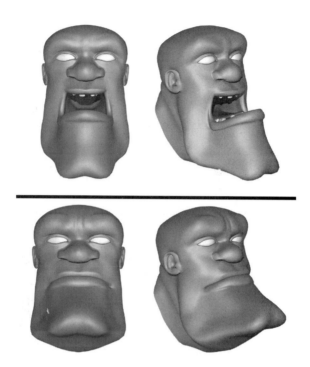

Distinguishing Features

Brows: The brows are lowered somewhat almost as if in anger, and brought together in the center. For cartoon characters, thinking is a painful process.

Eyes: The eyes are lowered somewhat.

Mouth: The mouth is relaxed.

Jaw: The jaw is closed.

MORPH TARGET GROUP	MORPH TARGET	PERCENTAGE
Brows	• Brows Anger	60
	• Brows Afraid	100
Eyes	• Eye Left Down	20
	• Eye Right Down	20
Mouth	• Closed	100

HUMAN FACIAL SHRUG

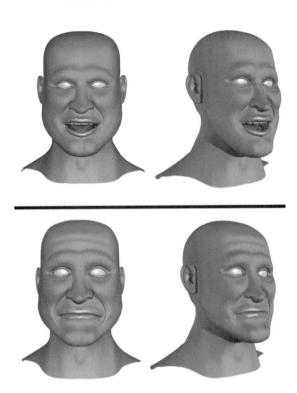

Distinguishing Features

Brows: The brows are raised straight upward to their limit.

Eyes: The eyes are open wide.

Mouth: The mouth is closed with the corners pulled down.

Jaw: The jaw may be closed, or opened fairly wide even though the mouth is closed.

MORPH TARGET GROUP	MORPH TARGET	PERCENTAGE
Brows	• Brows Arched	100
	• Brows Middle Up	90
Eyes	• Eyes Wide	100
Mouth	• Suppressed Sadness	60
Jaw	• Jaw Closed	100

CARTOON FACIAL SHRUG

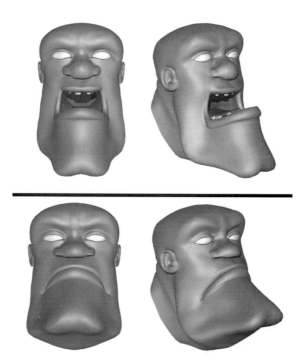

Distinguishing Features

Brows: The brows are raised straight upward to their limit.

Eyes: The eyes are open wide.

Mouth: The mouth is closed with the corners pulled down.

Jaw: The jaw may be closed, or opened fairly wide even though the mouth is closed.

MORPH TARGET GROUP	MORPH TARGET	PERCENTAGE
Brows	• Brows Left Raised	50
	• Brows Right Raised	50
Eyes	• Eye Left Down	20
	• Eye Right Down	20
Mouth	• Closed	100
	• Frown	50

HUMAN SURPRISE

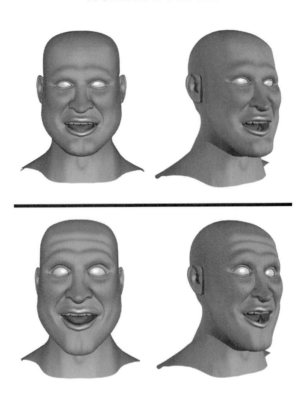

Distinguishing Features

Brows: The brows are raised high, causing wrinkles on the forehead.

Eyes: The eyes are opened wider than usual.

Mouth: The mouth is open but slack. How wide it opens depends on the severity of the surprise.

Jaw: The jaw is opened about one-third to one-half its limit.

MORPH TARGET GROUP	MORPH TARGET	PERCENTAGE
Brows	• Brows Arched	100
Eyes	• Eyes Wide	100
Mouth	• Mouth Surprise	100
Jaw	• Jaw Open	75

CARTOON SURPRISE

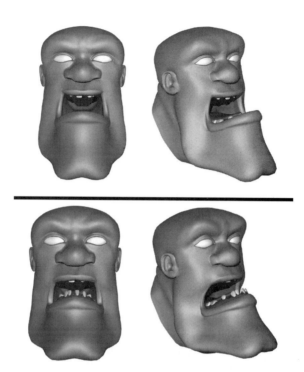

Distinguishing Features

Brows: The brows are raised high, causing wrinkles on the forehead.

Eyes: The eyes are opened wider than usual.

Mouth: The mouth is open but slack. How wide it opens depends on the severity of the surprise.

Jaw: The jaw is opened about one-third to one-half its limit.

MORPH TARGET GROUP	MORPH TARGET	PERCENTAGE
Brows	• Brows Right Raised	50
	• Brows Left Raised	50
Eyes	• NONE	N/A
Mouth	• Surprise	100

HUMAN DROWSINESS

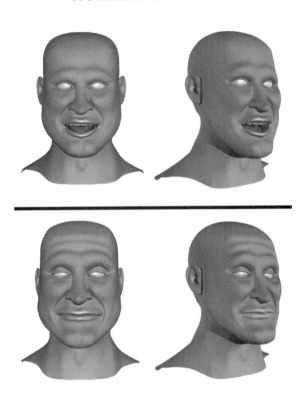

Distinguishing Features

Brows: The brows may be relaxed, or raised in an attempt to keep the lids from shutting.

Eyes: The eyelids are lowered. When animating, eye blinks may be slower in this condition.

Mouth: The mouth is relaxed. Any emotional expression will be greatly watered down.

Jaw: The jaw is closed.

MORPH TARGET GROUP	MORPH TARGET	PERCENTAGE
Brows	• Brows Arched	80
Eyes	• Eye Left Down	30
	• Eye Right Down	30
Mouth	• Mouth Smile Closed	60
	• Suppressed Sadness	60
Jaw	• Jaw Closed	70

CARTOON DROWSINESS

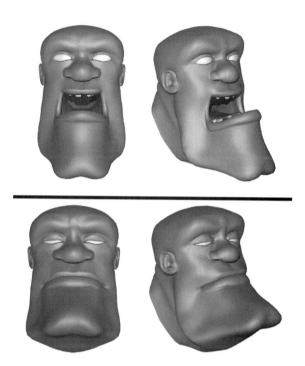

Distinguishing Features

Brows: The brows may be relaxed, or raised in an attempt to keep the lids from shutting.
Eyes: The eyelids are lowered. Eye blinks may be slower in this condition.
Mouth: The mouth is relaxed. Any emotional expression will be greatly watered down.
Jaw: The jaw is closed.

MORPH TARGET GROUP	MORPH TARGET	PERCENTAGE
Brows	• Brows Middle Raised	50
	• Brows Right Raised	50
	• Brows Left Raised	50
Eyes	• Eye Left Down	60
	• Eye Right Down	60
Mouth	• Closed	100

HUMAN SUPPRESSED SADNESS

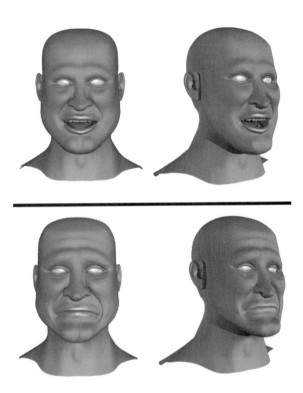

Distinguishing Features

Brows: The middle of the brow is raised.

Eyes: The eyes can be open or slightly shut. Bags may appear under the eyes if the condition is prolonged.

Mouth: The lips are pressed together, and the space between the gums and lower teeth may be filled with air.

Jaw: The jaw is closed.

MORPH TARGET GROUP	MORPH TARGET	PERCENTAGE
Brows	• Brows Middle Up	70
Eyes	• Eye Left Down	25
	• Eye Right Down	25
Mouth	• Suppressed Sadness	80
Jaw	• Jaw Closed	100

CARTOON SUPPRESSED SADNESS

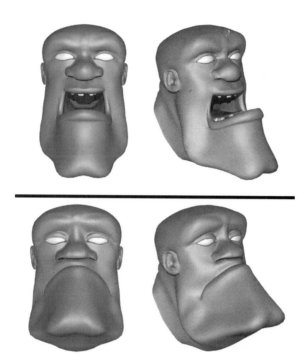

Distinguishing Features

Brows: The middle of the brow is raised.

Eyes: The eyes can be open or slightly shut. Bags may appear under the eyes if the condition is prolonged.

Mouth: The lips are pressed together, and the space between the gums and lower teeth may be filled with air.

Jaw: The jaw is closed.

MORPH TARGET GROUP	MORPH TARGET	PERCENTAGE
Brows	• Brows Middle Raised	80
Eyes	• Eye Left Down	30
	• Eye Right Down	30
Mouth	• Mouth Suppressed Sadness	100

HUMAN YAWN

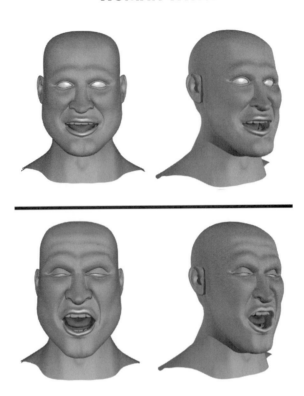

Distinguishing Features

Brows: The brows can be raised straight up, raised in the middle, or lowered.

Eyes: The eyes may be clamped shut or may be straining open.

Mouth: The mouth is open as wide as possible.

Jaw: The jaw is opened to its fullest extent.

MORPH TARGET GROUP	MORPH TARGET	PERCENTAGE
Brows	• Brows Angry	90
	• Brows Arched	100
Eyes	• Eye Left Down	50
	• Eye Right Down	50
Mouth	• Yawn	70
Jaw	• Jaw Open	120

CARTOON YAWN

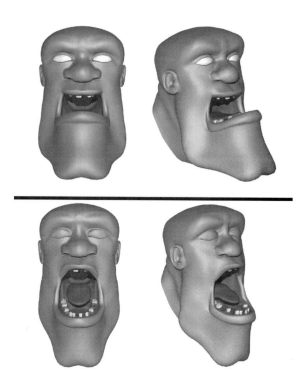

Distinguishing Features

Brows: The brows can be raised straight up, raised in the middle, or lowered.

Eyes: The eyes are clamped shut, or may be straining open.

Mouth: The mouth is open as wide as possible. Only the tips of the upper and lower teeth appear.

Jaw: The jaw is opened to its fullest extent.

MORPH TARGET GROUP	MORPH TARGET	PERCENTAGE
Brows	• Brows Middle Raised	60
Eyes	• Eye Left Down	100
	• Eye Right Down	100
Mouth	• Yawn	100

HUMAN DAZED

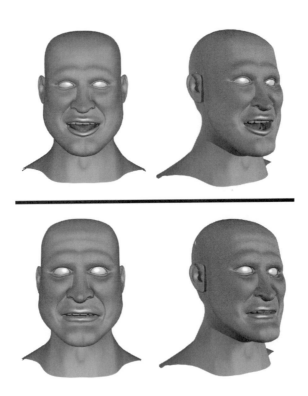

Distinguishing Features

Brows: The brows may be relaxed or raised a bit.

Eyes: The lids are opened wider than normal. The eyes stare straight-ahead and unfocused. In animation, they might swim about lazily.

Mouth: The mouth is relaxed.

Jaw: The jaw is closed.

MORPH TARGET GROUP	MORPH TARGET	PERCENTAGE
Brows	• Brows Arched	100
	• Brows Middle Up	90
Eyes	• Eyes Wide	100
Mouth	• Suppressed Sadness	60
	• Surprise	60
Jaw	• Jaw Closed	60

CARTOON DAZED

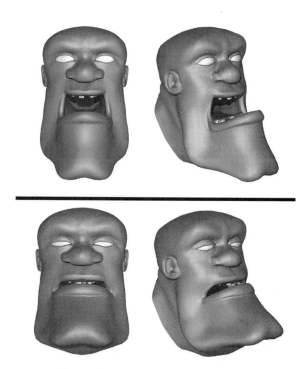

Distinguishing Features

Brows: The brows may be relaxed or raised a bit.

Eyes: The lids are opened wider than normal. The eyes stare straight ahead and are unfocused. In animation, they might swim about lazily.

Mouth: The mouth is relaxed.

Jaw: The jaw is closed.

MORPH TARGET GROUP	MORPH TARGET	PERCENTAGE
Brows	• NONE	N/A
Eyes	• Eye Left Down	45
	• Eye Right Down	45
Mouth	• Closed	100
	• Frightened	40

HUMAN SLEEP

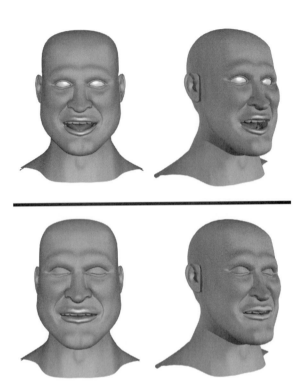

Distinguishing Features

Brows: The brows are relaxed.

Eyes: The eyes are closed.

Mouth: The mouth is either shut or slightly opened and relaxed.

Jaw: The jaw is either closed or slightly open.

MORPH TARGET GROUP	MORPH TARGET	PERCENTAGE
Brows	• NONE	N/A
Eyes	• Eye Left Down	100
	• Eye Right Down	100
Mouth	• Mouth Purse	20
Jaw	• Jaw Closed	20

CARTOON SLEEP

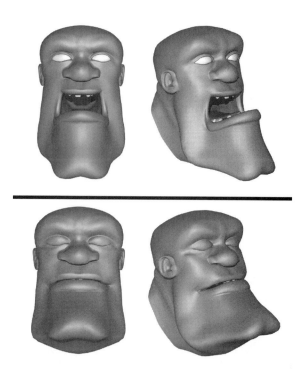

Distinguishing Features

Brows: The brows are relaxed.

Eyes: The eyes are closed.

Mouth: The mouth is either shut or slightly opened and relaxed.

Jaw: The jaw is either closed or slightly open.

MORPH TARGET GROUP	MORPH TARGET	PERCENTAGE
Brows	• NONE	N/A
Eyes	• Eye Left Down	100
	• Eye Right Down	100
Mouth	• Smile	90

HUMAN DRUNK OR TIRED LAUGHTER

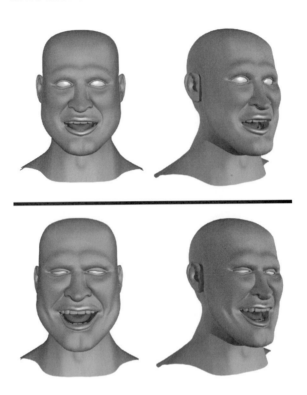

Distinguishing Features

Brows: The brows are either relaxed or raised in an attempt to raise the eyelids.

Eyes: The eyelids are drooping almost to their halfway position.

Mouth: The mouth is open and pulled back toward the ears, tightening the lips against the teeth. The cheeks bunch up and dimples appear, but these are not as severe as most other laughs.

Jaw: The jaw is open.

MORPH TARGET GROUP	MORPH TARGET	PERCENTAGE
Brows	• NONE	N/A
Eyes	• Eye Left Down	50
	• Eye Right Down	50
Mouth	• Laughter	100
Jaw	• Jaw Open	50

Cartoon Drunk or Tired Laughter

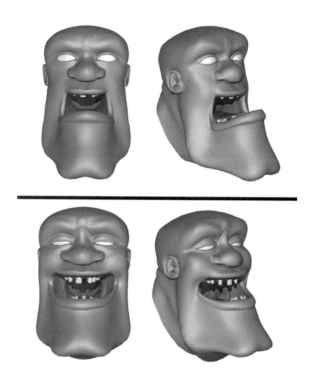

Distinguishing Features

Brows: The brows are either relaxed or raised in an attempt to raise the eyelids.

Eyes: The eyelids are drooping almost to their halfway position.

Mouth: The mouth is open and pulled back toward the ears, tightening the lips against the teeth. The cheeks bunch up and dimples appear, but these are not as severe as most other laughs.

Jaw: The jaw is open.

MORPH TARGET GROUP	MORPH TARGET	PERCENTAGE
Brows	• Brows Left Raised	100
	• Brows Right Raised	100
	• Brows Middle Raised	70
Eyes	• Eye Left Down	50
	• Eye Right Down	50
Mouth	• Laughter	75
	• Smile Open	100

HUMAN "I THINK YOU'RE NUTS" SMILE

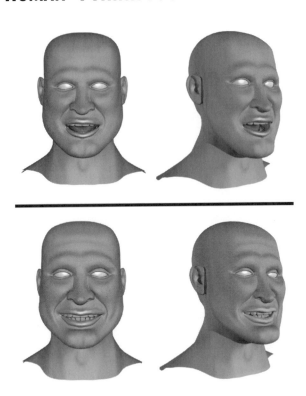

Distinguishing Features

Brows: The brows are raised straight up.

Eyes: The lids are lowered slightly.

Mouth: The mouth is opened, pulled back toward the ears, and stretched tightly against the teeth.

Jaw: The jaw is closed or slightly open.

MORPH TARGET GROUP	MORPH TARGET	PERCENTAGE
Brows	• Brows Arched	45
	• Brows Middle Up	35
Eyes	• Eye Left Down	15
	• Eye Right Down	15
Mouth	• Laughter	70
	• Smile Closed	60
Jaw	• Jaw Closed	70

CARTOON "I THINK YOU'RE NUTS" SMILE

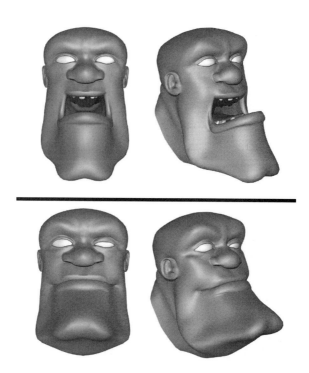

Distinguishing Features

Brows: The brows are raised straight up.

Eyes: The lids are lowered slightly.

Mouth: The mouth is opened, pulled back toward the ears, and stretched tightly against the teeth.

Jaw: The jaw is closed or slightly open.

MORPH TARGET GROUP	MORPH TARGET	PERCENTAGE
Brows	• Brows Left Raised	100
Eyes	• Eye Right Down	100
Mouth	• Smile	100

HUMAN BAD ODOR

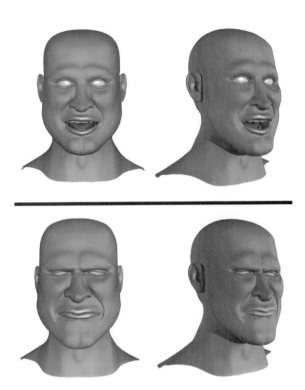

Distinguishing Features

Brows: The brows are lowered as if angered.

Eyes: The eyes are open or partly shut.

Mouth: The mouth is closed, with the upper lip raised in a sneer.

Jaw: The jaw is closed or slightly parted.

MORPH TARGET GROUP	MORPH TARGET	PERCENTAGE
Brows	• Brows Compressed	80
Eyes	• NONE	N/A
Mouth	• Crying	100
	• Closed	100
Jaw	• Jaw Closed	100

CARTOON BAD ODOR

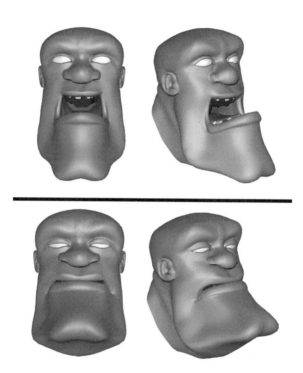

Distinguishing Features

Brows: The brows are lowered as if angered.

Eyes: The eyes are open or partly shut.

Mouth: The mouth is closed, with the upper lip raised in a sneer.

Jaw: The jaw is closed or slightly parted.

MORPH TARGET GROUP	MORPH TARGET	PERCENTAGE
Brows	• Brows Left Raised	100
Eyes	• Eye Left Down	50
	• Eye Right Down	50
Mouth	• Closed	90
	• Repulsion	100

JUST FOR FUN—
CARTOON EXPRESSIONS

In addition to animating humans realistically, there may be times when you need over-the-top animation with stylized humans and cartoon characters. Cartoon characters have the advantage of doing just about anything they want and are not limited to the physical restraints of realistic human animation. Cartoons can exaggerate every expression and often transform their appearance to suit the expressions. Many classic cartoon character emotions and expressions have been developed over the years by Warner Brothers, Disney, and Hanna-Barbera. These expressions, along with many others, are provided in this appendix to give you a visual reference of common cartoon character expressions.

For this appendix, Butch the alley dog will be used. Our first figure shows Butch in a neutral facial pose, which will be the starting point for this character's facial animation expressions. All the expressions in this appendix start with this pose. With each facial expression, the neutral pose is at the top of the image, with the expression pose in the lower half of the image, making comparison of the expression and neutral pose easier.

AFRAID

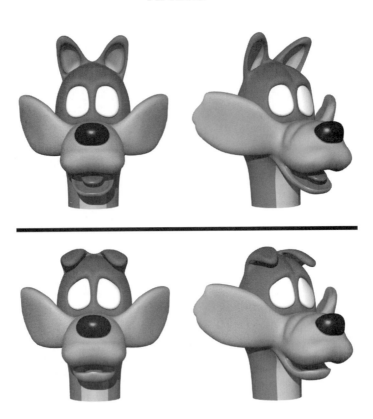

Distinguishing Features

Ears: The ears droop forward over the brow.

Brows: The brows are drawn toward the center.

Eyes: No change.

Whiskers: No change.

Mouth: The mouth is slightly open, with the lower lip curled inward and the tongue resting against the lower gum.

ANGER

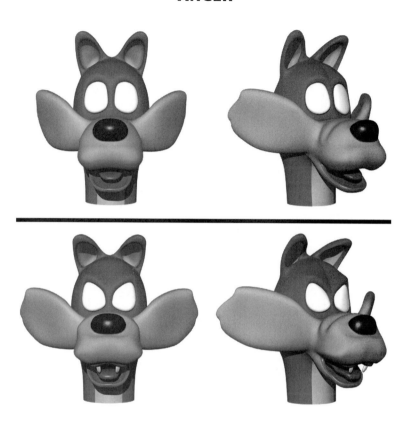

Distinguishing Features

Ears: The ears are bent forward slightly.

Brows: The inner portion of brow is drawn down toward the nose.

Eyes: No change.

Whiskers: The whiskers move forward a bit.

Mouth: The upper lip is pulled up in a snarl. The nose is crumpled, creating wrinkles along the muzzle. The tongue curls, making it wavy. Finally, fangs appear in the gums. It's generally acceptable for cartoon characters to spontaneously generate body parts that enhance an expression. In this case, the fangs help to make him appear more frightening.

ASLEEP

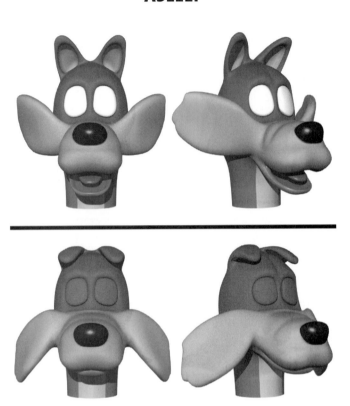

Distinguishing Features

Ears: The ears flop forward over the brow.

Brows: No change.

Eyes: The eyelids are lowered 100%, showing an eyelid seam.

Whiskers: The whiskers droop down in a relaxed position.

Mouth: The mouth is closed and relaxed.

CRYING

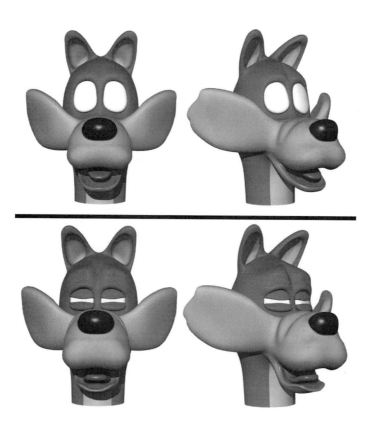

Distinguishing Features

Ears: No change.

Brows: The brow is pushed forward.

Eyes: The eyes are compressed, with the upper and lower eyelids nearly meeting in the middle.

Whiskers: No change.

Mouth: The jaw and tongue are curled and drawn back, while the nose and top of the muzzle are pulled up slightly.

DOOM

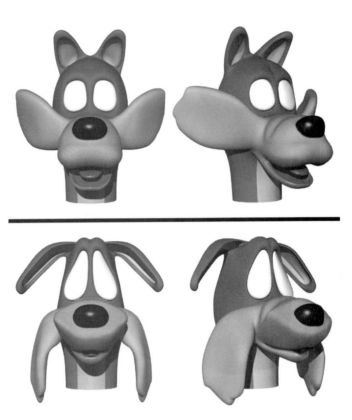

Distinguishing Features

Ears: The ears are rotated out to the side, drooped down, and stretched out.

Brows: The brows are drawn up and in toward the center, with the brow rising above the top of the head. The top of the head is compressed inward with the brow.

Eyes: The eyes are stretched upward and inward.

Whiskers: The whiskers droop down completely.

Mouth: The mouth is partially closed. The upper lip is tightened and pulled up, and the lower lip is drawn to a point, with the top of the tongue is curled to a point.

Common Uses

Anticipation is one of the key animation principles. This is a great expression to use when your character sees its impending doom, such as when a piano or anvil is about to drop onto its head.

DUH?

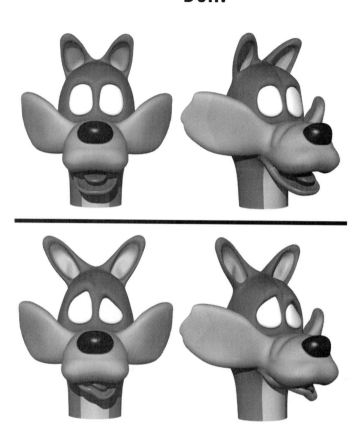

Distinguishing Features

Ears: The ears are spread wide and remain upright.

Brows: The brows are asymmetrically drawn in toward the center, with one lowered.

Eyes: The eyes are deformed asymmetrically, one squinting more than the other.

Whiskers: No change.

Mouth: The mouth is closed on one side and drooped downward on the other.

Common Uses

For dimwitted characters, this expression is a classic example of a basic confused look. When the character is faced with a situation or conversation he can't comprehend, use this expression.

FALSE SMILE

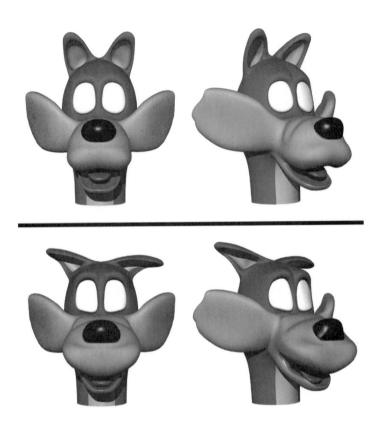

Distinguishing Features

Ears: The ears are rotated sideways and lowered to nearly parallel with the top of the head.

Brows: The brows are raised straight up so they are parallel with the top of the head.

Eyes: The inner, lower corners of the eyes are drawn down toward the muzzle.

Whiskers: No change.

Mouth: The corners of the mouth are drawn up in a smile, and the rest of the mouth, betraying a lack of sincerity, is rippled.

HAPPY

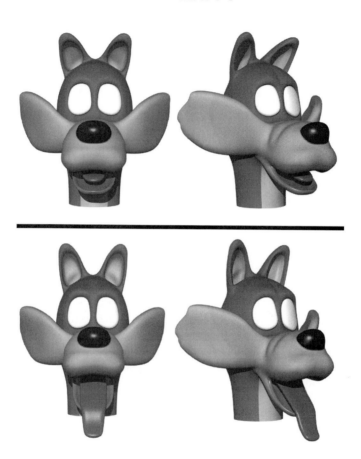

Distinguishing Features

Ears: No change.

Brows: The brows are raised slightly.

Eyes: No change.

Whiskers: No change.

Mouth: The mouth is dropped open and the tongue hangs out.

LAUGHTER

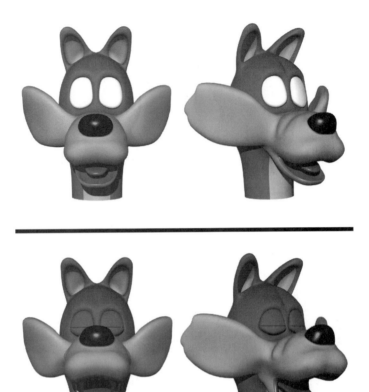

Distinguishing Features

Ears: No change.

Brows: No change.

Eyes: The eyes are closed showing a seam where the eyelids meet in the middle. The cheeks are pushed up against the lower portion of the eye.

Whiskers: No change.

Mouth: The mouth is open wide with the upper muzzle being raised. The tongue hovers above the lower gums.

PAIN

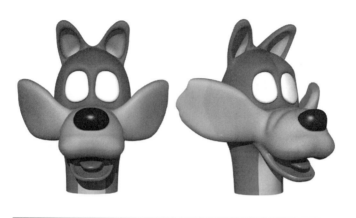

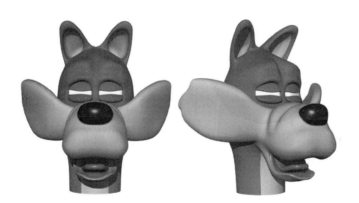

Distinguishing Features

Ears: No change.

Brows: The brow raised and pushed forward.

Eyes: The eyes are squeezed vertically, and the lids are partly shut, showing a gap in the middle.

Whiskers: No change.

Mouth: The muzzle is crumpled, with the lower lip and tongue curled upward at the tip.

SAD

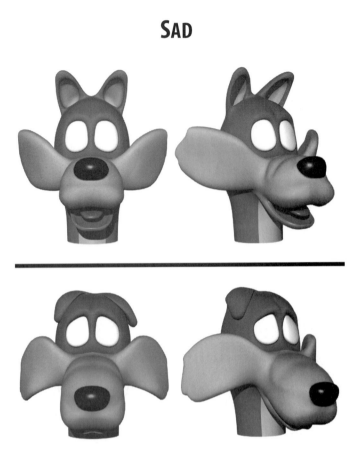

Distinguishing Features

Ears: The ears droop down and lay flat against the side of the head.

Brows: The brows are drawn up in the center and slightly forward.

Eyes: No change.

Whiskers: The whiskers droop down.

Mouth: The jaw is closed, leaving only a slight gap. The muzzle droops downward, and the lower lip is pulled down on either side.

SATISFACTION

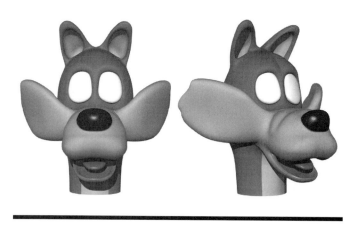

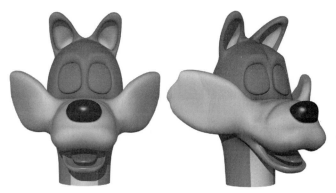

Distinguishing Features

Ears: No change.

Brows: The brows are lifted slightly.

Eyes: The eyes are completely closed showing no seams.

Whiskers: No change.

Mouth: No change.

SLEEPY

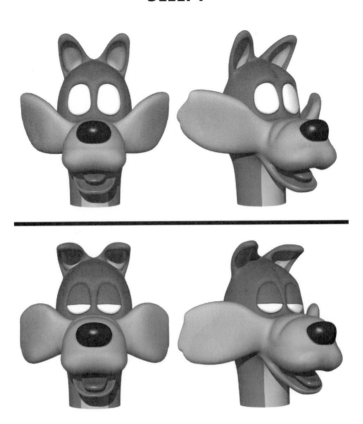

Distinguishing Features

Ears: The ears are drooped over the brow slightly.

Brows: No change.

Eyes: The upper eyelids are pulled down leaving only a small gap. There are no lower eyelids present.

Whiskers: The whiskers are drooped downward at the tips.

Mouth: The muzzle is puffed up slightly.

SNEER

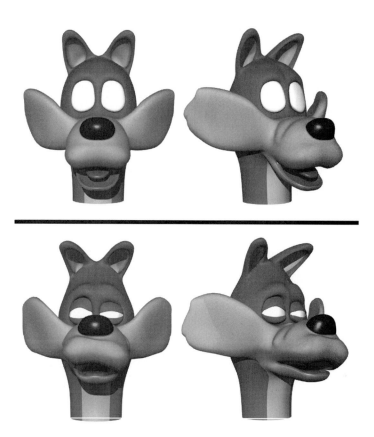

Distinguishing Features

Ears: The ears are rotated outward and downward slightly. The top of the head is tapered to a rounded point.

Brows: The brows are lowered dramatically and pushed forward. One is lowered more than the other.

Eyes: The eyes are closed, leaving only a small gap between the eyelids. The upper eyelid of the larger eye is pulled upward in the middle.

Whiskers: The whiskers are rotated down slightly at the tips.

Mouth: The upper muzzle is compressed and raised up slightly on the side of the larger eye. The lower jaw is pulled upward to become parallel with the muzzle, and the tongue rests flat on the lower gums.

SNOBBISH

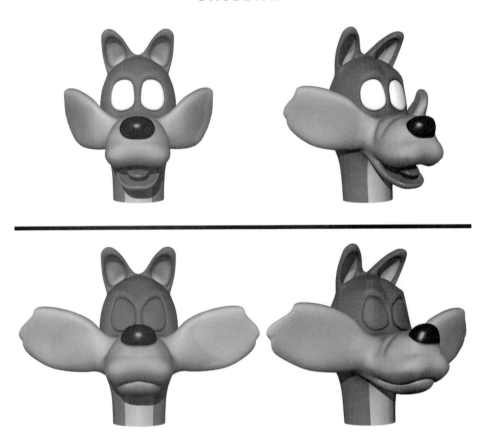

Distinguishing Features

Ears: No change.

Brows: The brows are raised on the outside of the eyes.

Eyes: The eyes are closed completely, showing no eyelid seam.

Whiskers: The whiskers are rotated forward to become parallel with one another.

Mouth: The mouth is closed with the muzzle curled upward at the tip.

YAWN

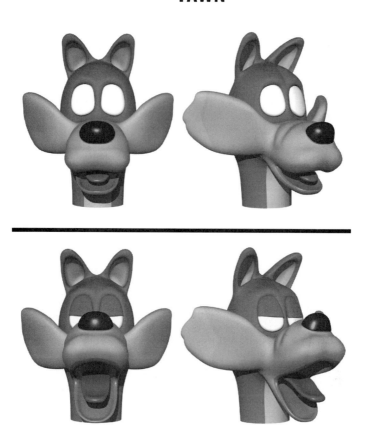

Distinguishing Features

Ears: No change.

Brows: No change.

Eyes: The upper lids of the eyes are lowered halfway down the eye. There is no lower eyelid visible.

Whiskers: No change.

Mouth: The upper muzzle is rotated upward and the mouth is wide open. The tongue remains in the middle of the mouth and curls slightly at the tip.

YELL

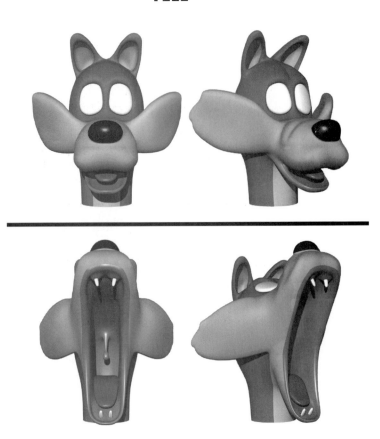

Distinguishing Features

Ears: No change.

Brows: No change.

Eyes: No change.

Whiskers: The whiskers are folded back against the head.

Mouth: The head is rotated backward significantly. The upper muzzle is rotated upward significantly. The lower jaw is dropped all the way down, and fangs appear in the upper and lower gums. The tongue lies flat on the lower gums.

ACCORDION

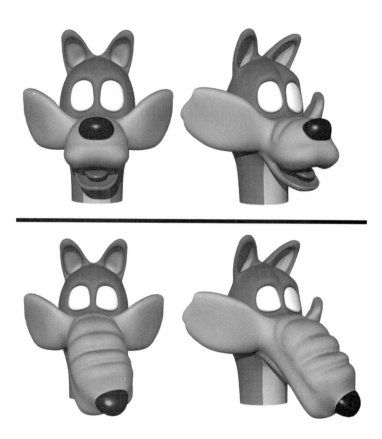

Distinguishing Features

Ears: No change.

Brows: No change.

Eyes: No change.

Whiskers: No change.

Mouth: The muzzle is stretched forward and drooped downward. The mouth is closed, and multiple creases are present on the top of the muzzle, creating the accordion appearance.

Common Uses

This is a great animated expression, where the nose recoils like an accordion. This is commonly used when the character runs into an immovable object like a wall or cliff. It's also used when the character is hit in the face with an object.

ANGUISH

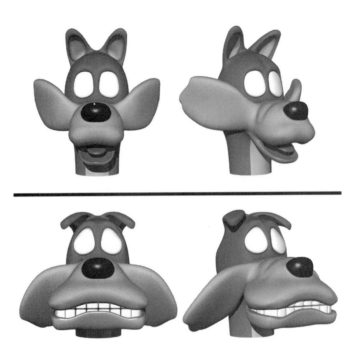

Distinguishing Features

Ears: The ears are drooped outward and down toward the brow.

Brows: The brows are raised inward to become parallel with the top of the head.

Eyes: The eyes are shaped like teardrops.

Whiskers: The whiskers are drooped downward.

Mouth: The sides of the mouth are pulled outward severely to form a square jaw. The lips are lowered, and the gums are parted and lowered on either side, exposing rows of teeth.

WACH THE BIRDIE

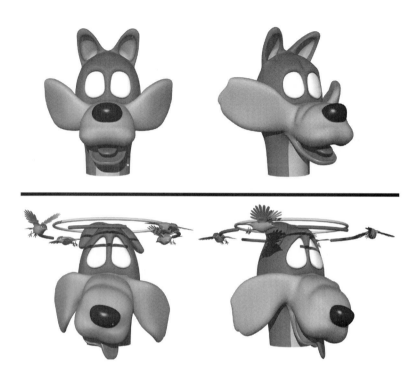

Distinguishing Features

Ears: The ears are lowered so they lay flat on the sides of the head.

Brows: The brows are pulled upward and inward until they are parallel with the head.

Eyes: The eyes are shaped like long teardrops.

Whiskers: The whiskers droop down to the sides of the head.

Mouth: The muzzle is drooped downward with the jaw open slightly, letting the tongue hang out.

Special: Little birds are added, flying in circles around the top of the head. The birds are accompanied by circular lines that also rotate around the top of the head.

Common Uses

Watch the Birdie is a very common expression for cartoon characters. It's unique, since it has supporting cast members and is heavily animated. The common uses for Watch the Birdie are situations in which the character is hit on the head with a smaller object that doesn't knock him unconscious, such as a brick, rock, or anvil. Typically, Spelunker expression precedes Watch the Birdie.

CLANG

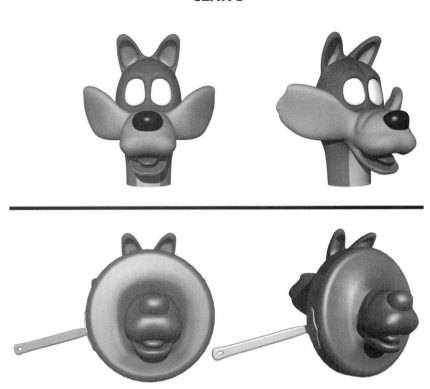

Distinguishing Features

Ears: No change.

Brows: No change.

Eyes: No change.

Whiskers: No change.

Mouth: The impact object is molded around the muzzle of the character, taking the on shape of the muzzle.

Common Uses

The Clang expression is used when an object sticks to the face of your character, taking on the shape of its face. This expression is often used when the character is hit with a frying pan, pie pan, or in many cases an object like a baseball bat. Whatever the object, it takes on the shape of the character's face. The Clang expression is typically followed by Watch the Birdie.

HUBBA-HUBBA

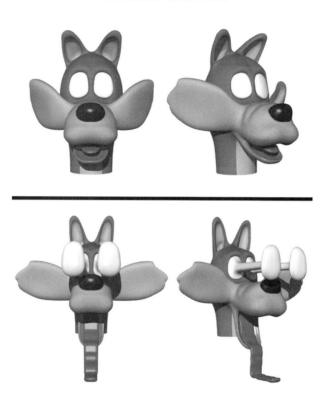

Distinguishing Features

Ears: The ears stand straight up and are stretched upward a bit.

Brows: The brows are moved forward a bit.

Eyes: The eyes pop out of the head and hang over the end of the muzzle.

Whiskers: The whiskers stand straight out to the sides of the muzzle.

Mouth: The lower jaw drops all the way down and the tongue unrolls like a carpet. The tongue in this expression is typically longer than normal.

Common Uses

Hubba-Hubba is a fun expression used to express extreme desire, and can be used for a number of situations. While it's commonly used when your character sees an attractive character of the opposite sex, it can also be used to express lust for an object such as money. It could be used when your character opens the door to a vault of money, or when a sultry character walks into the shot. This expression typically involves extreme body deformation as well, such as an over-exaggerated beating heart.

IMPACT

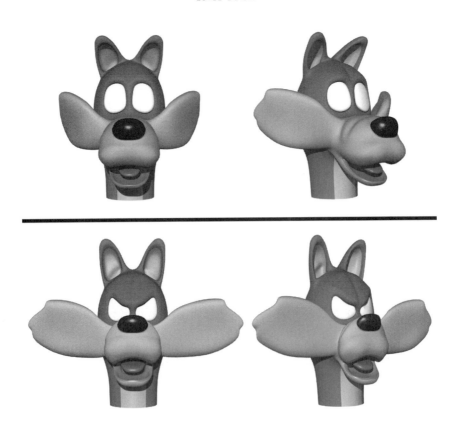

Distinguishing Features

Ears: The ears stand straight up and are stretched upward a bit.

Brows: The center of the brows is pushed downward to the center of the eye.

Eyes: Only changed by the brow movement.

Whiskers: The whiskers stand straight out to the sides of the muzzle.

Mouth: The muzzle is pushed flat against the head.

Common Uses

This expression is used similar to Clang, but the object doesn't stick to the face. It's used when the impact is less severe; for example, if your character is hit in the face with a board, falls flat on its face, or runs into a wall. It's a great expression to use when a door is slammed in the face.

GRIN

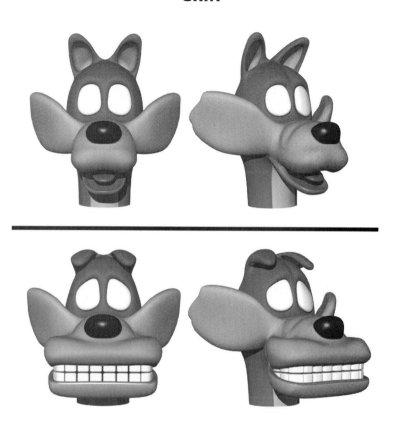

Distinguishing Features

Ears: The ears drooped forward over the brow.

Brows: The outside edge of the brow is lowered slightly.

Eyes: The eyes are shaped like teardrops.

Whiskers: The whiskers are pulled upward at the tips.

Mouth: The sides of the mouth are pulled outward severely to form a square jaw. The lips are parted, exposing a wide gap that shows rows of teeth.

Common Uses

Cartoon characters are very flexible and develop features on the fly to accentuate expressions. Grin is a perfect example of this. The character has developed a full set of teeth to facilitate the Grin expression. This expression is used when the character has irritated a larger character and is trying to weasel out of it with a grin.

LOVE

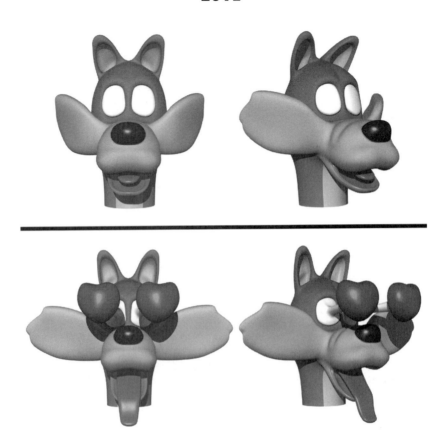

Distinguishing Features

Ears: The ears are raised upward.

Brows: No change.

Eyes: The eyes are pulled out over the muzzle and shaped like hearts.

Whiskers: The whiskers are pulled upward at the tips.

Mouth: The lower jaw is dropped downward, and the tongue hangs out of the mouth, lying against the lower gums.

PUMMELED

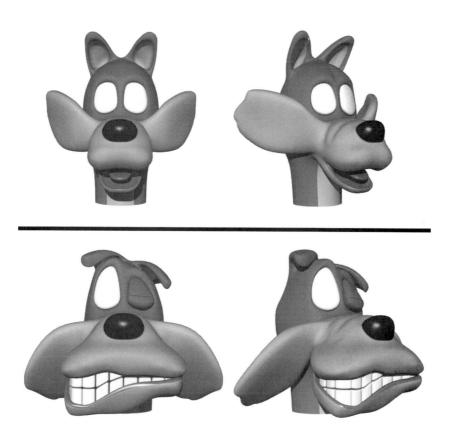

Distinguishing Features

Ears: The ears are drooped over the sides of the head.

Brows: The brows are raised with one passing the top of the head.

Eyes: The high brow eye is unchanged, while the lower-brow eye is closed with a seam in the middle where the eyelids meet. The smaller eye is also puffed outward to appear swollen.

Whiskers: The whiskers are rotated forward and drooped down against the sides of the head.

Mouth: The sides of the mouth are pulled outward severely to form a square jaw. The lips are parted, exposing a wide gap that shows rows of teeth—the gap is widest on one side tapering to a small gap on the opposite side. The largest gap is on the same side as the larger eye. The jaw is lowered on the side with the greatest gap.

BLINDS

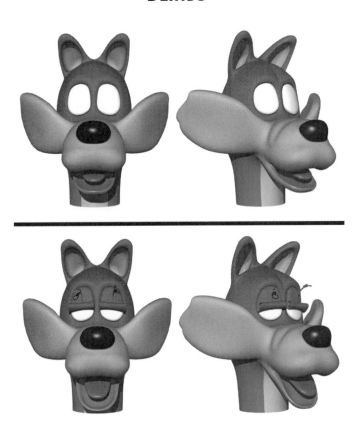

Distinguishing Features

Ears: No change.

Brows: The brow is pulled forward slightly.

Eyes: The upper eyelids are closed two-thirds of the way down the eye and curled at the tip. A string and ring are attached to the eyelid to create the appearance of blinds.

Whiskers: No change.

Mouth: The lower jaw is dropped open, and the tongue hovers above the lower gums.

Common Uses

The Blinds expression is usually the result of another character pulling your character's eyelids down like shutters. It's the cartoon equivalent of poking someone in the eyes.

SPELUNKER

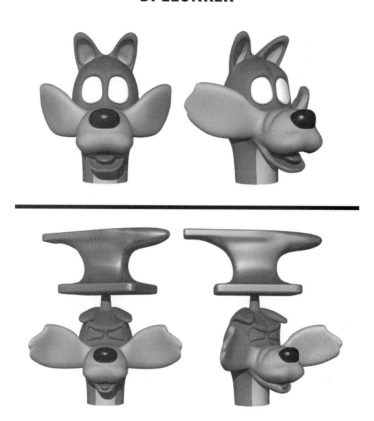

Distinguishing Features

Ears: The ears lie flat on the brow. A large bump is raised between the ears where the object that struck the character sits.

Brows: The brows are compressed downward in the middle.

Eyes: The eyes are closed, showing a seam where the eyelids meet.

Whiskers: The whiskers are rotated forward, curling past the parallel point.

Mouth: The mouth is nearly closed, and the lower jaw is curled inward with the tongue curled inward as well.

Special: An object sits atop the bump between the ears.

Common Uses

The Spelunker is the moment of impact, when an object of significant weight has been dropped on the character's head. This expression usually precedes Watch the Birdie.

STAR STRUCK

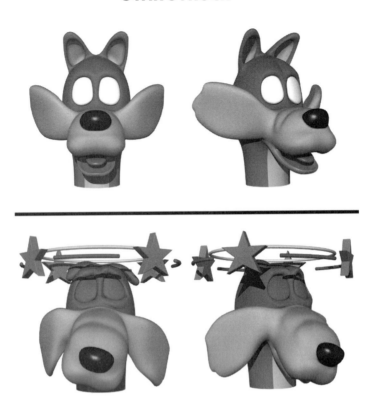

Distinguishing Features

Ears: The ears lie flat on the sides of the head and the top of the head is compressed flat.

Brows: The brows are pushed forward.

Eyes: The eyes are closed with no visible eyelid seam, and there are puffy bags below the eyes.

Whiskers: The whiskers droop against the sides of the head.

Mouth: The mouth is closed and the muzzle droops downward.

Special: Little stars are added, flying in circles around the top of the head. The stars are accompanied by circular lines that also rotate around the top of the head.

Common Uses

Star Struck is very similar to Watch the Birdie. It involves supporting cast members rotating around the character's head while it is unconscious. While Watch the Birdie is used when a small object is dropped on the character's head, Star Struck is used when large objects like pianos and safes are dropped, knocking the character out.

TRAIN WHISTLE

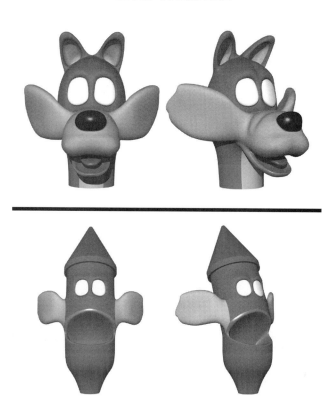

Distinguishing Features

Ears: The ears are removed.

Brows: The brows remain unchanged.

Eyes: No change.

Whiskers: The whiskers are rotated backward.

Mouth: The mouth is turned into a gaping wedge.

Special: The head is shaped like a train whistle, cylindrical with a cone top.

Common Uses

Train Whistle is a severe morphing expression where the character's head takes on the shape of a train whistle. This is often used to express having eaten something hot such as chili or hot liquid.

TRUMPET

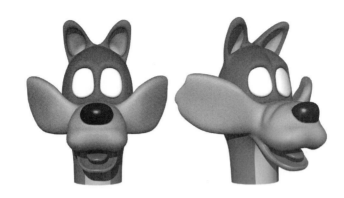

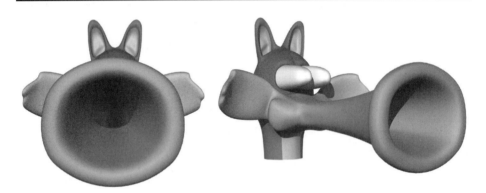

Distinguishing Features

Ears: The ears stand straight up.

Brows: No change.

Eyes: The eyes bug out of the head and stop at the end of the cheeks.

Whiskers: The whiskers stand straight out to the sides of the head and are curled forward at the tips.

Mouth: The cheeks are puffed full of air, and the muzzle is stretched outward and shaped like a horn.

Common Uses

The Trumpet expression is often used to express a loud yell, calling another character, or warning it of danger. It is sometimes used to express lust, typically as a transitional expression preceding Hubba-Hubba.

WHISTLE

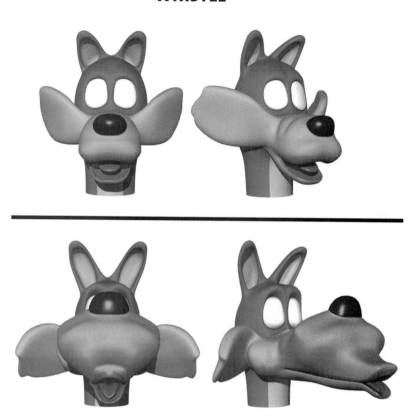

Distinguishing Features

Ears: The ears stand upward and are stretched a bit.

Brows: The brows are raised upward and forward over the eyes until they are parallel with the top of the head.

Eyes: No change.

Whiskers: The whiskers are rotated forward until the tips curl around the cheeks.

Mouth: The cheeks are puffed full of air, and the muzzle is stretched outward, tapering larger at the tip. The mouth is closed, and the lips are pulled forward and parted.

Common Uses

Whistle is a common expression used in the early days of cartoon animation to express interests in a good-looking character walking by. It's the equivalent of the construction worker's catcall. It can also be used to express interest in other things such as money. It's not as severe as the lust of the Hubba-Hubba expression, although it often precedes it.

ABOUT THE CD-ROM

The CD-ROM that accompanies this book includes animated samples of phonemes, facial expressions, color versions of all the figures, and over 100 Facial Expression and Phoneme templates.

SYSTEM REQUIREMENTS

- Win/Mac compatible
- QuickTime
- No special hardware or software requirements, although having a 3D program installed (sold separately) would be most beneficial to explore all the resources explained in the book. 3ds Max or Maya recommended.

FOLDERS

The files on the disc are organized into the following folders:

Figures: All the figures from the book, organized in folders by chapter.

Chapters: Contains the QuickTime movies referenced throughout the chapters.

Expression Templates: JPEG format image files depicting all the expressions explained in the book.

Phoneme Templates: JPEG format image files depicting 32 common phonemes.

INDEX